POSITIVE PSYCHOTHERAPY

POSITIVE PSYCHOTHERAPY
WORKBOOK

Tayyab Rashid

and

Martin Seligman

OXFORD
UNIVERSITY PRESS

Oxford University Press is a department of the University of Oxford. It furthers
the University's objective of excellence in research, scholarship, and education
by publishing worldwide. Oxford is a registered trade mark of Oxford University
Press in the UK and certain other countries.

Published in the United States of America by Oxford University Press
198 Madison Avenue, New York, NY 10016, United States of America.

CIP data is on file at the Library of Congress
ISBN 978–0–19–092024–1

9 8 7 6 5

Printed by Sheridan Books, Inc., United States of America

CONTENTS

PREFACE

An unspoken and untested premise of psychotherapy-as-usual is that when a client is encouraged to talk at length about what is wrong, this client will somehow recover. Positive psychotherapy (PPT) takes the opposite approach. It encourages clients to recognize fully what is right and strong and good in their lives and to deploy what is best about them in order to buffer against mental disorders. Consider the following examples:

- *Emma, a young woman obsessed with memories of trauma, musters the courage to consider that forgiveness helps as well as hurts.*
- *Alejandro, a middle-aged man with depression and suicidal ideation, sits in the psychiatric emergency room. He comes to notice that almost everyone else sitting there is worse off than he is, and he realizes that he has enough internal resources to manage his situation.*
- *Myriam, a female graduate student in her late 20s, experiences visual and auditory hallucinations that do not neatly fit into any diagnostic category. She goes back into therapy having been referred to numerous specialists who cannot agree on a definitive diagnosis.*

Over the past 15 years, these individuals, and hundreds of others, have come to PPT because this approach does not view them merely as wounded souls, fatigued bodies, and listless spirits. PPT assesses, appreciates, and amplifies what is good about clients—without minimizing their distress—and uses these strengths as the levers of healing.

- When Emma was ready to look at her trauma, PPT became a process of understanding the nuances of forgiveness—where it can help or hurt. She discovered that her strength of forgiveness defines her as a kind and empathic person.
- During PPT, Alejandro discovered that perspective is one of his signature strengths. He was able to determine that others are worse off than he is, and this understanding gave him the strength to look at the positives in his own situation.
- When asked what brings her back to therapy (despite the fact that she was referred to numerous other services), Myriam says that PPT is the only place in the world that sees her beyond her symptoms and appreciates that her creativity and perseverance will carry her to the completion of her degree.

Psychotherapy evolved as a discipline centered on fixing, repairing, and remediating. In this workbook, you will learn that psychotherapy can, in contrast, be centered on exploring and cultivating kindness, love, gratitude, hope, and curiosity.

ACKNOWLEDGMENTS

Numerous helping hands and kind hearts have contributed in curating this workbook. We are thankful to Sarah Harrington of Oxford University Press, for spearheading this project with the thoughtfulness and care it needed. Kate Scheinman's editorial acumen polished the manuscript immensely. The following individuals have helped in their own unique ways: Our heartfelt thanks go to Diane Ostermann, Therese Ostermann, Jane Gillham, David Cooperrider, Denise Quinlan, George Vaillant, Barbara Fredrickson, Donna & Neal Mayerson, Ryan Neimeic, Robert McGrath, Karen Reivich, Robert Bernstein, Angela Duckworth, Acacia Parks, Lea Waters, Judith Moskowitz, Jenny Brennan, Leona Bradwene, Phillip Streit, Carmelo Vazquez, Antonia Csillik, Charles Martin-Krumm, John Hendry, Charlie Scudamore, Milad Hadchiti, Hamid Peseschkian, Dan Strunk, Nicolas Troyano, Robert Fazio, Jorden Peterson, Ruth Louden, Curtis Cole, Miriam Shuchman, Fahim Kazemi, Amanda Uliaszek, Jennifer Hamilton, Bruce Kidd, David Newman, Jeanne Robb, Peter Cornish, Lina Di Genova, Vera Romano, Shadi Laghai, Amina Shabeen, Andilib Sajid, Meghan Kizuik, Shafik Kamani, Ahmed Ashraf, Gjylena Nexhipi, Jim Cheston, Noman Siddique, Arun & Rashmi Sahni, Michael Alexander, Abdul Rauf, Faisal Nisar, Asif Saeed, Eman Bente Syed, Mehreen Raza, Zeib & Imraan Jeeva, Samira Kanji, Timothy Gianotti, Peter Vlaovic, Rashaad Vahed, Muhammad Munshi, Yaseen & Summayah Poonah and to our clients who taught us how to heal amidst hurts.

Tayyab Rashid
Martin Seligman

POSITIVE PSYCHOTHERAPY

INTRODUCTION TO THIS WORKBOOK

WHAT IS POSITIVE PSYCHOTHERAPY?

Positive psychotherapy (PPT) is a therapeutic approach that attempts to counteract your symptoms with strengths, weaknesses with virtues, and deficits with skills, to help you understand complex situations and experiences in a balanced way.

The human brain pays more attention and responds more strongly to negatives than to positives. However, PPT helps by teaching us to build up our positives. To deal with the toughest challenges in life, we need our toughest internal resources, which in turn will build our resilience. Much like health is better than sickness, mastery is better than stress, cooperation is better than conflict, hope is better than despair, and strengths are better than weaknesses.

The positives in PPT are primarily based on Dr. Martin Seligman's ideas of well-being. Dr. Seligman organized happiness and well-being into five scientifically measurable and teachable parts: (a) **P**ositive emotion, (b) **E**ngagement, (c) **R**elationships, (d) **M**eaning, and (e) **A**ccomplishment, with the first letters of each part forming the mnemonic **PERMA** (Seligman, 2012). These elements are neither exhaustive nor exclusive, but it has been shown that fulfillment of these elements is associated with lower rates of distress and higher rates of life satisfaction.

PPT practices will help you assess your strengths from multiple perspectives, followed by a series of practices that will help you develop what we call "practical wisdom." Examples include how to decide between taking a risky new initiative versus relying on the tried and tested; how to strike a balance between fairness and kindness; and how to show empathy to a friend but also be objective. The goal of practical wisdom is to help you better deal with challenging situations, that is, to choose the wise way when there are many options for how to deal with a challenge.

PPT teaches about strengths, but in context. In fact, under some circumstances, negatives such as sadness and anxiety may be more adaptive than positives, especially when survival is at stake. Similarly, anger—expressed as protest to work toward a greater good—is more adaptive than compliance. You and your clinician will work together to understand your pain and hurts, and you will also be looking to find meaning from this pain.

PPT can be divided into three phases:

- Phase One focuses on helping you to come up with a balanced narrative by exploring your strengths from multiple perspectives. You will create meaningful goals using your signature strengths.
- Phase Two focuses on building positive emotions and, with support, dealing with negative memories, negative experiences, and negative feelings. These negatives may be keeping you stuck and not allowing you to move forward.
- Phase Three focuses on exploring your positive relationships and strengthening the processes that nurture these relationships. This final phase of PPT also allows you to explore the meaning and purpose of your life.

THE SESSIONS AND PRACTICES

Table I.1 outlines the PPT sessions and main practices. Not everyone completes every practice, and your clinician may decide to work with you in a different session order.

THE STRUCTURE OF THE SESSIONS

There is a general pattern to how the sessions unfold, although your clinician has flexibility to structure the sessions to work best for you and your needs. Table I.2 provides an outline of a typical PPT session.

Table I.1.

POSITIVE PSYCHOTHERAPY: SESSION-BY-SESSION DESCRIPTION

Session Number and Title	Content	Main Practices
Phase One		
1: Positive Introduction and Gratitude Journal	Session One explains the clinical environment and clarifies both your and your clinician's roles and responsibilities. This session also teaches you how to start the ongoing practice of cultivating gratitude through journaling positive experiences and appreciating the impact of gratitude on well-being.	*Positive Introduction:* You will recall, reflect on, and write a one-page story (that called for the best in you) with a beginning, middle, and positive end. *Gratitude Journal:* You will start an ongoing journal to record three good things every night (big or small) and also write about what made these good things happen.
2: Character Strengths and Signature Strengths	This is the first of three sessions focusing on character strengths and signature strengths, which are positive traits that can be developed through practice and can contribute to personal growth and wellness.	*Character Strengths:* You will compile your signature strengths profile by collecting information from multiple resources including self-report, an online measure, a family member, and a friend.
3: Practical Wisdom	This session presents the skills of practical wisdom. These skills teach you how to apply your signature strengths in a balanced way to solve problems.	*Know How of Strengths:* You will learn how to apply practical wisdom strategies (seeking specificity, finding relevance, resolving conflict, reflection, and calibration) to resolve three specific scenarios.
4: A Better Version of Me	This session looks at articulating and implementing a written plan of positive, pragmatic, and persistent self-development.	*A Better Version of Me:* You will create a self-development plan called *A Better Version of Me* that uses your strengths through specific, measurable, and achievable goals.
Phase Two		
5: Open and Closed Memories	In this session, you will learn to recall, write about, and process your open (negative) and closed (positively resolved) memories. You will learn to develop skills for dealing with open memories.	*Positive Appraisal:* After practicing relaxation, you will write about bitter memories and explore four ways to deal with them adaptively.

Table I.1.

CONTINUED

Session Number and Title	Content	Main Practices
6: Forgiveness	This session teaches that forgiveness is a process for change, rather than an event. This session explains what forgiveness is and what it is not.	*REACH:* You will learn about REACH—a process of forgiveness; and/or: *Forgiveness Letter:* You will write a letter of forgiveness, but you may not necessarily deliver it.
7: Maximizing versus Satisficing	This session presents the concepts of maximizing (aiming to make the best possible choice) and satisficing (making a "good enough" choice).	*Toward Satisficing:* You will explore in which areas of life you maximize or satisfice. You will then draft a plan to increase satisficing.
8: Gratitude	This session expands the concept of gratitude by having you recall and write to someone who is alive now and who in the past did something positive but who you have never fully thanked.	*Gratitude Letter:* You will reflect on and write a letter of gratitude to someone who helped you during a time of need and who you have not thanked properly. *Gratitude Visit:* You may invite the person to whom you wrote the *Gratitude Letter,* for a one-on-one meeting. Without explaining in advance, you read the letter in person.
Phase Three		
9: Hope and Optimism	In this session, you will learn to see the best possible, realistic outcomes. You will see that challenges are temporary and learn how to develop a sense of hope.	*One Door Closes, Another Door Opens:* You will reflect on and write about three doors that have closed in your life and three doors that have opened.
10: Posttraumatic Growth	This session invites you to explore deep feelings and thoughts about a traumatic experience that continues to bother you.	*Expressive Writing:* You can complete an optional exercise of transporting troubling and traumatic experiences to a piece of paper, with the assurance that this writing is for your eyes only. The practice is done after you have developed healthy coping skills and are no longer overwhelmed by current stressors.
11: Slowness and Savoring	In this session, you will learn how to deliberately slow down and develop an awareness of how to savor. In so doing, you will learn to attend mindfully to positives.	*Slow* and *Savor:* You will select one slowness technique and one savoring technique to try that fit your personality and life circumstances.

(continued)

Table I.1.
CONTINUED

Session Number and Title	Content	Main Practices
12: Positive Relationships	In this session, you will learn about the significance of recognizing the strengths of your loved ones.	*Tree of Positive Relationships:* You will assess and plot your strengths on a large "tree," drawn on paper. You will then discuss with your loved ones ways of enriching your relationships by celebrating one another's strengths.
13: Positive Communication	In this session, you will learn about four styles of responding to good news and which of these predicts relationship satisfaction.	*Active Constructive Responding:* You will practice responding to a positive event shared by your loved one in a lively and authentic way.
14: Altruism	In this session, you will learn how being altruistic helps both you and others.	*Gift of Time:* You will plan to give the gift of time by doing something meaningful that also uses your signature strengths.
15: Meaning and Purpose	This session focuses on the search and pursuit of meaningful endeavors for the greater good.	*Positive Legacy:* You will write about how you would like to be remembered, especially in terms of your positive footprints.

Table I.2.
POSITIVE PSYCHOTHERAPY: GENERIC SESSION STRUCTURE

Core Concepts	Your clinician may begin sessions by describing evidence-based core concepts in easy-to-understand language. These concepts explain why each session is important.
Relaxation Practice	Each session begins with a relaxation practice; typically you will be guided through a three- to five-minute relaxation practice.
Gratitude Journal	Following the relaxation practice, your clinician will ask you to share a few positives events or experiences noted in your *Gratitude Journal* from the past week.
Review	You and your clinician will review the previous session's core concept/s and practice. Your clinician will encourage you to share your experiences, reactions, and reflections regarding the concepts discussed and practiced during the previous session.
In-Session Practice	Each session has at least one in-session practice that continues between sessions with the hope that you will continue to practice at home.
Reflect and Discuss	These are questions to encourage you to reflect on and discuss the in-session practices.
Relaxation	We recommend that each session end with the same brief relaxation practice that started the session.

IS PPT RIGHT FOR YOU?

If you have been experiencing problems, seeking psychotherapy is most likely to be beneficial for you. Since there are many varieties of psychotherapy, you may wonder if PPT is right for you. The following five questions and answers will help you make an informed and thoughtful decision.

1. *Is PPT an evidence-based treatment?* More than 10 randomized controlled studies, mostly conducted by clinical researchers not affiliated with the authors of this workbook, have demonstrated that PPT is effective when compared to no treatment, and comparably effective when compared to an active treatment such as cognitive behavior therapy (Rashid & Seligman, 2018).

2. *Is PPT right for my psychological problems?* PPT has been applied with a number of clinical conditions. PPT has also been shown to be effective with a range of psychological disorders, including depression (Csillik, Aguerre, & Bay, 2012), addiction (Akhtar & Boniwell, 2010), borderline personality disorder (Uliaszek, Rashid, Williams, & Gulamani, 2016), posttraumatic stress (Gilman, Schumm, & Chard, 2012), and psychosis (Meyer, Johnson, Parks, Iwanski, & Penn, 2012; Schrank et al., 2015).

3. *Which mode is more effective—individual or group?* Both can be helpful. It depends on your level of comfort regarding the issues you want to tackle in therapy. For example, individual therapy enables you to discuss highly personalized concerns within the confidential and safe confines of a one-on-one therapy setting. Group PPT will allow you to listen to the strengths-based narratives and stories of resilience that the other members of the group are likely to share, and this sharing will allow you to review and appraise your own concerns in perspective. In addition, this process of sharing can lead to an environment of trust that often creates therapeutic synergy that helps group members bond in support of one another's well-being. You can also switch from individual to group and vice versa.

4. *I have significant problems, and PPT seems like it is all about positives. Do I understand correctly?* Because of its name, PPT may give this impression that is all about positives. Unlike its name, PPT fully attends to your distressing experiences without dismissing, ignoring, or, most importantly, minimizing them. However, PPT attempts to give equal weight to your strengths. For example, if you discuss a painful memory, the PPT trained clinician—using basic therapeutic skills such as warmth, genuineness, and positive regard—will attend to your feelings and thoughts. However, whenever appropriate, the clinician will also help you recall your joys and pleasant memories. You will be encouraged to think about moments of isolation as well as when you felt connected. Within the safe therapeutic environment, PPT will offer you space and time to express your resentments and also what you may appreciate. PPT will process the harsh criticism you may have encountered and will balance it with recalling instances when you were genuinely complemented.

5. *Will I be expected to do homework? My schedule is so busy that I hardly have time to come in for therapy. I don't think that I will have time to do any homework.* PPT sessions generally do not include homework. There is a practice to be done within each session, followed by reflections and discussion. The aim is to prepare you to apply the skills learned in session in your everyday life. For example, the *Gratitude Journal* practice will ask you to notice and record (in a manner convenient to you) positive things that happen. *Signature Strengths* will help you to use your already intact and positive resources in a more focused manner. *Active-Constructive Responding* will teach you ways to respond to your loved one's good news in a positive and constructive manner. In summary, you are

not expected to start a new set of behaviors and habits. You will apply skills and perspective to behaviors already in place.

STARTING THE JOURNEY

Seeking therapy is an act of courage. Sustaining it is act of persistence. Both courage and persistence need your motivation, willingness to change, and openness to try things differently. If your clinician presents specific rules pertaining to the clinical setting, please review them and discuss, should you have any concerns. This will help you to understand the structure and sequence of the treatment. Like all clients, you will not be starting therapy as blank slate. Rather, you are likely to bring "heavy baggage" (issues) with you. Like most clients, you may have previously tried to resolve these issues, in ways you thought might work—because when we are stressed, we try to alleviate it. Sometimes the ways we try work, and sometimes they don't. If the latter is true for you, please do not feel inadequate! The fact that you are seeking treatment shows your adequacy in that you are willing to solve your problems. However, as you embark on this journey, keep the following tips in mind:

1. **Expect some discomfort:** Engaging in PPT, like any treatment, is not easy.
    Therapy is supposed to shake up your equilibrium, which can cause temporary
    disruptions. Therefore it is helpful from the start to expect some disruption.
    However, if you persist, you will most likely be able to find a balance that works
    for you and those around you. Please keep in close contact with your clinician
    about your progress throughout the PPT process.
2. **Motivation:** As you start this journey, please understand that treatment cannot be
    forced or coerced. If you are attending the treatment on your own volition, build
    on this initiative by seeing yourself as an agent of change in your life. From the
    start, try to connect the concepts and practices from your PPT sessions to your
    everyday life. For example, through the practice of the *Gratitude Journal* (which
    will be covered in your first PPT session), begin to look at positive events and
    experiences: If someone holds a door for you, smiles at you, or does a favor for
    you that you were not expecting, briefly pause and think about this. Such pause
    and reflection will gradually help you cement changes in your daily life—for the
    better.
3. **PPT is not a panacea:** PPT is not universally applicable, relevant, or appropriate
    for every clinical condition. If you have chronic, complex, and severe mental
    health concerns, it is important that you seek an appropriate level of care,
    including psychiatric, medical, and vocational. Developing a positive outlook,
    learning to more effectively use your character strengths, and developing a
    sense of purpose or meaning may not be sufficient or even relevant to all of your
    psychological problems. Setting realistic expectations from the start regarding the
    extent to which PPT can be helpful is an important consideration.
4. **Progression is not linear:** Changing behaviors, especially those developed
    and cemented over many years, takes time, and we highly recommend that you
    and your clinician periodically monitor your progress using a valid and reliable
    feedback system. Also, a number of external factors over which you may have
    little or no control—such as conditions at work; mental health issues of a loved
    one; or social, economic, or political challenges (e.g., economic depression,
    unexpected climate-related disasters, cyber-bullying, or terrorist attacks)—may
    adversely impact or derail your therapeutic progress. Please make sure that
    your clinician is aware of any such factors that may impact your progress. Such
    communication will help to develop a shared understanding and also help the
    clinician understand your circumstances. Furthermore, some PPT practices. Such

as *Positive Appraisal* (which looks at open/negative memories) and *Expressive Writing* (which looks at posttraumatic growth), can potentially trigger unpleasant memories. Therefore, it is important to discuss your therapeutic progress with your clinician on a regular basis and make ant necessary changes.

5. **PPT is not for everyone:** Individuals with some acute psychological conditions such as severe and frequently experienced symptoms of panic disorder, those with an entrenched sense of perceiving themselves as a victim, or those who have experienced severe and prolong abuse may need another specific treatment protocol to first deal with the acute symptoms. After stabilizing, such clients can consider pursuing PPT.

1

SESSION ONE: *POSITIVE INTRODUCTION* AND *GRATITUDE JOURNAL*

SESSION ONE EXPLAINS THE CLINICAL ENVIRONMENT AND clarifies both your and your clinician's roles and responsibilities. This session also teaches you how to start the ongoing practice of cultivating gratitude through journaling positive experiences and appreciating the impact of gratitude on well-being. The two positive psychotherapy (PPT) practices covered in this session are *Positive Introduction* and *Gratitude Journal*.

THREE THINGS TO KNOW ABOUT THE *POSITIVE INTRODUCTION*

1. **Recalling and reflecting on a time when you prevailed:** Psychotherapy may be one of the few times when you have the opportunity to share your life story in a way you may not have shared it before. Unfortunately, psychotherapy is largely seen as a process for "unloading" your stories, which are often stories of hurt, guilt, or betrayal. The *Positive Introduction*, however, is a practice that will ask you to recall, reflect on, write about, and hopefully, over the course of treatment, also reframe an experience from your life in which, despite challenges, you prevailed.

2. **Restoring a healthier and resilient self:** By mindfully recalling a meaningful experience, weaving it into a story (with a beginning, middle, and end), writing it down, and potentially sharing it, you will have the opportunity to reframe, reappraise, and refile important parts of the self from which you can draw personal strength. We start PPT with the *Positive Introduction* practice as it can be a catalyst for you to construct or restore a healthier and resilient self-concept. This practice will allow you to explore a holistic snapshot of your personality.

3. **Distress is not ignored or dismissed:** The *Positive Introduction* practice doesn't mean that your story of hurts or distress will not be attended to. You are always welcome to share what is bothering you. Rest assured that this exercise is not meant to encourage you to look only at the sunny side. Instead, the intent of this practice is to help you take a deeper look at your past and focus on an experience that was quite difficult, yet somehow you overcame it. Starting therapy with such an experience, we believe, will help you transfer skills used in the past to present problems—that is, how the resilience you exhibited in the past can possibly help your present and future. In this way, the *Positive Introduction* practice is a guidepost from the past that you can use to steer your life in the desired direction.

START-OF-SESSION RELAXATION

At the start of the session, your clinician may begin with a brief relaxation exercise. To discover some of these practices on your own, go to Appendix A: Relaxation & Mindfulness Practices, which can be found at the end of this workbook.

IN-SESSION PRACTICE: *POSITIVE INTRODUCTION*

Your clinician will be working with you on the in-session practices. Refer to Worksheet 1.1.

Think about a time when you handled a tough situation in a positive way. You don't need to come up with a huge, life-changing event. Perhaps what comes to mind is a small event that called forth the best in you. Write about this situation. Make it in the form of a story with a clear beginning, middle, and a positive end. If you need more space, write on an additional piece of paper.

_____

_____

_____

_____

_____

_____

_____

_____

_____

_____

_____

_____

_____

_____

_____

_____

This worksheet was originally published in Rashid and Seligman's *Positive Psychotherapy: Clinician Manual.*

Reflect & Discuss

Reflect on and discuss the following:

- Some stories become part of the way we perceive ourselves. How might this story have impacted your self-concept?
- What helped you to deal with the situation? Please describe specifics, such as:
  - Personal attributes, including persistence, optimism, or faith.
  - Environmental attributes, such as support from close friends, family members, or professional relationships.
- Are significant others in your life aware of this story in the same spirit or way that you recall it?

In Real Life: Kevin, 20, male, Caucasian[1]

When I was in 10th grade, I was diagnosed with a rare form of cancer. I was told that it is a type of cancer generally found in the knee, but it was detected in my throat. My parents took long-term leave from their full-time jobs, and, during a grueling 14-hour surgery, my throat was reconstructed. The hospital became my home as I moved between treatment, recovery, and rehabilitation. At first, I was afraid that I wouldn't graduate with peers, but this fear mattered less when I came to know that my father had also been diagnosed with cancer, one that was in the terminal phase. I succeeded in graduating from high school, but my father lost his battle with cancer. Then, two years later, in martial arts practice, one of my lungs collapsed, and I went through another round of surgery. I am not a person who complains. I tend to face problems head on, yet I couldn't help asking, "Why me?" My reserved disposition hasn't helped me to open up to anyone, not even to my mom, with whom I am very close. I don't want to add to her list of worries; she already has a lot on her plate. However, I have been particularly self-conscious that the surgical scars on my neck will make dating awkward for me—so I don't like to talk about myself. Writing about my challenges in a Positive Introduction *and discussing them with my therapist has helped me value my experiences more than I have. More importantly, I feel that if I can deal with such big challenges, finding a date is not such a big deal. "There is always someone worse off than me."*

Tips to Maintain Your Progress

Discuss the following tips with your clinician to help you maintain your progress:

- A *Positive Introduction* can help you recall other stories of growth and triumph. We encourage you to share other similar stories. Sometimes the most important story comes after you and your clinician get to know one another better and you are more comfortable with the therapeutic process.
- Stories you tell about yourself are different parts of yourself. To extend the benefit of this practice, reflect on stories you tell to yourself and others about yourself. Explore if there is an underlying theme to your story. For example, do you see yourself as a resilient person? If so, from where do you draw your resilience? Also, would you have told your story in the same way, let's say, six months or a year ago? We change over time, and circumstance around us change. Do these changes also change the way you recall and tell (yourself) your story?
- Stories that we tell ourselves are shaped by the culture in which stories take place. One way to seek in-depth understanding of your culture is by exploring and sharing your stories, especially those of resilience, with your loved ones. Similarly, invite them to share their stories with you. This process will most likely cement your relationships with others and you will also learn different ways of handling the same challenge.

THREE THINGS TO KNOW ABOUT THE *GRATITUDE JOURNAL*

1. **We remember negatives more than positives:** The human brain has developed such that we remember failures more readily than successes. Negatives stick with us, and often keep us stuck, while positives swiftly pass, without staying very long in our attention and memory. We complain and criticize easily but struggle to complement and express gratitude. The goal of the *Gratitude Journal* practice is to help you cultivate a regular practice of expressing gratitude.

2. **Gratitude provides perspective:** Gratitude is expressing and enacting a sense of thankfulness, including a deliberate effort to observe, be aware of, and appreciate positive things in life. We assume that positive things just happen, and, therefore, we take them for granted. Cultivating gratitude helps us to not take things for granted. When we don't take things for granted, we value them, which in turn helps us to perceive both the positives and the negatives in our lives in perspective.

3. **Benefits of gratitude:** Gratitude has numerous benefits. It helps to offset our negativity and also enables us to appreciate what we have. Therefore, we are less likely to compare ourselves with others in regard to material goods. Gratitude also engenders appreciation of others, especially their kindness, care, and affection. When we express our gratitude toward others, it naturally builds and cements our relationships.

IN-SESSION PRACTICE: *GRATITUDE JOURNAL*

Your clinician will be working with you on the in-session practices.

Reflect & Discuss

Reflect on and discuss the following:

- Did you have any difficulty recalling specific good events? If so, please specify.
- Did you notice any patterns in your good events or blessings? Family, friends, work, or nature?
- Was any aspect of your life clearly not represented in the good events or blessings, such as work or friends?
- Did you have an active role in the occurrence of good events or blessings, or did they mostly just happen to you?
- Do you find yourself reflecting more about good things after this practice?
- Do you find it a new way of looking at situations and people?
- Have you shared your good events or blessings with others?
- Did you find it hard to write them down? If so, why?

In Real Life: Roseanne, 19, female, multiethnic

When I was in high school, every day my eastern European mother put tremendous pressure on me to be a ballerina, and she also wanted me to do well academically. And I was doing all of this. However, the pressure to be selected for a state competition was immense, and I started caving in to this pressure. First, I developed an eating disorder. I would binge and then purge. Episodes of binging and purging left me empty. I filled the void at first with occasional recreational drugs. Then, gradually, my drug use became more regular, as my tolerance increased. I resorted to delinquent behavior, and within a year I found myself on the streets—homeless, hungry, and cold. The warm rays of sunshine woke me, one day, lying on a sidewalk. The sky was blue—crisp, clean, and filled with fresh air. I started crying because I felt that that day might be the last day I could appreciate this blue sky. I realized that I could die any day from an overdose or something else. I got up and made up with my family, and I am now back in school.[2]

Tips to Maintain Your Progress

Expressing gratitude every day maintains and enhances well-being. This expression can be as simple as a conscious and sincere "thank you" to someone who holds the door open for you or getting a positive email from a friend. We encourage you to make a habit of building gratitude into your daily schedule.

Discuss the following tips with your clinician to help you maintain your progress:

- Grateful people are less envious of others and are less likely to measure their success in terms of material gains. When we are genuinely thankful and appreciative for what we have (e.g., family, friends, health, home), we are less likely to pay close attention to what our neighbors have (Finlay & Lyons, 2000; Froh, Emmons, Card, Bono, & Wilson, 2011). Grateful people are also more likely to help others. When we become aware of the kind and caring acts of others, we naturally feel like reciprocating (Watkins, 2010). In this way, gratitude reinforces other favorable consequences, increasing and strengthening it. What other favorable changes happen when you start practicing gratitude?
- A pervasive sense of gratitude contributes to positive interpretations of life events. That is, grateful people tend to look at life events in a more positive way. After practicing gratitude (by consistently maintaining a *Gratitude Journal*), whenever you recall past hurts and painful memories, we encourage you to discuss with your clinician if your interpretation of these events have changed after practicing gratitude.
- Observe if a blessing or a good thing is related to your strengths, qualities, or talents; that is, has being grateful also helped you to appreciate your other attributes, such as kindness, social and personal intelligence, and appreciation of beauty?
- You can express your gratitude through art (e.g., painting, sketching, photography, collage, or scrapbooking).
- Instead of writing, for a few weeks you can share your blessings with your partner and encourage him or her to share with you.
- On days you may be gripped by a negative or sad mood and don't feel like writing in your *Gratitude Journal*, just review previous entries.

RESOURCES FOR *POSITIVE INTRODUCTION*

Readings
- Denborough, D. (2014). *Retelling the Stories of Our Lives: Everyday Narrative Therapy to Draw Inspiration and Transform Experience*. New York: W. W. Norton.
- Martin, L. (2017). *Telling Stories: The Craft of Narrative and the Writing Life*. Lincoln: University of Nebraska Press.
- McAdams, D. P. (2006). *The Redemptive Self: Stories Americans Live By*. New York: Oxford University Press.

Videos
- First author's positive introduction: Tayyab Rashid on Using Strengths at a Time of Trauma: https://youtu.be/Pucs6MUpKng

Websites
- Readers' Digest section on true and inspiring stories: http://www.rd.com/true-stories/
- Inspiring stories including amazing, short, moral, funny, positive, touching, and spiritual stories: http://www.inspirationalstories.eu

RESOURCES FOR *GRATITUDE JOURNAL*

Readings

- Dziurda, K. (2017). *Gratitude Journal: A 52 Week Challenge to Mastering the Art of Gratitude and Positively Transforming Your Life*. First Publication.
- Emmons, R. (2007). *Thanks! How the New Science of Gratitude Can Make You Happier*. New York: Houghton Mifflin.
- Fredrickson, B. (2009). *Positivity: Discover the Ratio That Tips Your Life Toward Flourishing*. New York: Three Rivers Press.

Videos

- Martin Seligman explains Three Blessing Exercise:
  https://youtu.be/RT2vKMyIQwc
- Robert Emmons on evidence-based practices of cultivating gratitude:
  https://youtu.be/8 964envYh58
- Louie Schwartzberg's TED Talk on gratitude showing stunning time-lapse photography, Title: Gratitude | Louie Schwartzberg | TEDxSF:
  https://youtu.be/gXDMoiEkyuQ

Websites

- Explore what good is happening in the world through these websites:
  www.selfgrowth.com/news
  www.happynews.com
  www.optimistworld.com

2

SESSION TWO: *CHARACTER STRENGTHS* AND *SIGNATURE STRENGTHS*

SESSION TWO IS THE FIRST OF THREE sessions focusing on *Character Strengths* and *Signature Strengths*, which are positive traits that can be developed through practice and can contribute to your personal growth and wellness. Taken together, Sessions Two to Four cover assessing what your strength are, understanding how and when you use them, and understanding how specific strengths can be used to help you create a desired or better version of yourself.

THREE THINGS TO KNOW ABOUT *CHARACTER STRENGTHS*

1. **Character strengths versus talents:** Character strengths are positive traits that manifest through your feelings, thoughts, and actions. Character strengths enable you to act in ways that contribute to your well-being and the well-being of those around you. Strengths are distinct from talents. Talents are expressions of natural abilities (e.g., musicality, dexterity, agility), whereas strengths are expression of character and tend to be more acquired. Examples include Malala Yousazai (bravery), Nelson Mandela (forgiveness), Oprah Winfrey (social intelligence), Steven Hawking (love of learning), Ellen Johnson Sirleaf (leadership), and singer Bono (kindness).
2. **Strengths and symptoms:** Whereas stressors, symptoms, deficits, dysfunctions, and disorders signal your psychological distress to you, character strengths, positive emotions, and meaning are desired anchors of your personality. They are ways for you to be good and to do good. All things being equal, our strengths elevate us, rather than diminish us.
3. **Strengths as dimensions versus categories:** Understanding that strengths are distinct from one another, such as creativity is distinct from curiosity, love from kindness, and fairness from integrity, may give you the impression that these strengths are naturally separate categories. Indeed, creativity is distinct from curiosity in many ways (see Appendix D: Building Your Strengths, for descriptions of each). However, strengths often overlap. Elements of curiosity spark creativity and vice versa. Curiosity and creativity may also need perseverance and self-regulation to turn the idea into reality. Fairness and integrity go hand in hand and often are supported by a dose of courage.

START-OF-SESSION RELAXATION

At the start of the session, your clinician may begin with a brief relaxation exercise. To discover some of these practices on your own, go to Appendix A: Relaxation & Mindfulness Practices, which can be found at the end of this workbook.

IN-SESSION PRACTICE: CHARACTER STRENGTHS ASSESSMENT

Your clinician will be working with you on the in-session practices. Refer to Worksheets 2.1 to 2.6.

You will watch a video showing pictures of the strengths listed here. Each picture will be labeled with the name of one of these strengths, and each picture will appear for a very brief period. Without focusing on whether the picture best represents the strength, please tune in to your emotions as sharply as you can. Keep your pen ready and with minimal thinking, if the strength represents your personality, please circle it or put an "x" in the right-hand column. Try to keep your selections limited to five strengths that best describe you. If you end up choosing more than five, you will have an opportunity to cross out any extra ones after the video is over.

	Character Strengths	**Represents You**
1	Creativity	
2	Curiosity	
3	Open-mindedness	
4	Love of Learning	
5	Perspective	
6	Bravery	
7	Persistence	
8	Integrity	
9	Vitality & Zest	
10	Love	
11	Kindness	
12	Social Intelligence	
13	Citizenship & Teamwork	
14	Fairness	
15	Leadership	
16	Forgiveness & Mercy	
17	Humility & Modesty	
18	Prudence	
19	Self-regulation	
20	Appreciation of Beauty and Excellence	
21	Gratitude	
22	Hope & Optimism	
23	Humor & Playfulness	
24	Spirituality	

When you have completed Worksheet 2.1, transfer the identified strengths to column 2 of Worksheet 2.6.

This worksheet was originally published in Rashid and Seligman's *Positive Psychotherapy: Clinician Manual.*

WORKSHEET 2.2   WHAT ARE YOUR "HEAD" STRENGTHS?

*Read the following descriptions of 24 positive character strengths. Select the **five** that **most often** characterize you, by placing a checkmark in the Signature Strengths column.*

	Description	Signature Strengths
1	I am good at thinking of new and better ways of doing things.	
2	I love to explore things, ask questions, and am open to different experiences and activities.	
3	I am flexible and open-minded; I think through and examine all sides before deciding.	
4	I love to learn new ideas, concepts, and facts in school or on my own.	
5	Friends consult with me on important matters, as they consider me to be wise beyond my age.	
6	I do not give up in the face of hardship or challenge, even when I am afraid.	
7	I finish most things, even if get distracted; I am able to refocus and complete the task.	
8	I consider myself to be a genuine and honest person, known to be trustworthy. I act consistent with my values.	
9	I am energetic, cheerful, and full of life.	
10	Showing and receiving genuine love and affection come naturally to me.	
11	I love to do kind acts for others, often without being asked.	
12	I manage myself well in social situations and am known to have good interpersonal skills.	
13	I am an active community or team member, and I contribute to the success of my group.	
14	I stand up for others when they are treated unfairly, bullied, or ridiculed.	
15	Others often choose me as a leader as I am known to lead well.	
16	I do not hold grudges; I forgive easily those who offend me.	
17	I don't like to be the center of attention and prefer others to shine.	
18	I am careful and cautious; I can anticipate risks and problems of my actions and respond accordingly.	
19	I manage my feelings and behaviors even in challenging situations; I generally follow rules and routines.	
20	I am moved deeply by beauty in nature, in art (e.g., painting, music, theatre) and/or in excellence in many fields of life.	
21	I express thankfulness for good things through words and actions.	
22	I hope and believe that more good things will happen than bad ones.	
23	I am playful and funny, and I use humor to connect with others.	
24	I believe in a higher power and participate in religious or spiritual practices (e.g., prayer, meditation) willingly.	

When you have completed Worksheet 2.2, transfer the identified strengths to column 3 of Worksheet 2.6.

This worksheet was originally published in Rashid and Seligman's *Positive Psychotherapy: Clinician Manual.*

Character Strength		Heart	Head
1	Creativity		
2	Curiosity		
3	Open-mindedness		
4	Love of Learning		
5	Perspective		
6	Bravery		
7	Persistence		
8	Integrity		
9	Vitality & Zest		
10	Love		
11	Kindness		
12	Social Intelligence		
13	Citizenship & Teamwork		
14	Fairness		
15	Leadership		
16	Forgiveness & Mercy		
17	Humility & Modesty		
18	Prudence		
19	Self-regulation		
20	Appreciation of Beauty and Excellence		
21	Gratitude		
22	Hope & Optimism		
23	Humor & Playfulness		
24	Spirituality		

In the heart column, mark the strengths identified on Worksheet 2.1, and in the head column, mark the strengths identified on Worksheet 2.2. There is no need to transfer these strengths to Worksheet 2.6. The purpose of Worksheet 2.3 is to allow you to see if there is any overlap between you heart and head strengths.

This worksheet was originally published in Rashid and Seligman's *Positive Psychotherapy: Clinician Manual.*

To be completed by a family member

Please read the following descriptions of 24 positive character traits. Then select with a checkmark exactly **five** (no less, no more) you find **most often** characterize _____.

	Description	Signature Strengths
1	Is good at thinking of new and better ways of doing things	
2	Loves to explore things, asks questions, is open to different experiences and activities	
3	Is flexible and open-minded; thinks through and examines all sides before deciding	
4	Loves to learn new ideas, concepts, and facts in school or on her/his own	
5	Friends consult him/her regarding important matters; is considered to be wise beyond age	
6	Does not give up in face of hardship or challenge, even when afraid	
7	Finishes most things; is able to refocus when distracted and complete the task	
8	Is a genuine and honest person, is known to be trustworthy; acts consistent with her/his values	
9	Is energetic, cheerful, and full of life	
10	Both loving and being loved comes natural to him/her; values close relationships with others	
11	Loves to do kind acts for others, often without being asked	
12	Manages her/himself well in social situations and is known to have good interpersonal skills	
13	Is an active community or team member, and contributes to the success of the group	
14	Stands up for others when they are treated unfairly, bullied, or ridiculed	
15	Is often chosen by others as a leader; is known to lead well	
16	Forgives easily those who offend him/her; does not hold grudges	
17	Doesn't like to be the center of attention and prefers others to shine	
18	Is careful and cautious, can anticipate risks and problems of his/her actions and responds accordingly	
19	Manages feelings and behaviors well in challenging situations; generally follows rules and routines	
20	Is moved deeply by beauty in nature, in art (e.g., painting, music, theatre) and/or in excellence in many fields of life	
21	Expresses thankfulness for good things through words and actions	
22	Hopes and believe that more good things will happen than bad ones	
23	Is playful and funny, and uses humor to connect with others	
24	Believes in a higher power and participates in religious or spiritual practices (e.g., prayer, meditation) willingly	

When you have completed Worksheet 2.4, transfer the identified strengths to column 4 of Worksheet 2.6.

This worksheet was originally published in Rashid and Seligman's *Positive Psychotherapy: Clinician Manual.*

WORKSHEET 2.5   YOUR *CHARACTER STRENGTHS*—AS OBSERVED BY A FRIEND

To be completed by a friend

*Please read the following descriptions of 24 positive character traits. Then select with a checkmark exactly **five** (no less, no more) you find **most often** characterize _____.*

	Description	Signature Strengths
1	Is good at thinking of new and better ways of doing things	
2	Loves to explore things, asks questions, is open to different experiences and activities	
3	Is flexible and open-minded; thinks through and examines all sides before deciding	
4	Loves to learn new ideas, concepts, and facts in school or on her/his own	
5	Friends consult him/her regarding important matters; is considered to be wise beyond age	
6	Does not give up in face of hardship or challenge, even when afraid	
7	Finishes most things; is able to refocus when distracted and complete the task	
8	Is a genuine and honest person, is known to be trustworthy; acts consistent with her/his values	
9	Is energetic, cheerful, and full of life	
10	Both loving and being loved comes natural to him/her; values close relationships with others	
11	Loves to do kind acts for others, often without being asked	
12	Manages her/himself well in social situations and is known to have good interpersonal skills	
13	Is an active community or team member, and contributes to the success of the group	
14	Stands up for others when they are treated unfairly, bullied, or ridiculed	
15	Is often chosen by others as a leader; is known to lead well	
16	Forgives easily those who offend him/her; does not hold grudges	
17	Doesn't like to be the center of attention and prefers others to shine	
18	Is careful and cautious, can anticipate risks and problems of his/her actions and responds accordingly	
19	Manages feelings and behaviors well in challenging situations; generally follows rules and routines	
20	Is moved deeply by beauty in nature, in art (e.g., painting, music, theatre) and/or in excellence in many fields of life	
21	Expresses thankfulness for good things through words and actions	
22	Hopes and believe that more good things will happen than bad ones	
23	Is playful and funny, and uses humor to connect with others	
24	Believes in a higher power and participates in religious or spiritual practices (e.g., prayer, meditation) willingly	

When you have completed Worksheet 2.5, transfer the identified strengths to column 5 of Worksheet 2.6.

This worksheet was originally published in Rashid and Seligman's *Positive Psychotherapy: Clinician Manual.*

WORKSHEET 2.6   COMPILE YOUR SIGNATURE STRENGTHS

This worksheet has columns for you to fill out. Each column is independent of the others.

Column 2 and 3: *Record the five strengths you self-identified from Worksheets 2.1 and 2.2.*

Column 4 and 5: *Record the five strengths identified by your family member from Worksheet 2.4 and the five strengths identified by your friend from Worksheet 2.5.*

Column 6: *Record your top five or six strengths identified from the Signature Strengths Questionnaire:* www.tayyabrashid.com.

Column 7: *Add the scores across each row.*

Column 8: *Identify five strengths that you may be lacking (Underuse) or have in excess (Overuse).*

Column 9: *Identify five strengths that you would like to possess.*

Signature Strengths Profile

Column 1		Column 2	Column 3	Column 4	Column 5	Column 6	Column 7	Column 8	Column 9
Strengths		WS2.1 Heart	WS2.2 Head	WS2.4 Family	WS2.5 Friend	SSQ- 72	Totals	U/O	Desired
1	Creativity & Originality								
2	Curiosity, Interest in the World								
3	Open-Mindedness, Critical Thinking								
4	Love of Learning								
5	Perspective & Wisdom								
6	Bravery & Valor								
7	Persistence, Diligence & Industry								
8	Integrity, Authenticity & Honesty								
9	Vitality, Zest, Enthusiasm & Energy								
10	Love: Capacity to Love and Be Loved								
11	Kindness & Generosity								
12	Social Intelligence								
13	Citizenship, Teamwork & Loyalty								
14	Fairness, Equity & Justice								
15	Leadership								
16	Forgiveness & Mercy								
17	Humility & Modesty								
18	Prudence, Caution & Discretion								
19	Self-Regulation & Self-Control								
20	Appreciation of Beauty								
21	Gratitude								
22	Hope & Optimism								
23	Humor & Playfulness								
24	Spirituality & Religiousness								

This worksheet was originally published in Rashid and Seligman's *Positive Psychotherapy: Clinician Manual.*

Reflect & Discuss

Reflect on and discuss the following:

- After considering various perspectives, how well do your signature strengths reflect your personality? Would your signature strengths adequately describe your personality to someone who knows nothing about you?
- Are there significant differences among your perspective and those of your family, friend, and the questionnaire (SSQ-72)? Did multiple people identify the same specific strengths? Explain.
- After compiling your profile, did you find out that you display specific strengths with specific people or in specific situations? Explain.
- When you think about your life thus far, which of your strengths have always existed? Which strengths are new? What can you learn from this?
- How do your strengths work together in synergy?

In the space provided, first list your signature strengths taken from your signature strengths profile. Next, using the provided questions, briefly write about specific experiences, including anecdotes about one or more of your signature strengths. Note that the questions will help to highlight key markers (authenticity) of your signature strengths.

My Signature Strengths, according to my profile are:
1.
2.
3.
4.
5.
6.
QUESTIONS to Determine Key Markers of Signature Strengths
1. **Authenticity:** Is this strength a core part of me?
2. **Excitement:** When I use my signature strength(s), do I feel excited?
3. **Learning:** Is it natural and effortless for me to use this strength?
4. **Finding new ways to use**: Do I yearn to find new ways to use my strength(s)?
5. **Persistence:** Do I find it difficult to stop an activity that fully uses this strength?
6. **Invigoration:** Does using this strength make me feel invigorated instead of exhausted?
7. **Projects to Use the Strength:** Do I create personal projects designed to make use of this strength?
8. **Enthusiastic:** Do I feel joyous, zestful, and enthusiastic while using this strength?

This worksheet was originally published in Rashid and Seligman's *Positive Psychotherapy: Clinician Manual.*

POSITIVE PSYCHOTHERAPY

Reflect & Discuss

Reflect on and discuss the following:

- Which signature strength stood out for you in terms of specific markers (e.g., authenticity, learning, or invigoration)? Explain why.
- After completing this worksheet, how confident do you feel about your signature strengths?
- Please review all 24 strengths. Are there strengths not identified by your profile that you feel should be there, in terms of the markers listed in Worksheet 2.7? Why did these strengths not make the list of your top five or six signature strengths?

Read the following description of the strengths. Put a minus sign next to three strengths you might be underusing (or lacking altogether). Put a plus sign next to three strengths you overuse. (Note that these strengths do not have to be one of your signature strengths.)

Then for each of your signature strengths, specify a corresponding lack/underuse and excess/overuse, if applicable.

Character Strength		Description	Underuse or Lacking	Overuse or Excess
1	Creativity & Originality	Thinking of new and better ways of doing things; not being content with doing things in conventional ways		
2	Curiosity & Openness to Experience	Being driven to explore things; asking questions, not tolerating ambiguity easily; being open to different experiences and activities		
3	Open-Mindedness & Critical Thinking	Thinking through and examining all sides before deciding; consulting with trusted others; being flexible to change one's mind when necessary		
4	Love of Learning	Loving to learn many things, concepts, ideas, and facts in school or on one's own		
5	Perspective (wisdom)	Putting things together to understand underlying meaning; settling disputes among friends; learning from mistakes		
6	Bravery & Valor	Overcoming fears to do what needs to be done; not giving up in the face of a hardship or challenge		
7	Perseverance, Persistence, & Industry	Finishing most things; being able to refocus when distracted and completing the task without complaining; overcoming challenges to complete the task		
8	Integrity, Authenticity, & Honesty	Not pretending to be someone one is not; coming across as a genuine and honest person		
9	Vitality, Zest, Enthusiasm, & Energy	Being energetic, cheerful, and full of life; being chosen by others to hang out with		
10	Love: Capacity to Love and Be Loved	Having warm and caring relationships with family and friends; showing genuine love and affection through actions regularly		
11	Kindness & Generosity	Doing kind deeds for others, often without asking; helping others regularly; being known as a kind person		
12	Social Intelligence	Easily understanding others' feelings; managing oneself well in social situations; displaying excellent interpersonal skills		
13	Citizenship, Teamwork, & Loyalty	Relating well with teammates or group members; contributing to the success of the group		
14	Fairness, Equity, & Justice	Standing up for others when they are treated unfairly, bullied, or ridiculed; day-to-day actions show a sense of fairness		
15	Leadership	Organizing activities that include others; being someone others like to follow; being often chosen to lead by peers		

Character Strength		Description	Underuse or Lacking	Overuse or Excess
16	Forgiveness & Mercy	Forgiving easily those who offend; not holding grudges		
17	Humility & Modesty	Not liking to be the center of attention; not acting special; admitting shortcomings readily; knowing what one can and cannot do. Letting others shine.		
18	Prudence, Caution, & Discretion	Being careful and cautious; avoid taking undue risks; not easily yielding to external pressures		
19	Self-Regulation & Self-Control	Managing feelings and behavior well; gladly following rules and routines		
20	Appreciation of Beauty & Excellence	Being moved deeply by beauty in nature, in art (painting, music, theatre, etc.), or in excellence in any field of life		
21	Gratitude	Expressing thankfulness for good things through words and actions; not taking things for granted		
22	Hope, Optimism, & Future-mindedness	Hoping and believing that more good things will happen than bad ones; recovering quickly from setbacks and taking concrete steps to overcome them		
23	Humor & Playfulness	Being playful, funny, and using humor to connect with others		
24	Religiousness & Spirituality	Believing in God or a higher power; liking to participate in religious or spiritual practices, e.g., prayer, meditation		

This worksheet was originally published in Rashid and Seligman's *Positive Psychotherapy: Clinician Manual*.

Reflect & Discuss

Reflect on and discuss the following:

1. Sometimes, what we think of as a negative behavior in others can be under- or overuse of strengths. Reflect on these common scenarios and discuss which might be a reflection of the under- or overusage of a strength:
   a. Someone feeling sad and slow
   b. Someone worrying too much about small things or worrying about minute details that may not be critical
   c. Someone always being in a playful and humorous mood
   d. Someone who fails to confront his friend for inappropriate behavior
   e. Someone who may be taking too many projects or assignments
2. Often it is not clear-cut or straightforward to distinguish a balanced use of a strength from its over- or underuse. Take curiosity as an example. Curiosity entails actively seeking knowledge to open oneself to new experiences. Its underuse (disinterest, apathy, or boredom) may be easily recognizable, but its overuse may be difficult to spot. One could actively seek knowledge for many purposes, including Facebook stalking others. The latter behavior would most likely be nosiness. Similarly, zest can range from displaying vitality and enthusiasm to manic, hysterical, or frantic behavior. Consider your signature strengths and reflect on what specific behaviors and actions may let you know if you are under- or overusing a strength.
3. Are there any specific situations or circumstances that reinforce under- or overuse of one of your signature strengths?
4. Are there some cultural factors that endorse under- or overuse of specific strengths? For example, some cultures put greater emphasis on humility, while others emphasize teamwork or social intelligence.
5. If you overuse one of your signature strengths—say, creativity—can you think of other strengths (such as self-regulation, modesty, or prudence) that may not be one of your signature strengths but can still help you to use creativity in a balanced way?

In Real Life: Rochelle, 32, female, Caucasian

I am considered quite a psychologically minded person. Many friends consult with me when they are in an emotional pickle. I did not have the best of childhoods. The lives and choices of people close to me unleashed many toxins, which affected many areas of my life. I spent a lot of time thinking about these toxins. In "thinking expeditions," upon which I often embarked after a setback, I focused on how emotionally fragile, weak, and vulnerable I felt. But it was the deeper and nuanced knowledge of my strengths—from multiple sources including friends and family—that helped me to convince myself that I am not merely a pile of weakness and past mishaps. Rather, I am a complex mosaic of weaknesses and strengths. This knowledge was very timely, because, awkwardly enough, I was becoming comfortable with my symptoms. Knowing and owning my strengths—which initially sounded weird—has helped me perceive myself more holistically, more humanely.

Tips to Maintain Your Progress

Discuss the following tips with your clinician to help you maintain your progress.

As human beings, our ability to spot negativity within ourselves—and around ourselves—is far sharper, deeper, and more stubborn than our ability to note positives. This tendency grows whenever we experience negative events.

If you don't do anything about this negativity bias, you will likely remain stuck in negativity and, in turn, it will stick with you, often manifesting through chronic anxiety, sadness, anger, ambivalence, and isolation. You probably assume, like most of us, that psychotherapy is the place to discuss these negatives, and indeed it is. However, psychotherapy is also a place where you can also explore what makes you resilient, without ignoring your vulnerabilities; where you can discover your hopes and dreams, without dismissing your despair and illusions; and where you can acquire skills to build your strengths, without ignoring your weaknesses. Engaging in such an effort in a sustained way can reset your negativity lens. The systematic ways you learn to spot and use your strengths can prepare you to apply this learning in other areas of your life such as at work and at home, and it can expand your general outlook toward life. Here is an example:

> Karen, a young female client, found it very difficult to think of herself in strengths terms. She perceived herself as an "undesirable package" with a history of hospitalization for chronic suicidal ideation, psychotic breaks, and a preoccupation with negative memories of the past, including emotional abuse and loss of close family members. After much skepticism, Karen began to explore her strengths. Love of learning, curiosity, creativity, bravery, and leadership turned out to be her signature strengths. When asked to share concrete experiences related to each strength, this young woman stated that she entered college as one of the top scholars in her province with a full scholarship. Despite all her challenges, Karen was able to maintain her academic standing and always made the Dean's List. She has given talks to many high school girls about overcoming the stigma of seeking timely help. Just sharing these concrete events shifted her mood, and she said, "I just realized, my life is not that bad. I can still do some things."

Can you identify with Karen in some ways? Ask yourself, what sorts of stories do you tell yourself? What is the underlying theme of your stories? Much like the *Positive Introduction* practice in which you recalled an event that brought out the best in you, and your daily *Gratitude Journal* practice of looking at good things that happen, this practice of acknowledging your strengths can help you orient your mindset toward more positive aspects within you and around you. We are good at attributing negatives (e.g., his dishonesty caused the embezzlement), and knowledge of strengths will help you make positive attributions in daily life (e.g., her kindness helped her friend with a place to stay after she had to leave an abusive relationship).

Positive psychotherapy practices will help you to know and understand your strengths in depth. From mere labels, you will learn to internalize your strengths. The following are some illustrations of client self-descriptions at the start of therapy and then after exploring strengths; these statements demonstrate how these clients internalized the strengths perspective into their personality.

Client 1
At the start of therapy

> I am hopeless, I don't think I will ever find a person who would understand me. Soon after a first date, I start seeing their real and negative side. . . . Perhaps I am only good at attracting the wrong person.

After exploring strengths

> I feel better that others have spotted some strengths in me. I never thought that, despite not being able to find the right person, I am perceived as a kind, socially intelligent, prudent, and humble person. This was quite helpful. As soon as I start dating, I know that I need not worry too much and overuse my prudence in judging the person too quickly. Instead, I will use my kindness and social intelligence to understand the other person.

Client 2
At the start of therapy

Many a times, I have asked myself, is that it?

After exploring strengths

I never realized that I get moved deeply by the wonders of nature. The last time I was close to nature, I was in absolute awe; my mind, body, and spirit were all at ease. Perhaps there is more to life than I think.

Client 3
At the start of therapy

I am known to be a lively person who never escapes from challenges; I embrace them. But lately, I cannot seem to get it right. . . . Often I do the right thing but at the wrong time or the right thing with the wrong person.

After exploring strengths

I can put things in perspective. . . . Knowing that zest is one of my signature strengths, and that others see it too, makes sense; I am easily inspired, passionate, and throw everything into the activities that I undertake. Perhaps a little prudence can serve me better.

Client 4
At the start of therapy

I deliberately hold off expressing my love and affection to my partner. Perhaps I am afraid I may come across to the person I am dating as weak, dependent, and insecure.

After exploring strengths

I didn't realize that I am overly cautious; I need to open up in order to give and receive love. I didn't realize that it is a strength. . . . I used to think that too much expression of love could make me vulnerable.

Client 5
At the start of therapy

I cannot grow until I get rid of all my faults.

After exploring strengths

I have spent hundreds, if not thousands, of hours with therapists, life coaches, amazing motivational speakers, and spiritual gurus to correct my weaknesses,. . . but always felt I couldn't get rid of them. . . . I always felt due to my weaknesses, I would never measure up to the expectations of my high achieving father. . . . Identifying my strengths has made a serious dent in my thinking . . . perhaps I would be better off building my strengths than trying to get rid of my faults.

RESOURCES

Readings

- Linley, A. (2008). *Average to A+: Realising Strengths in Yourself and Others*. Coventry, UK: CAPP Press.
- Niemiec, R. M., & Wedding, D. (2014). *Positive Psychology at the Movies: Using Films to Build Character Strengths and Well-Being* (2nd ed.). Boston: Hogrefe.
- Polly, S., & Britton, K. (2015). *Character Strengths Matter: How to Live a Full Life*. Washington, DC: Positive Psychology News.

Videos

- What Are Your Character Strengths? A brief video to assess character strengths (Worksheet 2.1: What Are Your "Heart" Strengths):
  https://youtu.be/K-3IjNr1gCg
- A TEDxUTSC Talk on importance of character strengths in psychotherapy by Tayyab Rashid:
  https://youtu.be/Q6W5IrZH7tc
- The Science of Character: an eight-minute documentary presenting a compelling case for character strengths toward a fulfilling life:
  https://youtu.be/p0fK4837Bgg

Websites

- The VIA Institute on Character Strengths offers invaluable resources on both the science and practice of character, with free measure of character strengths:
  http://www.viacharacter.org

3

SESSION THREE: PRACTICAL WISDOM

SESSION THREE PRESENTS THE SKILLS OF PRACTICAL wisdom. These skills teach us how to apply our signature strengths in a balanced way to solve problems. The central positive psychotherapy (PPT) practice covered in this session is *Know-How of Strengths*.

THREE THINGS TO KNOW ABOUT *PRACTICAL WISDOM*

1. **Use strengths adaptively:** Practical wisdom is about using character strengths adaptively (in a healthy, positive way). The strengths you identified in the previous session don't pop up in daily life in isolation. Rather, they are embedded (or ought to be) in everyday situations that range from relatively straight forward to complex. Depending on the dynamics of the situation, using more of a strength (e.g., kindness, creativity, optimism, forgiveness, or bravery) may not necessarily achieve the best outcome for you. In other words, through the use of practical wisdom, you can figure out which of your strengths to use and how best to use them in a given situation.
2. **Reflect:** Utilizing practical wisdom skills also requires you to reflect on the impact of your strengths on others. You need to take into account the moral implications of exercising your signature strengths on a larger scale. For example, exercising spirituality from a specific tradition in the public realm may alienate those who don't subscribe to those beliefs. Exercising love of learning may negatively impact the self-confidence of those who struggle with learning due to a learning disability. Showing kindness selectively may create feelings of discrimination.
3. **Calibrate:** Keep your fingers on the pulse of the situation. Stay tuned in to the situation so that you can sense any change, and calibrate and recalibrate the use of your strengths as situational dynamics may require you to make changes. Think of strengths not as categories but as dimensions; that is, situational dynamics may require varying degrees of a strength. For example, specific dimensions or degrees of kindness or self-regulation may be needed to manage a particular situation. Likewise, some situations may be resolved by restraining your impulse, while others by managing or exerting control over irrelevant factors to stay focused to finish the task.

START-OF-SESSION RELAXATION

At the start of the session, your clinician may begin with a brief relaxation exercise. To discover some of these practices on your own, go to Appendix A: Relaxation & Mindfulness Practices, which can be found at the end of this workbook.

IN-SESSION PRACTICE: *KNOW-HOW OF STRENGTHS*

Your clinician will be working with you on the in-session practices. Refer to Worksheets 3.1 to 3.3.

Use the following illustration to diagram your strengths by turning your strengths into behaviors (the actions, activities, and habits you do when displaying your strengths). Select larger circles to indicate the strengths you overuse and smaller circles for strengths you underuse. Use intersecting circles to indicate strengths that overlap with one another.

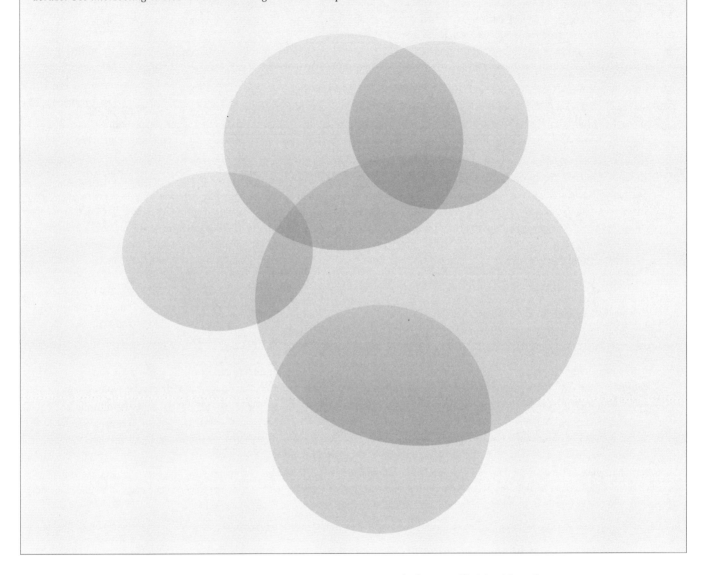

This worksheet was originally published in Rashid and Seligman's *Positive Psychotherapy: Clinician Manual.*

Following are five strategies for building practical wisdom, or Know-How of Strengths:

1. **Seek Specificity:** Complex real-life situations and challenges do not present themselves with clear instructions for which actions best represent a specific strength. One way to seek specificity is to consider the outcome. For example, if for you the outcome of using your love of learning is to increase knowledge, you can translate the outcome in specific terms, such as reading a specific number of books or articles to increase knowledge.

    To help you grasp the nuances of signature strengths and translate them into concrete actions, consult Appendix D: Building Your Strengths, which appears at the end of this workbook. This appendix offers multiple behavioral ways of using strengths.

2. **Find Relevance:** Explore if your signature strength is relevant to the situation at hand. For example, kindness and forgiveness may not be relevant in situations that need to be dealt with using fairness or courage. In some situations, your signature strengths of humility or playfulness may be very relevant, but in situations that need you to assert your rights, humility may not work; in situations that require us to empathize with others who may have just experienced a trauma, playfulness may not be appropriate.

3. **Resolve Conflict:** The third skill is understanding how to resolve a situation in which the use of two signature strengths may conflict with one another. For example, you are doing a project and want to do the best possible job. You want to utilize your signature strength of creativity or persistence. At the same time, your closest friend needs your time and company (signature strength: love). Or your signature strengths of zest and self-regulation may pull you in different directions. Resolve these conflicts by deciding which signature strength is more closely aligned with your core values or which signature strength will yield the optimal outcome.

4. **Reflect:** Practical Wisdom entails ability to take multiple perspectives anticipating and imaging the impact of your actions one others.

    It is also important that you reflect upon the goal, aim or purpose of your actions. How your goals impact you and or others. For example, if you want to exercise your strengths of bravery, reflect if your action of bravery doesn't jeopardize wellbeing of others. On the other hand, reflect how humor can lighten up a tense situation.

5. **Calibrate:** To nurture practical wisdom skills, you also need to regularly stay attuned to the situation, sense change, and calibrate and recalibrate (i.e., fine-tune) your use of strengths to suit the demands of the situation. Many people are unable to solve their problems, as they keep trying ineffective solutions or do not change their approach as the situation changes.

Now read the following three scenarios and under each one write the specific advice you would give to each person:

Accommodating and Considerate: Early in Jane's relationship with Jimmy, Jane understood that Jimmy becomes insecure and jealous as soon as he sees her talking to another guy, especially someone who Jimmy feels is "better" than he. But Jane is finding it hard to break up with Jimmy as she is known to be one of the most "accommodating" and "considerate" people around.

> ***Your Advice:***
>
> _____
>
> _____
>
> _____

All I want is to be happy: Lee, a young man in his mid-20s, often repeated the same thing in therapy. Followed by a long list of positives, such as "I work very hard; I was hired even before I finished my undergraduate degree; I am told that I am good-looking, funny, sporty, and helpful. I never hurt anyone, I have never argued with anyone (in my adult life) . . .," Lee would conclude with, "but I don't feel happy."

Your Advice:

_____

_____

_____

Just Talking Helps: Heena, a 21-year-old female, is making no progress in therapy—by all indicators (objective and clinical). Heena continues to report suicidal ideation although she has never made any attempt, and she resists any change and wants to continue therapy. She states that "just talking to someone helps."

Your Advice:

_____

_____

_____

This worksheet was originally published in Rashid and Seligman's *Positive Psychotherapy: Clinician Manual.*

Write about a current challenge you are facing and may have been trying to resolve. Describe it in concrete terms: What it is? When did it start, and how long has it been going on? In what ways has it been challenging?

The Challenge	Your Reflections
Describe a current challenge that needs to be solved.	
When did it start? How long has it lasted?	
What are its effects?	
Is it due to overuse of your strengths? Which ones? How?	
What aspects of this challenge would you like to change?	
Which specific practical wisdom strategy can you use to make adaptive changes?	

This worksheet was originally published in Rashid and Seligman's *Positive Psychotherapy: Clinician Manual.*

Reflect & Discuss

- Reflect on and discuss the following: Let's assume that you are able to use one of the practical wisdom strategies effectively in resolving the problem identified in Worksheet 3.3. What would it look like if this problem is resolved? What specific behaviors you would be doing? And what behaviors would stop? Try to answer as concretely as possible.
- Keeping the desirable behaviors in mind, what small, manageable, specific, and concrete steps can help you remain engaged and motivated in these behaviors?
- The practical wisdom strategy or strategies you have identified here will most likely require support from others. Who will support you? If you are unable to get this support, what alternative supports can you think of?

In Real Life: James, 42, male, Caucasian

James, a manager in a tech company, participated in a PPT-based workshop, during which he focused on self-development and compiled his signature strengths profile. After tabulating all sources, James felt that he was overusing his strength of leadership, and he was unsure of how to use his signature strength of authenticity, especially at work. The following are excerpts from his self-development plan, which required him to use practical wisdom strategies toward an adaptive use of his signature strengths:

I found practical wisdom strategies quite interesting. I will use them as follows:

- *Relevance: Relevant and useful to my situation. For example, my strength of being authentic and honest can lead to panicking under certain stressful situations. I am gradually learning the "where, when, and with whom" I should exercise my authenticity. I have learned that I am comfortable being totally authentic with my best friend—my wife. We have only been together for five years or so, but during these five years, we have grown together in such a way that I feel comfortable being myself and vice versa. However, using the strategy of relevance, I feel it is not helpful to be totally authentic at my workplace. I don't mean that I should act in a superficial way, but being a leader requires me to adhere to certain standards. For example, I do react strongly with a few staff members who I think are not fully on board with my company's strategic goals. And there are others who go above and beyond. In appreciating them, I cannot be fully "authentic," as this will give the impression that I favor those who are in agreement with me.*
- *Reflect: The signature strengths profile and the part related to under- and overuse of strengths has also helped me to understand that I sometimes use my strength of leadership in situations where it brings out negativity, instead of solving problems. I am leader of this company, but there are staff members who have been in this field much longer than I have. Reflection has helped me to see that although I am aware of newer technologies and smarter ways of doing things, I need to be sensitive to the fact that senior staff members may feel that my leadership diminishes their roles. By utilizing reflection, I have started consulting with them as to where their strengths can help the company and how they can take on some initiatives. Likewise, at family gatherings for Christmas and Easter, instead of taking charge of a lot of the preparations, I have, and will continue to, distribute various tasks among family members, especially as my nieces and nephews are growing up and can plan and execute things well.*
- *Calibrate: Calibration seems to be the most important skill, and also the toughest one to develop. While I promptly respond to acute situations at home and at work, I still need to develop the skills of how to calibrate my strengths*

as situations change. For example, when and where do I lead, and when and where do I follow? Or in which situations should I be kind and courteous to my employees who need to take time off, and when do I confront them if I feel that they are taking off too many days and not utilizing other resources provided by the company, such as supplementary medical benefits to help a family member, rather than staying home to be with them.

Tips to Maintain Your Progress

Blaine Fowers (2005) offers specific strategies which can help us to reinforce practical wisdom. Discuss the following tips with your clinician to help you maintain your progress:

- Sometimes your signature strengths may conflict with one another. For example, your courage may want you to take risks and explore a new and unknown route, and your prudence may caution against it. You may want to be kind to your friend, and your fairness demands that you ought to confront him over an ethical violation that impacts others. You want be empathic with your subordinate, and also feel compelled to let her know that her job may be cut. Or you want to be authentic with yourself, and social and cultural norms force you against it. Use the strategies listed in Worksheet 3.2 to resolve these conflicts through the use of practical wisdom strategies. Also, use your signature (and other) strengths to build perspective, one you may not see from simply following rules and regulations.
- When unsure which signature strength to use in a given context, rely on emotions to first hear and feel what the situation demands. Before acting, make emotion a partner with reason; educate emotions through other strengths.
- Make sure that you are using your signature strengths to do the right thing. Consult with wise minds about what is the right thing to do, within the circumstances.
- Understand that not every situation can be resolved by using signature strengths. Don't be afraid to experiment with your alternative strengths, skills, abilities, and talents.

RESOURCES
Readings
- Lama, D., & Tutu, D. (2016). *The Book of Joy: Lasting Happiness in a Changing World*. New York: Penguin Random House.
- Schwartz, B., & Sharpe, K. E. (2010). *Practical Wisdom: The Right Way to Do the Right Thing*. New York: Penguin.
- Sternberg, R. J. (Ed.). (1990). *Wisdom: Its Nature, Origins, and Development*. Cambridge: Cambridge University Press.

Videos
- TED Talk: Barry Schwartz: Using our Practical Wisdom: https://youtu.be/IDS-ieLCmS4
- TED Talk: Joshua Prager: Wisdom from Great Writers on Every Year of Our Life: https://www.ted.com/talks/joshua_prager_wisdom_from_great_writers_on_every_year_of_life

Websites
- Centre for Practical Wisdom: University of Chicago: http://wisdomresearch.org/
- Podcast: A Word to the Wise: Canadian Broadcasting Cooperation's Program, Ideas: http://www.cbc.ca/radio/ideas/a-word-to-the-wise-part-1-1.2913730

SESSION FOUR: *A BETTER VERSION OF ME*

4

SESSION FOUR, THE LAST OF THE SESSIONS focusing on character strengths, looks at articulating and implementing a written plan of positive, pragmatic, and persistent self-development. The central positive psychotherapy (PPT) practice covered in this session is *A Better Version of Me*.

THREE THINGS TO KNOW ABOUT *A BETTER VERSION OF ME*

Like many of us, you may want to improve yourself, to overcome challenges or to improve your level of happiness and well-being.

1. **Self-improvement:** Self-improvement is an age-old goal, and, like many other folks, you may want to improve yourself. Perhaps you want to be more relaxed, grounded, engaged, energized, creative, connected, reflective, social, satisfied, happier, or healthier. This desire for self-improvement—with a specific vision— can connect your motivation with specific action or vice versa. This specific PPT practice can help you to take actions toward creating a better version of yourself that optimally utilizes your strengths, skills, and abilities.
2. **Values and behavior:** A "best self" is created by imagining and then striving toward personal goals. What are your goals—personal and professional? Before charting a course to accomplish them, it might be helpful if you also clarify your values and day-to-day behavior.
3. **Refraining:** Creating a better version of yourself may also include cultivating positive and desirable actions and may require you to refrain, abstain, reduce, or replace some old and undesirable habits (e.g., giving up junk food, smoking, alcohol, being sedentary, staying up late, brooding, or obsessing). A balance between refraining from old habits and engaging in actions which use your strengths and yield positive emotions is likely to help you succeed in creating a better version of yourself.

START-OF-SESSION RELAXATION
At the start of the session, your clinician may begin with a brief relaxation exercise. To discover some of these practices on your own, go to Appendix A: Relaxation & Mindfulness Practices, which can be found at the end of this workbook.

IN-SESSION PRACTICE: *A BETTER VERSION OF ME*
Your clinician will be working with you on the in-session practices. Refer to Worksheet 4.1.

The Plan

Set Realistic Goals

What would be a better version of me on [Day,   Month,   Year   ]?

Set goals that are: • Concrete and observable through behaviors, actions, and habits • Well integrated with your current life situation • Not in conflict with your values • Supported by your social networks	Specify some changes you want to see: • More relaxed? More grounded? • More enthusiastic? More energized? • More engaged? More creative? • More connected? More reflective? • More social? More relaxed? • Happier? Healthier?

Complete these Sentences

This *Better Version of Me* will make me happier or more satisfied because

_____

It is something good for me because

_____

It is someone I always wanted to be because

_____

It is someone I have to be because

_____

Create a Timeline

Date of Plan: _____

Date of Anticipated Completion: _____

Mid-point (insert approximate date): _____

Partner with Someone

Name of friend who is willing to support me: _____

How frequently will the person check with me about my progress? _____

How will we communicate?   By Phone?   By Email?   In Person?

Examples of Goals for A Better Version of Me

Emotional Resilience	Social Resilience
More relaxed/grounded	More deeply connected with friends
• I will start a relaxation routine (e.g., breathe deeply a couple times a day, attend a weekly yoga/meditation class) • I will incorporate deliberate idle time (at least 15 minutes daily) when I will do nothing • Next time I become upset, I will take a break before reacting, breathe deeply, consult with someone who can give me an impartial perspective, or try to ask more questions to understand the context • I will eliminate at least one thing that distracts me from being focused and productive • I will take time to do/play something that I really enjoy	• I will spot the specific strengths, abilities, skills of others and compliment them • I will ask a friend who I care about, yet have not emotionally understood, specific ways in which I can better connect with him or her • I will engage in a meaningful yet fun activity with my friend which is mutually appealing to us (e.g., snow shoeing, rock climbing, playing a board game, going to a sporting event/ performance together) • I will have a one-on-one lunch or dinner date with my close friend, during which electronic devices will be off • I will do one kind act (big or small) for my friend without being asked
Physical Resilience	Work Place Resilience
More Energized/Healthier	More Engaged
• I will create an exercise routine that I can maintain on a regular basis (three times a week) • I will add at least one healthy snack to my daily eating plan • I will vow not to sit for X amount of time, and will incorporate physical activity every X (hour) into my routine • I will improve my sleep by doing at least one thing consistently (e.g., stop eating at least two hours before bedtime, stop looking at a screen at least one hour before going to bed, say no to events/activities that consistently impact my sleep adversely) • I will adopt at least one habit that will improve my physical health (e.g., wash hands, have regular checkups)	• I will familiarize myself with my work/job requirements by reviewing tasks required, deadlines, etc. • I will give each project the time and effort it deserves and will make it optimally engaging • If procrastination is a problem, I will change my inner dialogue for at least two of these: I have to TO *I choose to* I must finish TO *Where and when can I start?* The project is too large TO *I can divide the assignment into small steps* My project must be perfect TO *Not all of my projects can be perfect, I will strive for what is humanly possible, not perfect*

This worksheet was originally published in Rashid and Seligman's *Positive Psychotherapy: Clinician Manual.*

Reflect & Discuss
Reflect on and discuss the following:

- The worksheet required a long visualization. How would you describe the overall experience of visualizing a better version of yourself? Were you able to follow along, or did you experienced some challenges? Please share.
- How was the experience of writing about what your visualized? Were you able to capture what you visualized or did you struggle?
- Did this exercise help you to generate concrete ideas for a better version of yourself?
- How concrete are the ideas you generated? This practice works better when you are able to formulate concreate ideas which are realistic and which you can manage reasonably well.
- In case you struggled to generate concrete ideas, having a clear picture of a better version of yourself can still work. In our experience, having a clear image or perception of what a person wants to be—even if he or she has difficulty coming up with concrete ideas of how to get there—allows that person to focus on the process and ultimate goal. For you, what worked—a clear image of a better version, or concrete paths that lead to this better version, or both?

In Real Life: De Veillies, 34, male, South African descent

De Veillies, a business executive, describes his experience with *A Better Version of Me*:

> *I have attended many retreats, workshops, and courses—every time with the desire to find the best of me. Each attempt started with unbridled optimism. Each attempt—without exception—ended with more ambivalence, as I found something new that I did not like about myself. Vacillating between dips of depression and jolts of mania, I always wanted to be the best in everything. I perceived anything less than the best as the worst. Used to this roller-coaster ride, the notion of "A Better Version of Me," seemed less than satisfactory from the endless pool of possibilities. However, my therapist motivated me to trust the process. With a less than flattering record of trusting myself, I yielded, rather begrudgingly. Instead of being the best, I was asked to strive to become better than my past week and month. I want to be a better version of myself in terms of controlling my anger and reactions—something I have struggled with all my life. Every week, during therapy, I reviewed my weekly progress and set weekly goals. I learned simple relaxation techniques that helped me manage my anger better—deep breathing, calming my hot thoughts with a one minute mindfulness practice. I learned that not responding immediately is also an option available to me. I learned that if I can calm myself, I can even remember and use my strengths of open-mindedness, finding a creative solution to the situation, by using perspective to focus on the forest, not on the trees. Hearing from my therapist that I can use, and possibly enhance, my strengths has been quite reassuring. I am not sure if I have found the best within me, but I am happy to find "A Better Version of Me." I am still a work in progress, although I feel I have made good progress in becoming a better version of myself.*

Tips to Maintain Your Progress
Discuss the following tips with your clinician to help you maintain your progress:

- We each have many selves, including some that we like and desire to develop further and others that we dislike and want to change (Markus & Nurius, 1986).

The practice of *A Better Version of Me* offers you a structured way to develop a self you want to develop. You can repeat or revise this practice as many times as you want as long as you are clear about *which* specific desirable self you are moving toward.

- In developing a better version of yourself, select activities that you find realistic and relevant, and ones you can sustain over a period of time. (For examples, see the suggestions toward the end of Worksheet 4.1.) Sustenance doesn't mean that you don't allow yourself to deviate. Some situations may require to you alter your routine. These may include skipping exercise to help a friend who needs timely help, being less creative if a project needs to be completed within a specific time and budget, and curtailing courageous actions if these bring more chaos than calm.

- Although *A Better Version of Me* requires specific details (concrete actions to be done, when, how, where, and with frequency), it is also okay that you initiate this process (of becoming a better person) without having all relevant details. Sometimes, the mere commitment to become a better person is sufficient, and you can add relevant details as you go along. In other words, it is fine that you enjoy the process, as long as you remain committed to the outcome.

- Sometimes your negativity bias, which may be well entrenched in your self-concept, can impede your progress—and may be something you cannot change. You can postpone this practice and move on to other PPT practices that may help you undo the negativity bias, hopefully motivating you to take on the challenge of creating a better version of yourself.

- You should also keep in mind that the *A Better Version of Me* practice encourages you to create a *better*—not necessarily the *best*—version of yourself. It may take a while to create the best version. In the meantime, you can create multiple better versions. The cumulative effects of these versions may help you eventually create and sustain the most desirable version of yourself.

- While pursuing this practice, a setback or an acute challenge may derail your progress. Remind yourself that the ultimate judge of your better version is *you*. As long as you are putting forth your best effort—a better version of yourself will take shape.

RESOURCES
Readings
- Rubin, G. (2015). *Better Than Before: What I Learned About Making and Breaking Habits—To Sleep More, Quit Sugar, Procrastinate Less, and Generally Build a Happier Life*. Toronto: Imprint.
- Seligman, M. E. P. (1993). *What You Can Change . . . and What You Can't: The Complete Guide to Successful Self-Improvement*. New York: Fawcett Columbine.
- Sheldon, K. M. (2004). *Optimal Human Being: An Integrated Multi-Level Perspective*. Mahwah, NJ: Erlbaum.

Videos
- Barry Schwartz makes a passionate call for "practical wisdom" as an antidote to a society gone mad with bureaucracy. He argues powerfully that rules often fail us, incentives often backfire, and practical, everyday wisdom will help rebuild our world:
  https://www.ted.com/talks/barry_schwartz_on_our_loss_of_wisdom
- You 2.0—What it REALLY Takes to Be the Best Version of Yourself! | Anthony Cheam | TEDxChathamKent. This presentation covers the basis of human transformation and the basic principles of taking command of your life.
  https://youtu.be/M45HDbaW1DI

Websites

- The Max Planck Society's website. Eighty-three institutes of this Germany-based society, including a wisdom institute, conduct basic research in the service of the general public in the natural sciences, life sciences, social sciences, and the humanities: http://www.mpg.de/institutes
- The Science of Older and Wiser: http://www.nytimes.com/2014/03/13/business/retirementspecial/the-science-of-older-and-wiser.html?_r=0
- This website discusses practical wisdom as the master virtue: http://www.artofmanliness.com/2011/12/19/practical-wisdom/
- The Best Possible Self Exercise (Boosts Hope), by Ryan M. Niemiec: http://blogs.psychcentral.com/character-strengths/2012/09/the-best-possible-self-exercise-boosts-hope/

SESSION FIVE: OPEN AND CLOSED MEMORIES

IN SESSION FIVE, WHICH IS THE START of Phase Two of positive psychotherapy (PPT), you will learn to recall, write, and process your open (negative) and closed (positively resolved) memories. You will learn to develop skills for dealing with open memories through the PPT practice of *Positive Appraisal*.

THREE THINGS TO KNOW ABOUT *OPEN MEMORIES*

1. **Open and closed memories:** Open memories are usually the memories of negative experiences and events that you may not have fully understood and for which you don't feel a sense of closure. Closed memories are also memories of negative events, but you feel that you have a sense of closure about these. One way to assess if you have a lot of open memories is to ask yourself, "*Do I feel I am carrying a lot of emotional baggage?*" or "*Does my past prevent me from moving forward?*" Open memories may be triggered unexpectedly and, when they are, they leave you emotionally drained, impacting your day-to-day functioning.

2. **Venting:** Compared to many other forms of psychotherapy that focus more on negative memories of the past (with an assumption that you need to release your pent-up anger), PPT takes a stance that merely letting the anger out is not sufficient for therapeutic change. In fact, elaborate recall of negative experiences may leave you even angrier or in more despair. Without dismissing, minimizing, or overly simplifying your negative experience, PPT—in a safe, collaborate manner—helps you recall negative memories and invites you to assess the impact that holding on to these negative memories has on your emotional and psychological health.

3. **Positive appraisal:** Through the practice of *Positive Appraisal*, you will be invited to try out specific strategies (listed in Worksheet 5.1) to deal adaptively with your open memories. The purpose of these strategies is not to change the event or the person for whom you hold negative memories. Instead, the purpose is to process these memories using your own strengths (such as perspective, open-mindedness, and self-regulation) to refile the memories in such a way that they don't drain you emotionally or psychologically.

START-OF-SESSION RELAXATION
At the start of the session, your clinician may begin with a brief relaxation exercise. To discover some of these practices on your own, go to Appendix A: Relaxation & Mindfulness Practices, which can be found at the end of this workbook.

IN-SESSION PRACTICE: *OPEN MEMORIES*
Your clinician will be working with you on the in-session practices.

Reflect & Discuss

Reflect on and discuss the following:

- If an open or negative memory entails harm and hurt done by someone else, do you find yourself thinking about this person or about the causes and consequences of his or her actions? Would you describe this process as reflective, brooding, wallowing, conclusive, or something else? What are the benefits and disadvantages of this process?
- Have you discussed this negative memory with someone else? If you have, what was the outcome? Did you get another's perspective or vent your feelings?
- What are the long-term effects on your emotional well-being of harboring this negative memory? What can you do to lessen these effects?

IN-SESSION PRACTICE: *CLOSED MEMORIES*

Your clinician will be working with you on the in-session practices.

Reflect & Discuss

Reflect on and discuss the following:

- How has this experience benefitted you as a person?
- Were there personal strengths that grew out of this experience?
- How has the event put your life into perspective?
- How has this event helped you appreciate the truly important people and things in your life? In sum, how can you be thankful for the beneficial consequences that have resulted from this event?

IN-SESSION PRACTICE: *POSITIVE APPRAISAL*

Your clinician will be working with you on the in-session practices. Refer to Worksheet 5.1.

1. **Create Psychological Space:** *You can create psychological space between your lingering negative memory and yourself. One way to do this is to describe the bitter memory from a third person's perspective—that is, without using "I." This will allow you to create some distance between yourself and the open memory, offering you an opportunity to revise your feelings and the meaning of the memory rather than rehashing it.*

    Practice: Imagine you are journalist, photographer, or documentary filmmaker, and in the following space, describe your open memory or grudge from a third-person vantage point. Try to keep the third-person expression less personalized and more neutral.

    _____

    _____

    _____

2. **Reconsolidation:** *When you are immersed in the negative memory, you are unlikely to pay attention to all aspects of the situation because your thinking becomes narrow. Do the following practice when you are in a calm state and not overwhelmed by a current stressor.*

    Practice: Take deep breaths. Recall all the finer and subtle aspects of your open and bitter memory. Try to reinterpret it in the following space, deliberately recalling any positive aspects that you might have missed. Keep negative aspects at bay—as much as you can—because the focus of the practice is to acknowledge and write about the positive aspects of the open memory that you might have missed initially. In doing so, think of your most important values in life, and infuse them in your revised memory (Folkman & Moskowitze, 2000; Van Dillen et al., 2007; Vázquez, 2015).

    _____

    _____

    _____

3. **Mindful Self-focus:** *This practice encourages you to develop a nonjudgmental and sustained mental state whenever an open memory pops up. With a receptive mind, shift your attention to internal and external events and experiences evoked by the negative memory. As the open and negative memory unfolds, try to observe it than react to it.*

    Practice: Step back, and let your open and negative memory unfold in front of your eyes, as if you are watching a film. Be an observer, rather than being swept away by the emotions of memory. Your job is to let unpleasant memories pass by. Repeat this practice a couple of times, and note in the following spaces if your observations help you get used to the open memory and feel less upset.

    _____

    _____

    _____

4. **Diversion:** *We encourage you to sharpen your antenna to promptly recognize cues that activate the recall of your open and bitter memories, and, as soon as that recall begins, immediately try to draw your attention away and engage in a physical or cognitive task that interests you. The sooner you move your attention to a different task, the easier it may be to stop the recall of your open memory. The more often you are able to divert your attention, the better you will learn to recognize the external cues that activate bitter memories. You will then be able to catch them quickly and steer your attention to healthier and more adaptive behaviors.*

    Practice: As soon as an open memory is triggered, try to draw your attention away and engage in a physical or cognitive task that interests you. In the following spaces, write down three experiential, engaging, hands-on, and complex activities that can divert your attention from negative memories.

    _____

    _____

    _____

This worksheet was originally published in Rashid and Seligman's *Positive Psychotherapy: Clinician Manual.*

Reflect & Discuss

Reflect on and discuss the following:

- Of the four positive appraisal strategies, which one(s) do you find to be the most relevant to your open memories?
- After reviewing these four strategies, do you feel that your open memories can be changed, modified, or repacked in a different way that could work for you?
- Reflect upon your open memories. Which ones do you feel are not amenable to *Positive Appraisal*? Remember, you don't have to force yourself to deal with an open memory through *Positive Appraisal*.
- In applying one or more of the *Positive Appraisal* strategies, what sort of social supports will you need? Can you think of an alternative, in case such a support is not available?
- In what ways can these strategies help you in the future, as you encounter complex, ambivalent, or conflictual situations?

In Real Life: Shyria, 26, female, East Asian cultural background

Shyria, a graduate student, was beset with negative memories of having been bullied and ridiculed by her peers for being uncoordinated. She considered herself to be "clumsy and a klutz." She could not participate in sports or the performing arts, despite being one of the brightest students in her class. Starting in elementary school, Shyria was teased and bullied, but she never shared this with her parents. Instead, as she progressed to the upper grades, she avoided activities that would reveal her "clumsiness."

In the safe and secure confines of therapy, she shared her experiences. Through Positive Appraisal strategies, Shyria processed her negative memories and wrote about them. The clinician encouraged her to share these with her mother, which she did. Upon hearing about her daughter's experiences and initially shocked, her mother told Shyria that at age seven, she had been diagnosed with a sensory-motor condition. Her parents had decided not to share the diagnosis with her as she was deemed to be a very sensitive girl. They did not want her to feel different from the other children. Also, as Shyria grew up, her coordination improved and her avoidance of sports and activities that required fine motor skills masked her challenges. Upon hearing this information from her mother, Shyria was able to put things into perspective; she felt that if she had been offered this information earlier, she would not have beaten herself up so much. Nonetheless, she felt a sense of release from her negative memories.

Tips to Maintain Your Progress

Discuss the following tips with your clinician to help you maintain your progress:

- When an open memory keeps revisiting you, especially if it pops up unexpectedly in situations where you least desire it, use the skills learned in this session. If your experience with the practice of *Positive Appraisal* has helped you, consider handling a different open memory—preferably something that still disturbs you but that is not too traumatic. Find a comfortable and quiet place. Start with a mindfulness practice of your choosing—something you have already been doing in PPT. Recall the open memory. Take a couple of deep breaths. Monitor your emotional state. If you are not feeling overwhelmed or emotionally numb, proceed. Remember, the goal is to focus on negative feelings without being overwhelmed by them. If you don't feel overwhelmed, through reflection, elaborate on the memory by adding context from the past (any historical reasons related to this negative experience), from the present (has the situation changed since the incidence?) and related to the future (what are odds that the incident will recur?). Write about any meaning you can extract from the experience that is personally relevant to your well-being. Ask yourself if you can relate to the negative experience in a different way.

- If the open memories keep on disturbing you, using the process described here, try to recall any positive aspects that you might have overlooked at the time of the incident due to stressful circumstances. Due to negativity biases, positive or adaptive aspects of the situation often escape our attention. Recall the details to explore if you overlooked any positives. You can also recall similar situations that may help you to spot overlooked positives.
- Going forward, in stressful or negative situations, try distraction as discussed in the practice of *Positive Appraisal*. Although distraction is not always easy to do, try to shift your focus to a moderately complex cognitive task that engages you (like reading or baking your favorite chocolate cake).

RESOURCES

Readings

- Nolen-Hoeksema, S. (2004). *Women Who Think Too Much: How to Break Free of Overthinking and Reclaim Your Life.* New York: Henry Holt.
- Shapiro, F. (2013). *Getting past your past: Take control of your life with self-help techniques from EMDR therapy.* New York: Macmillan.
- Viscott, D. (1996). *Emotional Resilience: Simple Truths for Dealing with the Unfinished Business of Your Past.* New York: Three Rivers Press.

Videos

- A role-play demonstration about dealing with negative memories and grudges: http://www.webmd.com/mental-health/features/forgive-forget
- Cognitive restructuring in cognitive behavioral therapy, a video from Beck Institute for Cognitive Therapy: https://youtu.be/orPPdMvaNGA
- Quiet Positive Distractions—Explained by Crabtree Innovations: https://youtu.be/GhMaliATDNI
- Author and therapist Paul Gilbert explores how awareness of how our own minds work can help break negative thought patterns and help us to become more compassionate: https://youtu.be/pz9Fr_v9Okw

Websites

- MIT Technology Review: Repairing Bad Memories, June 17, 2013: http://www.technologyreview.com/featuredstory/515981/repairing-bad-memories/
- The Science of Happiness—An Experiment in Gratitude: https://youtu.be/oHv6vTKD6lg?list=PL373A068F767AD185

6

SESSION SIX: FORGIVENESS

SESSION SIX TEACHES THAT FORGIVENESS IS A process for change rather than an event. This session explains what forgiveness is and what it is not. The central positive psychotherapy (PPT) practices covered in this session are *REACH*, which is an approach to forgiveness, and writing a *Forgiveness Letter*.

THREE THINGS TO KNOW ABOUT *FORGIVENESS*

1. **Forgiveness is a choice:** Forgiveness offers you a choice to stop the longing to get back at someone who has hurt you. Thinking about the hurt, offence, or transgression naturally evokes the feeling of wanting to get back at the person who hurt you. However, think about the times you were able to take revenge and whether those actions resulted in halting the cycle of negativity. Instead, think about choosing forgiveness as a process of forsaking or abandoning those who have hurt you. By forgiving, not only will you give the offender a second chance, but you may also free up your own emotional and mental spaces that are being occupied by thoughts, memories, images, and desires of enacting revenge.

2. **Understand the nuances of the choice:** Forgiveness is not an easy choice. You need to explore if it is a choice you can enact and hold onto. This exploration needs to be deep and nuanced in the sense that you should not confuse forgiveness with other things that may look like forgiveness.

3. **Forgiveness is gradual:** If you continue to feel strong revenge-related emotions and cannot bring yourself to forgive the person, don't force yourself. Understand that forgiveness is a gradual process, rather than a switch to turn on or off. Even when you forgive, it takes time to fully acknowledge, accept, and stay committed to the decision. Therefore, rather than moving fast through the process, move deeper, reflecting on potential benefits of forgiving and also on the effects of not forgiving. Also understand that forgiveness is essentially a gift from you to the offender that doesn't necessarily require an admission or confession by the offender. You, however, need to ensure that the offense is forgivable. That is, forgiving offenses such as chronic abuse, ongoing discrimination, or exploitation could be harmful.

START-OF-SESSION RELAXATION
At the start of the session, your clinician may begin with a brief relaxation exercise. To discover some of these practices on your own, go to Appendix A: Relaxation & Mindfulness Practices, which can be found at the end of this workbook.

IN-SESSION PRACTICE: *REACH*
Your clinician will be working with you on the in-session practices. Refer to Worksheet 6.1.

Step One: *R = Recall* *an event:* You can close your eyes if you feel comfortable. Think of a person who hurt you and you continue to feel the ill effect of the hurt. Do not wallow in self-pity. Take deep, slow, and calming breaths as you visualize the event. When you are ready, open your eyes, and in the following spaces, describe the event, incident, or offense. You don't have to use actual names. You can use the person's initials or a pseudonym that you can remember.

_____

_____

_____

_____

_____

Step Two: *E = Empathize* *from the perpetrator's point of view:* When survival is being threatened, a perpetrator may hurt innocent people. Keep in mind that *empathy* is a key ingredient of forgiveness. Empathy involves identifying emotionally and experientially with the other—without evaluating. To help you do this, remember the following:

- When others feel their survival is threatened, they may hurt innocent people.
- People who attack others are themselves usually in a state of fear, worry, and hurt.
- The situation people find themselves in—not necessarily their underlying personalities—can lead to hurting.
- People often don't think when they hurt others; they just lash out.

Step Two is not easy to accomplish, but try to make up a plausible story that the perpetrator might tell if challenged to justify his or her actions. In the following spaces, please write down what you think your offender was thinking.

_____

_____

_____

_____

_____

Step Three: *A = Altruistic* *gift of forgiveness:* This is another difficult step. First, recall a time when you transgressed, felt guilty, and were forgiven. This was a gift you were given by another person because you needed it, and you were grateful for this gift. In the following spaces, please write a description of the event.

_____

_____

_____

_____

_____

Step Four: *C = **Commit** yourself to forgive publicly:* Ways to forgive yourself publicly include writing a "certificate of forgiveness," writing a letter of forgiveness, writing it in your diary, writing a poem or song, or telling a trusted friend what you have done. These are all contracts of forgiveness that lead to the final step in the *REACH* process. Of these, which contract are you willing to undertake publicly to express your commitment to forgiveness? In the following spaces, write how you would like to publicly show your commitment to forgiveness.

_____

_____

_____

_____

Step Five: *H = **Hold** onto forgiveness:* This is another difficult step because memories of the event will certainly recur. Forgiveness is not erasure; rather it is a change in the tag lines that a memory carries. It is important to realize that the memories do not mean that you have not forgiven that person. Don't dwell vengefully on the memories, and don't allow yourself to wallow in them. Remind yourself that you have forgiven, and read the document you composed in Step Four.

Then in the following spaces, list things that may help you to hold on to your forgiveness as well as things that may interfere with or weaken your resolve to hold on to forgiveness.

List things that may help you to hold on to your forgiveness:

1. _____

2. _____

3. _____

List things that may interfere with or weaken your resolve to hold on to forgiveness:

1. _____

2. _____

3. _____

This worksheet was originally published in Rashid and Seligman's *Positive Psychotherapy: Clinician Manual.*

Reflect & Discuss

Reflect on and discuss the following:

- How honestly and thoroughly were you able to follow the *REACH* practice?
- During the steps outlined, did anger, disappointment, and/or hostility arise? If you felt any of these emotions, what specific step of the practice, or anything else, helped you to keep moving forward?
- Which step of the practice did you find most difficult?
- If you can anticipate any experience that could derail your resolve to forgive, what might it be?
- Some people forgive but don't act in a forgiving way. How would you describe your forgiveness?
- How would you compare superficial forgiveness with genuine forgiveness?
- If you feel that you could not forgive fully at this point, what might help you achieve a greater level of forgiveness?

A SECOND PRACTICE: THE *FORGIVENESS LETTER*

PPT also offers a second practice of forgiveness, as described in Worksheet 6.2.

WORKSHEET 6.2   WRITING A *FORGIVENESS LETTER*

For this practice, think of people who have wronged you in the past and who you have never explicitly forgiven. Which of these experiences persist in your memory and generate negative emotions from which you would like to free yourself? Choose one person you would like to forgive, and write a letter of forgiveness to that person. Do not mail the letter—this practice is for you, not for him or her. You may even write to a person no longer living.

In the letter describe in concrete terms how you were wronged by this person. How were you affected by the original transgression? How have you continued to be hurt by the memory of the event? Be sure to end with an explicit declaration of forgiveness.

To consolidate this practice, consider two further options:

1. *You can design a ceremony in which you symbolically forgive the perpetrator/ transgressor and get rid of your rage or bitterness. For example, you may read the letter out loud (to yourself) and then bury it in the backyard or place it in a special envelope and seal it.*
2. *If you would like to continue your work on forgiveness, keep a Forgiveness Journal. In this journal, record those instances when painful memories of past wrongdoing intrude into the present. Reflect on how your life might be different if you were free of the anger and resentment that accompanies these memories. Use your journal to write forgiveness letters or briefer forgiveness declarations as needed.*

This worksheet was originally published in Rashid and Seligman's *Positive Psychotherapy: Clinician Manual.*

Reflect & Discuss

Reflect on and discuss the following:

- Writing about difficult memories and difficult situations, although challenging, is eventually therapeutic. In what ways was this process therapeutic for you?
- What was the most difficult part of writing this letter?
- In what ways is the writing process different from just holding onto the memories of the offense in your head?

In Real Life: Nico, 43, male, South American descent

Nico attended a PPT workshop that encouraged participants to complete an *Forgiveness* exercise. He submitted the following process report after completing this practice:

> *For this exercise I chose to write a Forgiveness Letter to a former romantic partner. Our relationship was strong, but as time passed, the strength shifted in the negative direction . . . and soon morphed into resentment. I resented my partner and also myself, for being so pathetic at relationships.*
>
> *Now, after almost a decade, this exercise forced me to revisit the memories out of the cold storage of time. A glance at the steps of the REACH exercise peaked my interest to try to revisit the experience. Recalling the hurt was easy. I felt hurt again. However, I was able to move on to find empathy, even though there was only a bit of it left. Since we separated, I have gone through a lot of shi*, which has taught me that there is no perfect relationship. Some of my subsequent partners had had similar or even worse issues.*
>
> *To emphasize deeply, I decided to write a letter, which I wrote in great detail. As I was writing, I became emotional. Along came anger, with compassion—which was utterly unexpected. I never thought I would feel compassion for my ex. Somehow feelings of compassion made me feel that we both were stupid and naïve. We both were unconventional—the very things that had brought us close initially, and which eventually drove us apart. I realized that I, too, made mistakes. Sure their mistakes, I still believe, damaged our relationship beyond repair. But then I think, in the long run, it was destined to happen.*
>
> *I finished writing the letter, folded it, put it in the envelope, and stamped and sealed it. Just before dropping it in the mailbox, I reopened the envelope and wrote, "Thank you for saving me from the embarrassment when I forgot the most important file that day, and you left everything and brought it to my office, just in time. That evening we fought about why I did not thank you properly. That file went a long way in bringing me where I am now, professionally. Thank you."*
>
> *Two weeks later, I received a very positive response from my ex.*

Tips to Maintain Your Progress

Discuss the following tips with your clinician to help you maintain your progress:

- Maintenance of forgiveness may depend on whether the perpetrator refrains from future offenses, especially if the victim and the offender are likely to see each other in the future. Solicited, weak, and insincere apologies may give the impression of forgiveness, but they may be insufficient to maintain forgiveness.
- If you are unable to forgive and continue to hold on to open and negative memories or grudges, note that those who hold grudges are likely to develop hypertension and have higher rates of heart disease, high blood pressure, heart attacks, and chronic pain. Choosing forgiveness is beneficial for your overall well-being.

- To maintain forgiveness, periodically review the five *REACH* steps (shown on Worksheet 6.1) and reaffirm your commitment, preferably with a trusted confidant.
- To maintain forgiveness or to extend its benefits, make a list of individuals against whom you hold a grudge and then either meet them personally to discuss it or visualize how you can apply *REACH* with them. Don't forget to put the original offense into its proper context and perspective.
- You may initially forgive an offense or offender but may not be able to maintain the forgiveness and may, in fact, resort to passive means of maintaining the grudge, offense, or hurt. Therefore, it is important to go through the forgiveness process for lasting change.

RESOURCES

Readings

- Enright, R. D. (2008). *Forgiveness Is a Choice: A Step-By-Step Process for Resolving Anger and Restoring Hope*. Washington, DC: American Psychological Association.
- McCullough, M. E., Sandage, S. J., & Worthington, E. (1997). *To Forgive is Human: How to Put Your Past in the Past*. Madison, WI: Intervarsity Press.
- Worthington, E. (2013). *Moving Forward: Six Steps to Forgiving Yourself and Breaking Free From the Past Paperback*. Colorado Springs: Waterbook Press.

Videos

- TED Talk: The mothers who found forgiveness and friendship, one lost her son on 9/11 and the other has a convicted son who played a role in the attacks: https://www.ted.com/talks/9_11_healing_the_mothers_who_found_forgiveness_friendship
- Nelson Mandela: Message of Forgiveness—The Making of Mandela: https://youtu.be/S2RyxVURHoY
- *Shawshank Redemption*: The moment when Red finally stands up to the system and asserts his own terms of redemption: https://youtu.be/KtwXlIwozog

Websites

- Psychologist Everett Worthington, a leader in the forgiveness research: http://www.evworthington-forgiveness.com/
- Ten Extraordinary Examples of Forgiveness: http://listverse.com/2013/10/31/10-extraordinary-examples-of-forgiveness/
- Valuable resources about forgiveness: www.forgiving.org/

Podcast

- A Better Way to Be Angry: advice from philosopher Martha Nussbaum: http://www.cbc.ca/radio/tapestry/anger-and-forgiveness-1.3997934/a-better-way-to-be-angry-advice-from-philosopher-martha-nussbaum-1.3997950

SESSION SEVEN: MAXIMIZING VERSUS SATISFICING

7

SESSION SEVEN PRESENTS THE CONCEPTS OF MAXIMIZING (aiming to make the best possible choice) and satisficing (making a "good enough" choice). The central positive psychotherapy (PPT) practice covered in this session is *Toward Satisficing.*

THREE THINGS TO KNOW ABOUT *MAXIMIZING* AND *SATISFICING*

1. **Choices:** Our lives present us with a wide range of choices, from everyday decisions such as what to eat, what to wear, and what image to set as a desktop background to more important decisions such as who to date, which university to attend, what career to pursue, and where to move or buy a house. According to Schwartz (2004), having more choices doesn't necessarily translate into higher well-being, because the more choices we have, the more rigorous standards we tend to apply in evaluating these choices and selecting the best one. If you select one that doesn't turn out to be the best, you are more likely to blame yourself for not selecting the best option. And if someone else's choice turns out to be the best one, you may feel threatened.

2. **Maximizers versus satisficers:** Are you a maximizer or a satisficer? A maximizer goes to great lengths to get the very best of out of every decision, choice, and opportunity. Barry Schwartz, in his book, *The Paradox of Choice* (Schwartz, 2004), posits that a maximizer strives to make the smartest and most well-informed decisions by comparing products; reading manuals and labels; consulting reviews, evaluations, ratings, and rankings; and exploring minor details. A satisficer, in contrast, takes into account his or her needs and options and settles for an option that meets the needs and is also available. Despite making the best possible decision, the maximizer is not satisfied and often suffers from regret, whereas after the decision has been made, the satisficer is less likely to experience regret, even if a better option comes up.

3. **Consequences:** Clearly maximizers invest a lot of time and effort in selecting, sifting through, and evaluating all possible choices. It is therefore not surprising that they may end up making a better decision on a rational basis. However, they are also more likely to feel regret after the purchase or selection if the product or decision disappoints them.

START-OF-SESSION RELAXATION

At the start of the session, your clinician may begin with a brief relaxation exercise. To discover some of these practices on your own, go to Appendix A: Relaxation & Mindfulness Practices, which can be found at the end of this workbook.

IN-SESSION PRACTICE: ARE YOU A MAXIMIZER OR A SATISFICER?

Your clinician will be working with you on the in-session practices. Refer to Worksheet 7.1.

WORKSHEET 7.1   ARE YOU A MAXIMIZER OR A SATISFICER?

Using the following scale, please rate yourself and explore where you fall on the Satisficer–Maximizer continuum.[1]

1 – Completely disagree   2 – Disagree   3 – Somewhat disagree

4 – Neutral   5 – Somewhat agree   6 – Agree   7 – Strongly agree

	Statement	Response
1	Whenever I'm faced with a choice, I try to imagine what all the other possibilities are, even ones that aren't present at the moment.	
2	No matter how satisfied I am with my job, it's only right for me to be on the lookout for better opportunities.	
3	When I am in the car listening to the radio, I often check other stations to see if something better is playing, even if I am relatively satisfied with what I'm listening to.	
4	When I watch TV, I channel surf, often scanning through the available options even while attempting to watch one program.	
5	I treat relationships like clothing; I expect to try a lot on before I get the perfect fit.	
6	I often find it difficult to shop for a gift for a friend.	
7	Renting videos is really difficult. I am always struggling to pick the best one.	
8	When shopping, I have a hard time finding clothing that I really love.	
9	I'm a big fan of lists that attempt to rank things (the best movies, the best singers, the best athletes, the best novels, etc.).	
10	I find that writing is very difficult, even if it's just writing a letter to a friend, because it's so hard to word things just right. I often do several drafts of even simple things.	
11	No matter what I do, I have the highest standard for myself.	
12	I never settle for second best.	
13	I often fantasize about living in ways that are quite different from my actual life.	

After completing the worksheet, compute the total score (the sum of all 13 items). The average score on this scale is 50. The high score is 75 or above and the low is 25 or below. There are no gender differences. If you scored 65 or higher, then you have maximizing behaviors or habits that have adverse impact on your well-being. If you scored 40 or lower, you are on the satisficing end of the scale.

[1] Reprinted with permission. Schwartz et al., 2002.

This worksheet was originally published in Rashid and Seligman's *Positive Psychotherapy: Clinician Manual.*

Reflect & Discuss

Reflect on and discuss the following:

- What does your score indicate about you?
- If you scored high (50 or higher), in what way will this awareness help you make some meaningful changes toward satisficing?
- If you scored high, how aware are you of the costs (economic, emotional, and physical) of maximizing?
- No one maximizes in all areas of life. In which do you maximize and in which do you satisfice? Please recall and compare your emotional reactions in both situations.
- Have you found yourself engaged in more product comparison than satisficers?
- Some people want to *have* choices, while others want to *make* choices. Which describes you better?

IN-SESSION PRACTICE: *TOWARD SATISFICING*

Your clinician will be working with you on the in-session practices. Refer to Worksheet 7.2.

No.	Strategy
1	***Be a Chooser, Not a Picker:*** Choosers are people who are able to reflect on what makes a decision important, on whether, perhaps, none of the options should be chosen, on whether a new option should be created, and on what a particular choice says about the chooser as an individual. *You can be a Chooser, not a Picker in following areas:* • Shorten or eliminate deliberations about decisions that are unimportant to you. • Use some of the time you have freed up to ask yourself what you really want in the areas of your life where decisions matters. If none of the options work, you will try: _____ _____
2	***Satisfice More and Maximize Less:*** To embrace satisficing, you will try to: • Think about occasions in life when you settled comfortably for "good enough." • Scrutinize how you chose in those areas. • Apply that strategy more broadly. If these options don't work, you will try: _____ _____
3	***Think about the Opportunity Costs:*** You can avoid the disappointment that comes from thinking about opportunity costs by trying the following: • Unless you are truly dissatisfied, you will stick with what you usually buy. • You will resist being tempted by "new and improved." • You will adopt the attitude "don't scratch unless there is an itch." • You will not worry that you'll miss out on all the new things that the world has to offer. If these strategies don't work, you will try: _____ _____
4	***Make Your Decision Nonreversible:*** When a decision is final, we engage in a variety of psychological processes that enhance our feelings about the choice we made relative to alternatives. If a decision is reversible, we don't engage these processes to the same degree. List examples of your reversible decisions: a. _____ b. _____ c. _____ Now list nonreversible decisions you will make in the following areas of your life: a. _____ b. _____ c. _____

POSITIVE PSYCHOTHERAPY

No.	Strategy
5	*Practice an "Attitude of Gratitude"*: You can vastly improve your subjective experience by consciously striving to be grateful more often for what is good about a choice and to be disappointed less by what is bad about it. You will practice an attitude of gratitude about your following choices: a. _____ b. _____ c. _____
6	*Regret Less:* The sting of regret (either actual or potential) colors many decisions and sometimes influences us to avoid making decisions at all. Although regret is often appropriate and instructive, when it becomes so pronounced that it poisons or even prevents decisions, you can make an effort to minimize it. You will lessen regret by trying to: • Adopt the standards of a satisficer rather than a maximizer. • Reduce the number of options you consider before making a decision. • Focus on what is good in a decision rather than focusing on your disappointments with what is bad. If these strategies don't work, you will try: _____ _____
7.	*Anticipate Adaptation:* We regularly adapt to almost everything we experience. In tough times, adaptation enables us to avoid the full brunt of the hardship; in good times, adaptation puts us on a "hedonic treadmill," robbing us of the full measure of satisfaction we expect from each positive experience. We can't prevent adaptation. You will develop realistic expectations about how experiences change with time: • If you buy a new gadget, you will be aware that the thrill won't last beyond two months. • You will spend less time looking for the perfect thing (maximizing), so that you won't have huge search costs to be "amortized" against the satisfaction you derive from what you choose. • You will remind yourself of how good things actually are instead of focusing on how they're less good than they were at first. If these strategies don't work, you will try: _____ _____
8	*Control Expectations:* Our evaluation of experience is substantially influenced by how it compares with our expectations. So what may be the easiest route to increasing satisfaction with the results of decisions is to lower excessively high expectations about them. To make the task of lowering expectations easier, you will: • Reduce the number of options you will consider. • Be a satisficer rather than a maximizer. • Allow for serendipity. If these strategies don't work, you will try: _____ _____

No.	Strategy
9	*Curtail Social Comparison*: We evaluate the quality of our experiences by social comparisons. Although useful, this often reduces our satisfaction. You will try the following: • You will remember that "He who dies with the most toys wins" is a bumper sticker, not wisdom. • You will focus on what makes you happy and what gives meaning to your life. If these strategies don't work, you will try: _____ _____
10	*Learn to Love Constraints:* As choices increase, freedom of choice eventually becomes a tyranny of choice. Routine decisions take so much time and attention that it becomes difficult to get through the day. In many circumstances, learn to view limits on possibilities as liberating, not constraining. Society provides rules, standards, and norms for making choices, and individual experience creates habits. By deciding to follow a rule (e.g., always wear a seat belt, never drink more than two glasses of wine in one evening), we avoid having to make a deliberate decision again and again. This kind of rule-following frees up time and attention that can be devoted to thinking about choices and decisions to which rules don't apply. You will follow these rules: a._____ b._____ c._____

[2] Schwartz (2004).

This worksheet was originally published in Rashid and Seligman's *Positive Psychotherapy: Clinician Manual.*

Reflect & Discuss

Reflect on and discuss the following:

- Of the satisficing strategies discussed earlier, which ones are you able to implement relatively independently?
- Of these satisficing strategies, for which ones do you need cooperation or support from others to succeed?
- Some choices or decisions such as where to move, which job to take, or who to marry would benefit from maximizing. What areas in your life would benefit from maximizing?
- Maximizing behavior and decision-making often rely on outside validation, such as something being highly ranked, recommended by experts, socially desirable, or favored or followed by many. Does your decision-making depend on these types of measures?

In Real Life: Sidhu, 24, male, South Asian cultural background

Sidhu is a student who used to be a varsity athlete and who also excelled in academics. He attended an elite private high school and went to college on a scholarship. His father (a successful businessman) and mother (an accomplished attorney) always focused on pursuing "excellence." Sidhu adopted this value exactly the way his parents wished.

Following a sports injury, however, Sidhu had to spend three months on crutches, and his sports and academics both suffered as a result. Although he passed all his classes, he missed an important state-level sports competition. Sidhu looked at this less than optimal result as a total failure. He slipped into a depression and sought PPT. In addition to practices such as Practical Wisdom, which taught him the contextualized use of strengths, the Maximizing and Satisficing practices helped him understand that while he can continue to pursue the best and maximize his options for success, he may not actually be the best because there might be someone better than him. Through satisficing strategies, Sidhu understood that he doesn't need to be the best when compared to rest. Rather, he needs to be his humanly best.

Tips to Maintain Your Progress

Discuss the following tips with your clinician to help you maintain your progress:

- Maximizers are more likely to engage in social comparisons, especially to assess standards and evaluate the relative status of their own experiences or possessions. To promote satisficing, rather than relying on external standards, develop your own anchors, that is, your own internal standards.
- To promote satisficing, savor experiences. Rather than trying to cultivate many experiences of very high quality (high in pleasure value), try to keep such experiences relatively rare and exclusive. This will thwart adaptation, and you will be less prone to up the ante after every pleasurable experience.
- By exploring a large number of options, maximizers tend to believe that they can control many areas of their lives—from their education to their employment, and from selecting partners to creating social identities. However, research shows that the net gain (in terms of additional information) has little or no impact on the outcome (Schwartz et al., 2002). In other words, the pursuit to control or manage a perfect outcome gives maximizers the impression that they are in control, but the result is almost inconsequential. Also, all of the effort used to manage the control process deprives maximizers of enjoying the process.

RESOURCES

Readings

- Iynger, S. (2010). *The Art of Choosing*. New York: Hachette.
- Luna, E. (2015). *The Crossroads of Should and Must: Find and Follow Your Passion*. New York: Workman.
- Schwartz, B. (2004). *The Paradox of Choice: Why More Is Less*. New York: ECCO.

Videos

- TED Talk: Barry Schwartz, author of *The Paradox of Choice* discusses how more choices paralyze us and deplete our happiness:
  https://www.ted.com/talks/barry_schwartz_on_the_paradox_of_choice
- TED Talk: Shyeena Iynger discusses how people choose and what makes us think that we are good at it:
  https://www.ted.com/speakers/sheena_iyengar
- TED Talk: Dan Gilbert discusses how our beliefs of what makes us happy are often wrong:
  http://www.ted.com/talks/dan_gilbert_researches_happiness
- To assess if you are maximizer or satisficer, take a free online test:
  http://www.nicholasreese.com/decide/

Websites

- *The Wall Street Journal*, How You Make Decisions Says a Lot About How Happy You Are: "Maximizers" Check All Options, "Satisficers" Make the Best Decision Quickly: Guess Who's Happier?, by Elizabeth Bernstein:
  http://www.wsj.com/articles/how-you-make-decisions-says-a-lot-about-how-happy-you-are-1412614997

SESSION EIGHT: GRATITUDE

8

SESSION EIGHT, WHICH IS THE FINAL SESSION in Phase Two of positive psychotherapy (PPT), expands the concept of gratitude—which was first introduced in Session One in the form of the *Gratitude Journal*. Session Eight facilitates recalling and writing to someone who is alive now and who in the past did something positive but who you have never fully thanked. The PPT practices covered in this session are the *Gratitude Letter* and *Gratitude Visit*.

THREE THINGS TO KNOW ABOUT *GRATITUDE*

1. **What is gratitude?** Gratitude is an experience of thankfulness, which includes noticing and appreciating the positive things in life. In so doing, you acknowledge the value and meaning of positives. Robert Emmons, in his book *THANKS* (Emmons, 2007), equates gratitude with a medicine that has no side effects.

2. **The undoing effect of gratitude:** Gratitude tends to have an "undoing effect" on negative emotions. Compared to positive emotions, negative emotions tend to be stronger, more pervasive, and longer lasting, and gratitude has the potential to undo them. For example, if you are feeling sad, hopeless, upset, and uncertain about the future, a deliberate effort to see realistic positive aspects of your life can help you put things in perspective. When you take stock of the good things in your life—small or big—through the practice of gratitude, you start realizing that your life may not be that bad after all.

3. **The other-orientation of gratitude:** Gratitude is often "other-oriented," which means that you express gratitude to someone, with someone, or for someone, and this process builds positive relationships. Gratitude also helps you re-examine the value of relationships that you may take for granted. When your loved one takes care of you when you are sick, delivers an important item just in time for your meeting or flight, consoles you when you face a setback, or tolerates or accommodates your idiosyncratic habits, you feel grateful to have that person in your life.

START-OF-SESSION RELAXATION
At the start of the session, your clinician may begin with a brief relaxation exercise. To discover some of these practices on your own, go to Appendix A: Relaxation & Mindfulness Practices, which can be found at the end of this workbook.

IN-SESSION PRACTICES: *GRATITUDE LETTER* AND *GRATITUDE VISIT*
Your clinician will be working with you on the in-session practices. Refer to Worksheet 8.1.

Write your initial draft:

Dear _____

_____

_____

_____

_____

_____

_____

_____

_____

_____

_____

_____

_____

_____

After you have completed the draft letter, please continue this exercise at home, as instructed:

Gratitude Letter and *Gratitude Visit*

- *Please polish the Gratitude Letter you drafted in session. Write and rewrite it, describing in specific terms why you are grateful. The letter should specify what the person did for you and clearly explain exactly how this action affected your life. In the letter, tell the person what you are doing now and how you often remember his or her efforts.*
- *Once you have finished the final version of the letter, sign and laminate it, to signify its importance.*
- *Next, make a date to visit that person. Invite her or him to your home, or travel to that person's home.*
- *It is important that you complete the next step of this exercise face to face, not just in writing or by phone. Do not explain the purpose of the visit in advance; a simple "I just want to see you" is enough.*
- *Wine and cheese do not matter, but bring the laminated version of your testimonial with you as a gift. When you and the person are all settled down, read your testimonial aloud slowly, with expression, and with eye contact. Then let other person react unhurriedly. Reminisce together about the concrete events that make this person so important to you.*

This worksheet was originally published in Rashid and Seligman's *Positive Psychotherapy: Clinician Manual.*

Reflect & Discuss

Reflect on and discuss the following:

- How did you feel as you wrote your letter?
- What was the easiest part to write and what was the toughest part?
- How did the other person react to your expression of gratitude? And how were you affected by their reaction?
- How long did these feelings last after you presented your letter?
- Did you recall the experience in the days that followed the reading of the letter? If so, how did this recollection affect your mood?

In Real Life: Reda, 47, female, Arabian background

Reda, who works in publishing in the Middle East, attended a PPT workshop and wrote this *Gratitude Letter* to her brother. Following the letter, Reda provides a reflection on her experience of reading the letter to her brother:

Dearest Brother:
I have been writing this letter in my mind for years, and the time has now come for me to let you know how much I love you, and how much I cherish you as a brother, friend, and father. You are my key bedrock of support. You are the one who has enabled me to deal with the many downs of life and to stand on my feet again.

My life has not been easy, having grown up in a broken family with a father who entered into one challenge after another—financial, legal, and personal. These challenges paralyzed his life and crippled ours in ways you know well. Your constant love, kindness, and care has helped me in these trying times.

- *By allowing me into your lovely family, and building a room for me in your new home, I know I have a family and I am not alone in life.*
- *By calling me regularly to check on my well-being--knowing how busy you are with your family and the stress of work in politically and economically unstable countries—I know I can always count on you.*
- *By always asking if I need anything, I know you are my guardian angel.*

Thank you for trying to mediate a potential predivorce solution by traveling to the Middle East three times in less than six months, when most people on the side of my ex were trying to maximize personal gains by fueling more trouble.
Thank you for loaning me the money that allowed me to move into the house of my dreams, to rebuild my life, and to feel secure again.
Thank you for traveling to stand by me when I underwent two surgeries in the past six years.
Thank you for inviting me to travel with your lovely family every year.
Thank you for spoiling me on every birthday and Christmas.
Thank you for offering to buy me a new car.
My thank you list is long. Your love, generosity, chivalry, care, and warmth give me an amazing feeling of belongingness and kindness that I have often missed in my life. The presence in my life of your children gives me a great sense of purpose in life other than work. They have compensated my sadness of not having my own children. What more can I ask for in life? You are my root, and in moments of doubt and gloom, I think of you, of our long talks, and trips.
I recall the fun days of our childhood that were filled with mischief. I know you will always be there for me. I feel grounded in your unconditional love. You have compensated me for lacking a father who stood by his kids, for lacking a dream family in my marriage,

and for lacking personal security. These three factors have fed a sense of low self-esteem that I continue to fight.

You are an amazing person, a gem, and a spot of continued sunshine in my life. I love you dearly, and I will always be there for you, for Monica, and for your three kids. You are one of a KIND. A dream brother, friend, and father.

REFLECTION

With permission of my therapist, I scheduled a skype visit with my brother Ahmed to express my heartfelt gratitude and thankfulness for all his support throughout my life. He thought we were going to having our regular chat. I asked if he was alone in the room and if he could close the door. He did so, but he got worried as to why I was asking these questions.

I asked him to be patient, to sit in the chair, and look at me. I told him I wanted to read a letter I wrote to him to express gratitude that god blessed me with a loving and caring brother like him. Right after I read the second line, I started crying. He started looking down at the floor and avoided eye contact. As I read further, I choked and tears streamed down my cheeks. I had to stop reading several times. Suddenly I saw him take a tissue, wipe his tears, and blow his nose. He looked at me and there were a few minutes of silence. "Thank you for this nice letter," he said, visibly moved. "Please forgive me for all those moments in which I hurt you as we were growing up." Then he admitted that I had often shamed him in our conservative society because "I was a rebel who wanted to live my life, dating men, and staying out late, when single females were supposed to be home early," but that he totally respects me and accepts me as a loving sister with a strong character who is self-dependent and makes him and his family proud.

He said he found it strange to be thanked for doing all these natural things. "You are the first one our immediate family to thank me . . . I never felt I have been properly thanked for something I did."

Our skype call lasted for 22 minutes, and I felt grace after hanging up. I felt how both of us were able to acknowledge the goodness in our lives, to accomplish a lot, and to move on although we had a very turbulent childhood. I also felt that we were both able to support one another during this encounter, which allowed my brother to open up and express clear emotions in front of me, something that had never happened before. He suddenly dropped his guard, which I felt helped de-stress him. It also allowed us to evaluate how our relationship had allowed us to keep each other strong in moments of weakness. We both were very grateful for having each other and treating each other as best friends in addition to being siblings. We were able to realize how both of us had touched each other's life in a genuine way. And we agreed to make gratitude a regular practice in our weekly skype calls because it will improve our well-being and allow us to deal with adversity and to nurture our strong relationship.

Tips to Maintain Your Progress

Discuss the following tips with your clinician to help you maintain your progress:

- Socialize more with people who are grateful and less with those who are not. An emotion expressed within a group has a ripple effect and becomes shared by the group. Happy and grateful people have a contagious effect.
- The words we use create reality. Grateful people have a particular linguistic style. They use a language of gifts, giving, fortune, abundance, satisfaction, blessing, and blessedness. Ungrateful people use expressions of deprivation, regrets, lack, need, scarcity, and loss. The expressions of depressed people who are low in gratitude are somewhat similar and focus on the self, such as, "I am a loser," and "no one loves me." If you want to cultivate gratitude, self-monitor your words. We are not suggesting that you inflate yourself with superficial

compliments but that you pay attention to the good things people have done for you.

- If your experience with the *Gratitude Letter* and *Visit* has been powerful, have you thought of others with whom you wish to share your gratitude? Think of the people—parents, friends, teachers, coaches, teammates, employers—who have been especially kind to you but have never heard you express your gratitude. Your gratitude may be long overdue.

- Express gratitude directly to another. Gratitude is an interpersonal attribute that is most effective when done directly—face to face, by phone, or by letter. Avoid the mere lip service of "thank you." Express your appreciation in concrete terms to, for example, the teacher who recognized your ability and connected with you in ways that brought out the best in you, or your favorite uncle who guided you through the tough terrain of adolescence when no else could understand you, or an old friend who stood by you when you were bullied. Write to them and express your gratitude in concrete terms. If it is appropriate and affordable, give that person a gift of something you two can do together, such as having dinner together, or going to see a musical, a concert, an art exhibition, or a sporting event.

RESOURCES

Readings

- Emmons, R. (2007). *Thanks! How the New Science of Gratitude Can Make You Happier*. New York: Houghton Mifflin.
- Pasricha, N. (2010). *The Book of Awesome*. New York: Penguin Random House.
- Sacks, O. (2015). *Gratitude*. New York: Alfred A. Knopf.

Videos

- Science of Happiness: An Experiment in Gratitude, the power of writing and sharing a gratitude letter:
  https://youtu.be/oHv6vTKD6lg
- Virtual *Gratitude Visit*: Dr. Daniel Tomasulo discusses how to conduct a virtual gratitude visit:
  https://youtu.be/iptEvstz6_M
- *Gratitude Letter*: Tal Ben-Shahar explains the *Gratitude Letter* exercise:
  https://youtu.be/W1GrLfmbiPE

Websites

- Robert Emmons' website, one of the most eminent researchers of gratitude:
  http://emmons.faculty.ucdavis.edu
- Stories of Gratitude: stories about the extraordinary power of gratitude:
  http://365grateful.com

9

SESSION NINE: HOPE AND OPTIMISM

IN SESSION NINE, WHICH IS THE START of Phase Three of positive psychotherapy (PPT), you will be learning to see the best possible, realistic outcomes. You will see that challenges are temporary and learn how to develop a sense of hope. The central PPT practice covered in this session is *One Door Closes, Another Door Opens.*

THREE THINGS TO KNOW ABOUT *HOPE* AND *OPTIMISM*

1. **Optimism and hope are similar and also distinct:** Optimism generally means that when you face a setback, you explain the causes of the setback in changeable terms (such as, the setback is not totally due to you, will not prevail forever, and it will not impact all aspects of your life [Seligman, 1991]). Optimism is also a generalized expectation that you will achieve your goals. Compared to optimism, hope places more emphasis on personal agency (the will) and identifies specific strategies (ways) to achieve those goals. Together, optimism and hope offer you ways to buffer yourself from sliding into pessimism, depression, and despair.
2. **Optimal use of optimism and hope:** Not every failure and setback needs a dose of optimism and hope. For example, repeated relationship failures, frequent loss of employment, or recurrent interpersonal arguments may first need critical analysis using strengths, such as open-mindedness, prudence, and self-regulation, followed by optimistic and hopeful future efforts.
3. **Hope and optimism in psychotherapy:** Optimism and hope are primary ingredients in psychotherapy. You seek treatment with the hope that doing so will help in alleviating your symptoms. That is, hope becomes a key element in therapeutic change. Your psychotherapist instills hope in you by listening and validating you and by connecting and empathizing with you. If your progress is derailed, your therapist reinstills hope in you to continue trying. Without hope, psychotherapy may not go too far.

START-OF-SESSION RELAXATION
At the start of the session, your clinician may begin with a brief relaxation exercise. To discover some of these practices on your own, go to Appendix A: Relaxation & Mindfulness Practices, which can be found at the end of this workbook.

IN-SESSION PRACTICE: ONE DOOR CLOSES, ANOTHER DOOR OPENS
Your clinician will be working with you on the in-session practices. Refer to Worksheet 9.1.

WORKSHEET 9.1   DOORS OPENING

Step One:

In the following blanks, write about your experiences with doors opening and closing. Did you see the open door immediately, or did it take a while? Did your disappointment, sadness, bitterness, or other negative feelings resulting from the closed door make it harder to find an open door? Are there things you can do in the future to find the open door more readily?

Consider three doors that closed on you. What other doors opened? Try to fill in the blanks:

(1) The most important door that ever closed on me was _____

     and the door that opened was _____

(2) A door that closed on me through bad luck or missed opportunity was _____

     and the door that opened was _____

(3) A door that closed on me through loss, rejection, or death was _____

     and the door that opened was _____

Step Two:

In this step, you will explore how you explain to yourself the reasoning behind why the door closed. Pick one of the three illustrations from Step One and respond to the statements by selecting a numeric response that best represents your reasoning for both closed and open doors. (On the scales, 1= Very untrue of you, while 7= Very true of you.)

The Door that Closed was Door Number____

1. This door closed mostly due to me	1. . . . . 3. . . . . 5. . . . . 7. . . . .
OR	
2. This door closed mostly due to other people or circumstances	1. . . . . 3. . . . . 5. . . . . 7. . . . .
3. This or similar doors will always remain closed	1. . . . . 3. . . . . 5. . . . . 7. . . . .
OR	
4. This door is closed temporarily	1. . . . . 3. . . . . 5. . . . . 7. . . . .
5. This closed door will ruin everything in my life	1. . . . . 3. . . . . 5. . . . . 7. . . . .
OR	
6. This door influences just this one aspect of my life	1. . . . . 3. . . . . 5. . . . . 7. . . . .

If you score high (12 or higher) on items 1, 3, and 5, this indicates that your explanations for closed doors (setbacks, failures, and adversities) are personalized (largely due to you), are permanent (will not change), and are pervasive (one closed door will close many other things in life).

If you score high on items 2, 4, and 6, this indicates that your explanations for closed doors are not personalized, are temporary, and are localized (not impacting all areas of your life). According to Seligman's theory of attributions (Forgeard & Seligman, 2012; Seligman, 1991), such explanations are associated with more adaptive functioning in the wake of negative experiences.

This worksheet was originally published in Rashid and Seligman's *Positive Psychotherapy: Clinician Manual.*

Reflect & Discuss

Reflect on and discuss the following:

- When people hold themselves solely responsible for a setback and perceive it as doom and gloom in almost all aspects of their lives that will last forever, they become vulnerable to depression and a host of other psychological problems. How do you explain causes of failure to yourself, especially when a door closes (i.e., a setback, missed opportunity, or adversity)?
- What was the impact of doors that closed? What were the negatives and positives regarding your happiness and well-being? Was the impact all-encompassing or long-lasting?
- Did this impact bring something positive to you? What was it?
- In what way has the *One Door Closes, Another Door Opens* practice enhanced your flexibility and adaptability?
- Do you think that deliberate focus on the brighter side (*Door Opens*) might encourage you to minimize or overlook tough realizations that you need to face?
- What led to a door closing, and what helped you to open another door?
- How easy or hard was it for you to see if a door opened, even just a crack?
- What does the closed door represent for you now?
- Did you grow from doors that opened? Is there room for more growth? What might this growth look like?
- Reflect on one or two people who helped you to open the doors or people who held the opened doors for you to enter.
- Would you still like the door that closed to be opened, or do you not care about it now?

In Real Life: Jenny, 25, female, marginalized background

Jenny presented with symptoms of emotional dysregulation, a history of abuse of all sorts, and an unending streak of unstable relationships. She was initially highly skeptical of the effectiveness of any positive emotions or character strengths, especially hope.

In one group session, while most participants shared positive emotions they'd experienced, Jenny was quiet. I (Dr. Rashid) looked at her, letting her know nonverbally that it was okay to pass if she didn't feel like sharing. Jenny sarcastically said, "My life only includes severe emotional abuse by my family, alcoholism, and negativity spewed at me by one of my parents—day in, day out. There isn't an iota of positivity in my life." As I felt the weight of Jenny's distress, I felt as though I had committed a therapeutic faux pas by asking participants to do this exercise. After an uncomfortable and long pause, another group member gently asked Jenny, "Why are you here in this group, every week?" Upon hearing this question, a stream of tears flowed from her eyes, and she quietly said, "This is my only hope . . . something I will never let go of." Everyone became silent, and we all were deeply moved. This silver lining of hope was more than enough for me to start the group discussing positive emotions and experiences.

Fast-forward to last year's graduation. At the convocation, Jenny's name was called. None of her family was in attendance. Before she even stepped onto the stage to receive her diploma, six people sitting on the stage themselves—faculty and staff, some in full academic regalia—spontaneously stood up, almost in unison, and cheered for Jenny. I was one of them. Jenny hugged each of us. Tears again streamed down her cheeks and those of many people around her. The entire audience was moved. Recently, Jenny obtained full-time employment with the university.

TIPS TO MAINTAIN YOUR PROGRESS

Discuss the following tips with your clinician to help you maintain your progress:

- The next time you help a friend with a problem, look for the positive aspects of the situation. Instead of using clichés like "look on the bright side," try to help your friend find specific, concrete opportunities that he or she might otherwise overlook.
- To maintain hope and optimism, especially in tough times after therapy, remember how you were able to benefit from psychotherapy—which is essentially a hope-enhancing process. People may seek therapy because they lack skills to change undesirable aspects of their behavior or because they have skills but lack confidence and how to creatively apply these skills. The therapeutic process, if effective, allows you to understand your skills and to harness or enhance them, if additional skills are needed. If you have skills, the therapeutic process will help you to gain or regain the confidence and motivation to apply those skills by devising a plan to accomplish specific goals. Next time you find yourself lacking hope and optimism, recall how psychotherapy effectively worked for you—if it did. Such a reflection will enable you to transfer skills learned in therapy to solve new challenges you may encounter in life.
- Maintaining hope and optimism also requires social support and a supportive social environment. Ensure that you surround yourself with people who are future-minded and optimistic. If you encounter a serious setback, failure, or adversity, an optimistic and hopeful friend can be an asset to help boost your mood. Likewise, if your friends encounter problems, you can lift their spirits.

RESOURCES

Readings
- Gillham, J. (2000). *The Science of Optimism and Hope*. West Conshohocken, PA: Templeton Press.
- Lopez, S. J. (2014). *Making Hope Happen: Create the Future You Want for Yourself and Others*. New York: Simon & Schuster.
- Seligman, M. (1991). *Learned Optimism: How to Change Your Mind and Your Life*. New York: Vintage Books.
- Snyder, C. R. (1994). *The Psychology of Hope: You Can Get There From Here*. New York: Free Press.

Videos
- Explanatory Style: Learn how your thinking habits can affect your ability to bounce back from stressful circumstances:
  https://youtu.be/q8UiXudooh8
- TED Talk: Neil Pasricha speaks on spreading little optimism everyday about things which make life worth living:
  http://www.ted.com/speakers/neil_pasricha
- Seligman on Optimism: at BBC's Hardtalk:
  https://youtu.be/nFzlaCGvoLY?list=PLB9036743C2E1866F
- Positive Emotions, by Barbara Fredrickson; positivity focuses on what "positivity" is and why it needs to be heartfelt to be effective:
  https://youtu.be/Ds_9Df6dK7c

Websites
- A website about awesome things:
  http://1000awesomethings.com
- Positive Psychology Daily News: To stay updated about positive psychology events:
  http://positivepsychologynews.com
- Positivity Ratio: Learn about your positive to negative emotion ratio, also called the positivity ratio, at Barbara Fredrickson's website:
  www.positivityratio.com

10 SESSION TEN: POSTTRAUMATIC GROWTH

SESSION TEN INVITES YOU TO EXPLORE YOUR deep feelings and thoughts about a traumatic experience that continues to bother you. The central positive psychotherapy practice covered in this session is *Expressive Writing*.

THREE THINGS TO KNOW ABOUT *POSTTRAUMATIC GROWTH (PTG)*

1. **What is PTG?** Following trauma, some individuals develop posttraumatic stress disorder, a serious condition requiring serious treatment. However, following trauma, many individuals also experience growth, generally known as PTG. Psychotherapy traditionally focuses on trauma and its short- and long-term impact, and this focus is essential because anyone who goes through trauma benefits from support in a safe, confidential, empathic, and caring milieu. Exploring the possibility of growth from trauma—at an appropriate time, without minimizing the pain—is a way that an individual can be helped to deal with the trauma.

2. **Benefits of PTG:** PTG often accompanies a change of insight into the meaning of life and the importance of relationships. This growth can mitigate negative feelings that are part and parcel of trauma. For example, trauma often leaves us with a strong feeling of loss of control. Knowing that you have lost control in one aspect of life but have grown in another area can lessen the pain of loss of control. Evidence (Jayawickreme & Blackie, 2014; Roepke, 2015) shows that people who experience PTG develop a renewed belief that they can endure and withstand challenges; explore, appreciate, and further cement relationships that stand the test of time; foster a deeper sense of empathy for other people who go through similar kinds of challenges; and develop a deeper, sophisticated, nuanced sense of meaning and purpose in life.

3. **PTG is not simple and straightforward:** As desirable as it sounds, PTG is not a simple and straightforward consequence. You have probably heard the axiom that time will heal. PTG is not something time will produce; rather, PTG is what you do within that time. PTG does not imply that one can and will withstand all future challenges adaptively. One can still be vulnerable, especially in areas associated with trauma. For example, one can survive cancer and can become resilient in many areas but can still be overwhelmed by relatively minor health problems.

START-OF-SESSION RELAXATION
At the start of the session, your clinician may begin with a brief relaxation exercise. To discover some of these practices on your own, go to Appendix A: Relaxation & Mindfulness Practices, which can be found at the end of this workbook.

IN-SESSION PRACTICE: *EXPRESSIVE WRITING*
Your clinician will be working with you on the in-session practices. Refer to Worksheet.

WORKSHEET 10.1 *EXPRESSIVE WRITING*

Using a note pad or journal, please write a detailed account of a trauma you experienced. Continue this exercise for at least 15 to 20 minutes a day for four consecutive days. Make sure you keep your writings in a safe, secure place that only you have access to.

In your writing, try to let go and explore your deepest thoughts and feelings about the traumatic experience in your life. You can tie this experience to other parts of your life, or keep it focused on one specific area. You can write about the same experience on all four days or you can write about different experiences.

At the end of four days, after describing the experience, please write if the experience has helped you:

- *understand what it means to you*
- *understand your ability to handle similar situations*
- *understand your relationships in a different light*

This worksheet was originally published in Rashid and Seligman's *Positive Psychotherapy: Clinician Manual.*

Reflect & Discuss

Reflect on and discuss the following:

- What was the most difficult part of writing? Do you agree that even though it may have been difficult, it still was worth writing?
- Some reactions to the trauma, adversity, or losses can be so strong that we deliberately avoid associated feelings. Did the writing process help you see this avoidance, if any?
- Did writing help you to visualize growth in terms of your perspective on life?
- Did you experience healing or growth, despite having the lingering pain of the trauma or loss?
- Write about some concrete actions or behaviors you have undertaken, or you plan to do, which signify PTG.
- Did the structure of the writing process help you to see the causal chain of the traumatic experience differently? If so, what different causal links did you discover?
- Do you see your character strengths reflected in your PTG?

In Real Life: Robert Fazio, male, mid 40s, Caucasian

This is the story of Dr. Rashid's dear friend, Rob Fazio. Rob lost his father during the September 11, 2001, terrorist attacks.

I lost my father at the World Trade Center on Tuesday, September 11th. There is not a day that goes by that I do not wish that he were here with us. The unfortunate reality is that our loved ones are somewhere else right now, and we are here. So what should we do and how can we go on? What I learned about my father after September 11th was that he was a person who reached beyond himself and made a difference in the world. He was a lifeline out of disaster, literally holding the door for others. His heroism, as well as many of other people's loved ones, is what has inspired me, my family, and friends to try to follow Dad's example and make a difference in people's lives. We have already begun to hold the door for others.

When I take the time to reflect upon what allowed me to honor the feelings of losing my dad, it is evident that I strive to live my life the way he lost his. I have a deep passion to put others first, especially in turbulent times. Interestingly enough, the best way to put others first is to first focus on yourself. What I mean by this is that to help others help themselves, you need to be healthy, strong, resilient, and emotionally intelligent. You need to be able to find a way to find the positive aspects in life when it seems that there are none.

I was fortunate to be studying psychology prior to the September 11, 2001, attacks. Throughout my training, as I worked with clients, I always felt strongly about practicing what I preach. When I would work with clients and invite them to practice behaviors and skills related to their emotional intelligence and self-awareness, I would do the same. This approach would provide me with the strength, balance, and energy to manage the fallout from my father's death as well as to maintain the pursuit of my dreams.

I remember the trip home from Richmond, Virginia, on September 12th. I wasn't able to get home on the 11th due to the highways, air traffic, and trains being shut down in certain areas. I can recall being on the way home and feeling extreme sadness and concern related to my missing dad.

I learned two things very quickly: I was going to need to be aware of the extreme feelings associated with the trauma of 9/11 and find the strength to rally and look for my dad on the streets of New York City. Personally, I attribute my ability to manage my feelings to my counseling training. The concepts that I had been studying and helping others to learn proved to be a huge resource for me as I cried at night while I thought of the idea that my dad would be gone forever, along with thousands of other Americans, and I hit the streets during the day determined to find him.

After looking for my dad, when I returned to school, to my group therapy class, I struggled with one question, "Is the strength in the crying and showing I am feeling the pain, or is the strength in the not crying and showing that I am okay and will be able to grow through the experience?" Dr. Craig Anderson, Virginia Commonwealth University's head of the group therapy program, said, "Rob, it is both." You know what, he was exactly right. To this day I share that story with people to illustrate how important it is to understand your feelings and experience and also to take steps toward self-reliance and strength.

Rob Fazio has spearheaded "Hold the Door," which is a non-profit organization with the aim to help people learning to grow through loss or adversity (e.g., loss of a loved one to cancer, divorce, or natural disaster). Through hands-on activities, expert speakers, and professionally designed workshops, Hold the Door programs teach participants to become more self-aware and learn practical skills to help them prepare for, live with, and grow through loss and adversity.

TIPS TO MAINTAIN YOUR PROGRESS
Discuss the following tips with your clinician to help you maintain your progress:

- Writing about a traumatic event can be extremely challenging. However, keeping the trauma inside—without expressing it in an adaptive manner—can be very harmful for you. Therefore, it is important that before and after the *Expressive Writing* practice, you remind yourself that your intent is to break the mental block, stop the cycle of thinking about the trauma, and, more importantly, explore if the trauma also brought about any positive changes in you.
- This practice is both individual and interpersonal. The therapeutic groundwork done so far, with the help of your clinician, is critical in preparing you to undertake this PTG endeavor. You will most likely use your strengths of courage, social intelligence, and self-regulation to undertake this work. However, to gain and maintain perspective, especially in interpreting its meaning and potential growth, you will greatly benefit from the continuation of therapeutic support. Confiding your feelings with your clinician, putting such feelings into words, and drawing insights about potential growth is best done in a safe, interpersonal context. We recommend that to maintain the benefits of this practice, you keep engaging in therapy for a while.
- It is also important that you do not force yourself to find growth or expect that surviving a trauma will yield major positive changes in your life. Growth from a trauma, although a more frequent phenomenon than acknowledged and recognized, may take its due time and course to manifest. Rather than searching for a discrete expression of growth, focus more on changes that might have organically occurred within you. For example, after surviving a traumatic event, most individuals report experiencing three things (Roepke, 2015):
  - Renewed belief in one's ability to endure and prevail.
  - Improved relationships—in particular, discovering who one's true friends are and on whom one can really count, and how critical one's relationships are, compared to material goods.
  - Feeling more comfortable with intimacy and feeling a greater sense of compassion for others who suffer.

Periodically reflect if these or similar changes have taken place in you.

RESOURCES

Readings

- Hass, M. (2015). *Bouncing Forward: Transforming Bad Breaks Into Breakthroughs*. New York: Simon & Shuster.
- Joseph, S. (2013). *What Doesn't Kill Us: The New Psychology of Posttraumatic Growth*. New York: Basic Books.
- Tedeschi, R. G., & Moore, B. A. (2016). *The Posttraumatic Growth Workbook: Coming Through Trauma Wiser, Stronger, and More Resilient*. Oakland, CA: New Harbinger.

Videos

- See Rob Fazio's story, described earlier in the section "In Real Life": https://youtu.be/RnTazUEzqt0
- Dr. Randy Pausch's inspirational speech: The Last Lecture: https://youtu.be/p1CEhH5gnvg
- Team Hoy: I Can Only Imagine, the story of Dick and Rick Hoyt, one of the most inspirational father and son teams to race in an Ironman competition: https://youtu.be/cxqe77-Am3w

Websites

- Home page of James Pennebaker: Pioneer in processing trauma through writing: https://liberalarts.utexas.edu/psychology/faculty/pennebak
- What doesn't kill us: http://www.huffingtonpost.com/stephen-joseph/what-doesnt-kill-us-post_b_2862726.html
- Mobile apps related to trauma: www.veterans.gc.ca/eng/stay-connected/mobile-app/ptsd-coach-canada
- Hold the Door for Others: A 9/11-inspired non-profit organization that offers invaluable free resources for those dealing with trauma, adversity, and bereavement: www.holdthedoor.com

SESSION ELEVEN: SLOWNESS AND SAVORING

11

IN SESSION ELEVEN, YOU WILL LEARN HOW to deliberately slow down and develop an awareness of how to savor. In so doing, you will learn to attend mindfully to the positives. The central positive psychotherapy (PPT) practices covered in this session are *Slow* and *Savor*.

THREE THINGS TO KNOW ABOUT *SLOW* AND *SAVOR*

1. **Turbo-charged world:** Speed dating, same-day delivery, drive-throughs, automated checkouts, instant fame (and infamy) through viral YouTubes and Tweets—all of these are indicators of our turbocharged lives in which every moment feels like a race against the clock. Instantaneousness and impatience have infected every corner of our lives—irrespective of where we live—and this speed is taking a toll on our health, diet, communication, relationships, politics, and environment Evidence shows that people who are cognitively busy are also more likely to act selfishly, use sexist language, and make erroneous judgment in social situations (Kahneman, 2011).

2. **Accomplished, yet not satisfied:** The pressures of our turbocharged world have enabled us to accomplish a lot. Multitasking—a ubiquitous phrase—has now become a desirable trait in our job descriptions. Speed, it seems, is becoming the most important ingredient in success. Going faster may be desirable, but, in most cases, it doesn't make us any happier or healthier.

3. **Slow and savor:** To reverse this cult of speed, it is important to explore the benefits of slowing down and savoring experiences. The latest neuroscience shows that when people are in a relaxed, mellow state, the brain slips into a deeper, richer, more nuanced mode of thought (Kahneman, 2011). Psychologists actually call this "Slow Thinking." Artists have always known that you cannot hurry the act of creation, and increasingly, businesses are realizing the same thing. Workers need moments to relax, unplug, and be silent in order to be creative and productive. Slowness is a prerequisite of savoring, which is mindfully combining the positive sensations, emotions, perceptions, thoughts, and beliefs to appreciate the experience.

START-OF-SESSION RELAXATION
At the start of the session, your clinician may begin with a brief relaxation exercise. To discover some of these practices on your own, go to Appendix A: Relaxation and Mindfulness Practices, which can be found at the end of this workbook.

IN-SESSION PRACTICE: *SLOW*
Your clinician will be working with you on the in-session practices. Refer to the Worksheet 11.1.

WORKSHEET 11.1 STRATEGIES TO SLOW DOWN

How can you shift gears and slow down a little? Here are some suggestions. Please select one that you feel you can easily implement. In the space at the end of this worksheet, indicate which option you selected. Then write about why you selected this option.

Start Small and Gradually Decelerate: An incremental and gradual slowing down of pace is better than screeching to a halt. Start with a small decrease and gradually decelerate.

Start with a Few Areas: Pick one or two areas you usually hurry through and slow those areas down. Some examples could be eating at least three meals slowly in a week, walking slowly at least once a week, or having a media/technology-free evening once a week.

Get Involved: Deliberately focus on peaceful experiences, such as following floating clouds with your eyes, watching the sunset, feeling the breeze, or hearing and enjoying wind chimes. You may find that the rhythms of nature are slow but deeply satisfying.

Educate: Talk to your family and friends about the adverse consequences of speed (e.g., accidents, injuries, stress, and anxiety).

Gadget-Free Zones: Create gadget-free times or zones (e.g., no cell phones after 6 PM or no TV in the bedroom).

Learn to Say No: Learn to say no and avoid overscheduling.

Selected Option:
Why did you select this option?

Actions:
What specific actions you will take?

How often?

What sort of social support do you think you need to implement this strategy?

If this strategy works, what would be different in three months?

This worksheet was originally published in Rashid and Seligman's *Positive Psychotherapy: Clinician Manual.*

POSITIVE PSYCHOTHERAPY

Reflect & Discuss

Reflect on and discuss the following:

- If you find yourself constantly busy, how does this business manifest in your daily life? Do you find yourself constantly short on time, and do you multitask?
- Do you feel that information overload, time crunch, overstimulation, underperforming, and multitasking are some of the signs of being busy and living life on the fast track? Which ones of these do you experience?
- What drives your busy behavior? Do you believe that these are internal, external, or a combination of both? Examples of internal behavior are anxious personality disposition and experiencing symptoms of anxiety.
- How does the slowness strategy you selected on Worksheet 11.1 relate to your specific signs?
- All of the strategies to slow down mentioned here require active engagement. What specific actions will you take, or who will support or inhibit your active engagement?
- Which strengths (either from your profile or otherwise) can you use to ensure that your selected strategy is successful?

IN-SESSION PRACTICE: *SAVOR*

Your clinician will be working with you on the in-session practices. Refer to Worksheet 11.2.

WORKSHEET 11.2   SAVORING EXPERIENCES AND TECHNIQUES

Savoring is mindfully combining the positive sensations, emotions, perceptions, thoughts, and beliefs to appreciate the experience. This worksheet lists different kinds of savoring experiences, followed by techniques you can use to savor. In the space at the end of this worksheet, select a savoring technique you would like to try. Then write about when, where, and how often you can use this technique in your daily life.

Kinds of Savoring Experiences
Basking: Taking great pleasure or satisfaction in one's accomplishments, good fortune, and blessings.
Thanksgiving: Giving thanks; expressing gratitude.
Luxuriating: Taking great pleasure (and showing no restraint) in enjoying physical comforts and sensations.
Marveling: Becoming filled with wonder or astonishment. Beauty often induces marveling. Exercising virtue may also inspire marveling. For example, one might marvel at a person's strength in facing and overcoming adversity.
Mindfulness: The state of being aware, attentive, and observant of oneself, one's surroundings and other people.
Savoring Techniques
Sharing With Others: You can seek out others to share an experience and tell others how much you value the moment. This is the single strongest predictor of pleasure.
Memory Building: Take mental photographs or even a physical souvenir of an event and reminisce about it later with others.
Self-praise: Don't be afraid of pride. Share your achievements with others. This is about being authentic and honest in celebrating your persistence in maintaining focus and verve in achieving something meaningful to you.
Sharpening Perceptions: This involves focusing on certain elements and blocking out others. For example, most people spend far more time thinking about how they can correct something that has gone wrong (or is about to go wrong) than they do basking in what has gone right. *Select one of these savoring techniques. When, where, and how frequently can you use it to increase positive emotions in your daily life?*

This worksheet was originally published in Rashid and Seligman's *Positive Psychotherapy: Clinician Manual.*

Reflect & Discuss

Reflect on and discuss the following:

- Of the four kinds of savoring (basking, thanksgiving, luxuriating, and marveling), which one would you use most frequently and in what situations?
- Is there any additional kind of savoring you utilized that is not listed here?
- Are there any factors that inhibit you from using any of the kinds of savoring listed in Worksheet 11.2?
- Savoring requires practice. What specific actions can you undertake to solidify your savoring practice?

IN-SESSION PRACTICE: PLANNED SAVORING ACTIVITY

If your clinician conducted a savoring activity during session, reflect on and discuss the following:

Reflect & Discuss

- How many of your senses did you involve as you were savoring the items of your choice?
- Did you try to focus on certain sensory properties of the items while blocking others?
- While you were savoring, did you feel the urge to leave one item and rush to another?
- Were you able to make yourself comfortable and relaxed to do this activity? What did you do to relax? Do you do this often?
- While savoring, did you think that the specific item could have been better? What prompted that thought?
- Did you have a good experience? What led to it?

HOMEWORK PRACTICE: *A SAVORING DATE*

If your clinician assigned a savoring date as homework, reflect on and discuss the following:

Reflect & Discuss

- How much did you enjoy your savoring date? If you didn't, what prevented you from enjoying it?
- Did deliberate planning affect the joy or pleasure? Do you think that doing this spontaneously would produce a different outcome?
- How rare is this type of date in your life?
- Did you try to take in every sensory property of the savoring date (sights, sounds, smells, etc.)?
- During the savoring date, did you think about other things that were hanging over you, such as problems, worries, or chores that you still must face?

In Real Life: Jin, 27, female, East Asian descent

Jin participated in group PPT and describes her experience with the practices of *Slow* and *Savor*:

"*I suffer from generalized anxiety—I worry about things I shouldn't—and when I am worried, I rush things that should not be rushed. I couldn't help it because I felt like a motor was driving me from inside at high speed. When the topic of slowness and savoring came up, my first reaction was, "I will even speed up the experiences that ought to be slow and ought to be savored." However, the worksheet I was using offered the option to start small and slow in just one area. I selected eating because I love good food. Before getting busy, I even used to cook, try new recipes, and invite friends over. I committed to two things:*

- *Taking at least eight minutes daily to eat one of my meals, and then gradually increasing it to 10.*
- *Cooking at least one meal from scratch, once a month, and inviting my boyfriend to share it with me.*

For the first one, I opted to try dinner. Initially it was a challenging because I usually rush through my dinner, often in front of the television or computer screen. However, the timer on my cell phone helped me, as I was able to slow down while keeping an eye on both my dinner plate and phone. After a week, I just started the timer, put my phone away, and ate slowly. For the first time in years, I began enjoying—--paying attention to what was I eating and how it tasted. Gradually it became a habit. Now I am unable to finish my dinner in less than 15 minutes.

The experience of cooking with my boyfriend has also been very positive. We take turns to select a recipe. We shop for ingredients together. Sometimes we are unable to find all the ingredients or one ingredient is too expensive or not available easily. We substitute it with something else, and usually it turns out fine. This experience has sharpened our savoring skills. We have started paying attention to specific smells, tastes, and textures. It has brought us closer together.

Tips to Maintain Your Progress

Discuss the following tips with your clinician to help you maintain your progress:

- Savoring requires practice. Reflect and write your personal list of actions which can sustain and enhance savoring.
- Some of us may struggle with savoring practices because we overthink experiences, which interferes with our ability to notice and attend to our senses, such as touch, smell, or hearing.
- Attend mindfully to all aspects of a savoring experience, including its cognitive, affective, and behavioral aspects. However, tuning in too much to feelings or thoughts may backfire and could interfere, eventually dampening the savoring experience.
- The focus of the *Slow* and *Savor* practices is positive. If you are feeling distressed, see if you are able to put aside your negative thoughts and feelings for a while, so that you will benefit more from these practices. You can use the diversion strategy (from Session Five: Open and Closed Memories) to optimally benefit from your savoring experience.
- One way to maintain savoring is to diversify it. Spend quality time with one of your favorite family members or friends. Pick an activity that both of you enjoy. It could be as simple as having a conversation in a distraction-free environment, watching a movie together, or going for a walk. Try to be in the "here and now" with that person without worrying about the past or the future.
- Spend some time by yourself. This could be for half an hour or an entire day. You could choose to listen to favorite songs, explore a park, go to a new restaurant, or simply read a book of your choice. Pay close attention to your senses while you are engaged in the activity. What do you see, smell, and hear around you?
- Speed is not always bad, nor always good. Sometimes it is good to work quickly, but, for the most part, when we work in a relaxed state, our brain becomes more creative and more productive in performing complex tasks.

- To maintain and enhance savoring, you can also replicate the in-session practice with friends and family members, especially on special occasions and celebrations.

The following is a suggested list of items to savor. The items on this list are designed to target each of the senses and to broaden the notion of savoring to include items beside food: Dark chocolate; smooth rocks and sea shells; bags of various ground coffees or loose teas; kaleidoscope; CDs with different genres of music such as opera, jazz, hip hop; various nuts; wind chimes; flowers; pine cones; honeysuckle; cotton; sandpaper, gauze; and a poem.

RESOURCES

Readings

- Bryant, F. B., & Veroff, J. (2007). *Savoring: A New Model of Positive Experience*. Mahwah, NJ: Erlbaum.
- Honore, C. (2004). *In Praise of Slowness: How a Worldwide Movement in Challenging the Cult of Speed*. San Francisco: Harper.
- Kahneman, D. (2011). *Thinking Fast and Slow*. London: Allen Lane.

Videos

- TED Talk: Nature. Beauty. Gratitude: Louis Schwartzberg's stunning time-lapse photography: http://www.ted.com/talks/louie_schwartzberg_nature_beauty_gratitude
- TED Talk: David Griffin: How photography connects us: http://www.ted.com/playlists/30/natural_wonder
- TED Talk: Julian Treasure lays out an eight-step plan to restore our relationship with sound: http://www.ted.com/talks/julian_treasure_shh_sound_health_in_8_steps

Websites

- National Geographic's official website: http://www.nationalgeographic.com
- The Slow Movement addresses "time poverty" through making connections: http://www.slowmovement.com/
- The World Institute of Slowness: Learn about slow consulting, slow brands, slow food, slow art, and more: http://www.theworldinstituteofslowness.com/

12

SESSION TWELVE: POSITIVE RELATIONSHIPS

IN SESSION TWELVE, YOU WILL LEARN ABOUT the significance of recognizing the strengths of your loved ones. The central positive psychotherapy (PPT) practice covered in this session is creating a *Tree of Positive Relationships*.

NAVIGATING PPT

So far, our PPT voyage has encouraged you to focus on unfolding your inner resourcefulness. We hope that these practices have helped you to be able to use your own positive resources to further build your own resilience. Together, you and your clinician have traveled the peaks and valleys of emotions and experiences—from spotting the good in the moment (*Gratitude Journal*) to revisiting experiences that brought out the goodness within; from calming meandering minds to composing a rich, textured, and holistic self-concept (signature strengths profile); from encountering with courage the pain of open and negative memories to expressing an enduring sense of thankfulness (*Gratitude Letter* and *Visit*). All of these positive emotions and experiences have helped to broaden your mindset. From this point onwards, the PPT practices focus primarily on interpersonal, social, and communal resourcefulness. We start with positive relationships.

THREE THINGS TO KNOW ABOUT *POSITIVE RELATIONSHIPS*

1. **Positive relationships and well-being:** Humans are essentially social beings. Think about your most critical, defining, and transformative moments—birth, first day in school, high school graduation, first job, first serious relationship, first house, first car, first heartbreak, significant sickness, significant losses, significant career achievement, memorable travels, and religious or cultural celebrations. For most of these occasions, if not all, you did not experience them alone. The fabric of our well-being is intricately interwoven within our social relationships. If these relationships have been largely positive, you are likely to be happy and healthy.
2. **Strength spotting:** Spotting, acknowledging, and leveraging strengths—as sources of well-being and happiness—are key to fostering positive relationships. From the vantage point of PPT, learning about one another's strengths is important because such understanding promotes empathy and fosters greater appreciation for each person's actions and intentions.
3. **Positive relationships buffer against stressors:** Positive relationships can be helpful in dealing with distress. If you feel stressed, sad, and indecisive, a strong and positive relationship allows you to share your worries, stressors, and confusion. Such sharing can help you make sense of complex situations. Likewise, if friends or loved ones are in a similar situation, you will probably offer them support, and this reciprocal care builds bonds that buffer you from loneliness and feelings of helplessness.

START-OF-SESSION RELAXATION

At the start of the session, your clinician may begin with a brief relaxation exercise. To discover some of these practices on your own, go to Appendix A: Relaxation & Mindfulness Practices, which can be found at the end of this workbook.

IN-SESSION PRACTICE: TREE OF POSITIVE RELATIONSHIPS

Your clinician will be working with you on the in-session practices. Refer to Worksheet 12.1.

One way to foster positive relationships is by realizing the importance of understanding and acknowledging the highest strengths of your loved ones and how you fit into your larger family and friend network. When you recognize the strengths of your friends and family members, you are more likely to appreciate them and to build stronger connections. In addition, learning about one another's strengths may potentially help you to gain new insights into the behavior of your loved ones that you previously misunderstood. For example, when Beverley discovers that several of her husband Jackson's top strengths are honesty, fairness, and bravery, she is better able to understand why he would drive all the way across town to return an extra dollar he was accidentally given when checking out at a grocery store— even though he will spend over a dollar in gas in the process of driving to and from the store. Rather than seeing Jackson's behavior as illogical, Beverley can see that he is simply acting according to his strengths of character. Likewise, parents who come to understand that a signature strength of their child is curiosity and interest in the world are better able to tolerate, and even come to enjoy, the abundance of questions posed by the child about how and why things work the way they do.

The Tree of Positive Relationships is designed to help you and people you are close with to gain greater insight into each other's strengths. In order to complete this homework, please ask your family members to complete the Signature Strengths Questionnaire (SSQ-72) available at: www.tayyabrashid.com, or the Values in Action survey available at: http://www.viacharacter.org/

After your loved ones have determined their strengths and have shared these results with you, please complete the blank tree here. We have provided an example of a completed tree for your reference.

Sample *Tree of Positive Relationships*

This worksheet was originally published in Rashid and Seligman's *Positive Psychotherapy: Clinician Manual.*

Reflect & Discuss

After you have finished Worksheet 12.1, move on to Worksheet 12.2, and share that with your clinician during your next session.

After you have completed your Tree of Positive Relationships, fill out this worksheet and bring it to your next session:

1.   What specific events exemplify strengths of your loved ones?
   •   Example 1: *My father is kind because he always tries to do nice things for me without me even asking for them.*
   •   Example 2: *My best friend is brave because she stands up for others when people say mean things.*

   Example:

   _____

   _____

   Example:

   _____

   _____

   Example:

   _____

   _____

2.   Can you identify people in your tree who have helped you develop your strengths?

   _____

   _____

3.   Do you have any strengths that are also in your loved ones' top five?

   _____

   _____

4.   Are there any specific patterns in terms of strengths among your close relationships?

   _____

   _____

5.   Do you have any strengths that no one else in your tree of strengths has?

   _____

   _____

6.   How can you use your strengths together to make relationships stronger?

   _____

   _____

This worksheet was originally published in Rashid and Seligman's *Positive Psychotherapy: Clinician Manual.*

In Real Life: Adina, 19, female, African-Canadian

Adina sought individual therapy to work on, among several other issues, her troubled relationship with her mother. Adina had a nonverbal learning difference; she presented as emotionally flat, with little expression on her face and minimal intonation in her responses, which were often short and interspersed by long and awkward pauses. In five sessions we made little progress. I (Dr. Rashid) was running out of ideas, but since Adina was compliant and came regularly to session, I asked her to complete the character strengths assessment, which she diligently completed. We tried many ways to use her strengths to improve her relationship with her mother, with no success. One day, I happened to remark, "Adina, has anyone ever told you that you look like a younger version of the tennis star, Serena Williams?" Adina blushed and then smiled—a rare therapeutic success—and, following a pause, she told me that many people have told her the same thing.

Adina's mother never wanted a daughter. She was afraid that a girl would be vulnerable, just as she was, and her mother started dressing Adina like a boy when Adina was very young. The mother took Adina to sports camps and martial arts classes, which Adina hated; she wanted to be a female, a fashion designer, and to celebrate her femininity. The mother's disapproval barred Adina from wearing any makeup or dressing according to her own tastes. When our session ended, I asked Adina to complete an assignment, using her character strengths, to write one-word descriptors to describe herself as a successful female, just like the famous person she resembles. Next session, Adina came with 27 descriptors, such as confident, committed, passionate, and caring.

With her permission, I invited her mother to join the following session, and both agreed. As the three of us met, I explained to her mother the task I had given Adina, who was willing to share each descriptor. I requested that Adina also describe how she personally relates to each descriptor, such as what makes her a confident female, what make her committed or disciplined. Adina started, in her soft voice, with minimal eye contact. With each descriptor, came a story, an anecdote, or a memory. Adina kept describing these positive traits without much variation in her tone. Her mother kept on listening, intently, and suddenly her eyes filled with tears. We barely finished six descriptors. Her mother got up and hugged Adina and said, "I am proud to have a daughter like you!"

TIPS TO MAINTAIN YOUR PROGRESS

Discuss the following tips with your clinician to help you maintain your progress:

- One way to build positive relationships is by spotting, naming, and celebrating the strengths of our loved ones. When you recognize the strengths of your loved ones, on the spot, it creates a positive resonance, which could, in turn, strengthen relationships.

- Focus on activities that develop bonds among family members; that establish routines, traditions, and communication patterns; and that happen on a regular basis. These are core family leisure activities.

- From spotting, acknowledging, and celebrating strengths, it is important to create both spontaneous and structured activities. Spontaneous activities are ones that require minimal planning, are informal, and are inclusive of everyone or most family members. Examples of spontaneous activities include family dinner in the park; shopping for ingredients together and then trying them in a new recipe; playing board or digital games; or casually doing sports together, such as shooting hoops in the driveway, playing badminton in the backyard, or enjoying ping pong in the basement. Examples of structured family activities include family vacations; outdoor adventures such as picnics, camping, attending sporting or cultural events; and visiting extended family or close friends in another city, state, province, or country (Morganson, Litano, & O'Neill, 2014).

For some families, structured activities may also include visiting specific places or sites of religious, spiritual, artistic, political, or cultural significance. Both spontaneous and structured activities that involve loved ones cement positive relationships like nothing else. Consider this quote from Kelly (1997):

Life is not composed of theme parks and cruises. It is composed of dinner table talk, vacations together, getting the home and yard in shape, kidding around, caring for each other, goofing off, dreaming, and all the minutiae of the day and the hour. That is the real life in real conditions that is important to us all (p. 3).

- Try to have an uninterrupted chat with every member of your family at least once a week. Periodically ask yourself, "Am I listening to my loved one the way I would like to be listened to?"
- Learning about one another's strengths may also help clients gain new insights into the behaviors of family members that they previously misunderstood. This knowledge will enable family members to know, acknowledge, and celebrate each other's strengths and promote interactions and family-centered activities around those strengths. For instance, if you learn that your partner has the strengths of appreciation of beauty and excellence, then a creative or performing arts center would be a great place to visit when you are on vacation. If some of your family members love sports, a family excursion around a sporting event may allow the display of multiple strengths, including playfulness and humor (having fun together), teamwork (coordination of the event), and love of learning (knowledge about sports).
- Investing in positive relationships within one's family, chosen family, and/or circle of significant others takes time, skill, and effort. This effort can lead to greater happiness.
- In cultivating positive relationships among significant others, it is important to recognize the strengths of these others and to engage in activities that allow all parties to use their strengths.
- Taking the time to remember the strengths and other positive qualities of loved ones is important for preserving positive relationships. Over time, we can get so used to these positive qualities that we do not notice them as much as we once did.

RESOURCES
Readings
- Durant, M. V., & Hieneman, M. (2008). *Helping Parents with Challenging Children Positive Family Intervention Guide*. New York: Oxford University Press.
- Lieberman, M. D. (2014). *Social: Why Our Brains Are Wired to Connect*. New York: Crown/ Random House.
- Reckmeyer, M. (2016). *Strengths Based Parenting: Developing Your Children's Innate Talents*. New York: Gallup Press.
- Waters, L. (2017). *The Strength Switch: How the New Science of Strength-Based Parenting Can Help Your Child and Your Teen to Flourish*. New York: Penguin Random House.

Videos
- YouTube: Let's Eat Rice Daddy: 2012 Chinese New Year commercial by BERNAS: https://youtu.be/LzP8E8KSgPc
- Positive Parenting: Lea Waters on Strength Based Parenting: https://youtu.be/RMhVopiQYzM
- TED Talk: Andrew Solomon: What Does Family Mean? https://www.ted.com/talks/andrew_solomon_love_no_matter_what?referrer=playlist-what_does_family_mean
- YouTube: Father, Son and a Sparrow: https://youtu.be/fOYpFhxEptE

Websites

- Institute of Family Studies:
  https://ifstudies.org/
- Better Together:
  http://robertdputnam.com/better-together/
- Centre for Family Studies, University of Oxford:
  https://www.cfr.cam.ac.uk/

SESSION THIRTEEN: POSITIVE COMMUNICATION

13

IN SESSION THIRTEEN, YOU WILL BE LEARNING about four styles of responding to good news. Of these styles, only *Active Constructive Responding (ACR)*—the central practice covered in this session—predicts relationship satisfaction.

THREE THINGS TO KNOW ABOUT *POSITIVE COMMUNICATION*

1. **Responding to negative and positive events:** When you experience an adversity, challenge, trauma, or setback, what are you most likely to do? You are most likely to seek support from your loved ones, friends, community, or professional resources. If you do, odds are that you will be able to better cope. What happens when you experience a success or accomplish something significant and you share it with your partner? Sharing positive events and experiences is as critical as sharing challenges and setbacks. When you share a positive event with your partner and he or she responds in a positive and constructive manner, it strengthens your relationship.

2. **Capitalization:** Shelly Gable and her colleagues (Gable, Reis, Impett, & Asher, 2004; Maisel & Gable, 2009) have explored the intrapersonal and interpersonal consequences of sharing a positive event or experience with loved ones. Their work is based on Langston (1994) who found that when people experience a positive event and share the news with others, this sharing makes them even happier. Langston termed this effect "capitalization," a term that Gable used to denote the process of sharing positive news with another person and thereby deriving additional benefit from it. Capitalization is a process of being seen, felt, valued, and expanded. The sum of these components is greater since both the sharer and the responder feel validated.

3. **Benefits and caveats about *ACR*:** If you share a significant positive event or experience with others and feel validated, it gives you the reassurance that you are important. In turn, the people who respond to you also feel happy, and this increases their positive emotions, thus strengthening your relationships. This communication process is about depth (listening well, asking pertinent questions) rather than volume (communicating with lots of people). Nonetheless, it is important that the respondent has sufficient time and space to respond actively and positively.

START-OF-SESSION RELAXATION
At the start of the session, your clinician may begin with a brief relaxation exercise. To discover some of these practices on your own, go to Appendix A: Relaxation & Mindfulness Practices, which can be found at the end of this workbook.

IN-SESSION PRACTICE: ACR
Your clinician will be working with you on the in-session practices. Refer to Worksheet 13.1.

WORKSHEET 13.1   EXAMPLES OF FOUR RESPONDING STYLES

Please read about the following different styles of responding and put an X in the Response column for the ones that apply to you most of the time.

Active/Constructive	Response
My partner usually reacts to my good fortune enthusiastically.	
I sometimes get the sense that my partner is even more happy and excited than I am.	
My partner often asks a lot of questions and shows genuine interest about the good event.	
Passive/Constructive	
My partner tries not to make a big deal out of it but is happy for me.	
My partner is usually silently supportive of the good things that occur to me.	
My partner says little, but I know he/she is happy for me.	
Active/Destructive	
My partner often finds a problem with it.	
My partner reminds me that most good things have their bad aspects as well.	
He/she points out the potential downsides of the good event.	
Passive/Destructive	
Sometimes I get the impression that he/she doesn't care much.	
My partner doesn't pay much attention to me.	
My partner often seems uninterested.	

- *Now it's your turn to try ACR today in-session. Take turns with a partner (or with your clinician if you are in individual therapy).*
- *As the **Sharer**, think of something meaningful and positive that happened to you, or that you noticed in the last week. Share this with your partner.*
- *As the **Responder**, think about your strengths and explore how you can use your strengths in the Active Constructive Responses you offer (e.g., curiosity to guide your question, optimism, social intelligence).*
- *Then switch roles between sharer and responder. When this practice is complete, your clinician will ask you some reflection questions.*

This worksheet was originally published in Rashid and Seligman's *Positive Psychotherapy: Clinician Manual.*

Reflect & Discuss

Reflect on and discuss the following:

- What was comfortable in doing this practice?
- What was uncomfortable in doing this practice?
- Are there any subjective or objective barriers (such as your personality style, preferences, family of origin, culture, beliefs, or interpersonal dynamics) that hinder you in engaging in *ACR*?
- If you already do some sort of *ACR*, what can you do to take it to a higher level?
- If you find that *ACR* doesn't come naturally to you, what small steps can you take to adopt some aspects of this practice that are consistent with your disposition?
- Identify individuals or situations that display all four responding styles. What effects do you notice of each style both on sharer and responder?
- What can you learn about yourself from identifying your response style?

HOMEWORK PRACTICE: IDENTIFY YOUR PARTNER'S STRENGTHS

If your clinician assigns this homework, please complete Worksheet 13.2.

Earlier in therapy, you completed practices that enabled you to determine your own signature strengths, and now you are quite familiar with these strengths. To complete this homework assignment, you will need two copies of this worksheet. Set aside at least 30 minutes for this practice with your partner. In a relaxed environment, ask your partner to fill out the worksheet by identifying five strengths that best represent you, without ranking them. While your partner is completing the worksheet, you complete one for your partner. When finished, exchange worksheets and continue with the Reflect & Discuss questions.

Description		**Signature Strengths**
1	Is good at thinking of new and better ways of doing things	
2	Loves to explore things, asks questions, is open to different experiences and activities	
3	Is flexible and open-minded; thinks through and examines all sides before deciding	
4	Loves to learn new ideas, concepts, and facts in school or on her/his own	
5	Friends consult him/her regarding important matters; is considered to be wise beyond age	
6	Does not give up in face of hardship or challenge, even when afraid	
7	Finishes most things; is able to refocus when distracted and complete the task	
8	Is a genuine and honest person, is known to be trustworthy; acts consistent with her/his values	
9	Is energetic, cheerful, and full of life	
10	Both loving and being loved comes natural to him/her; values close relationships with others	
11	Loves to do kind acts for others, often without being asked	
12	Manages her/himself well in social situations and is known to have good interpersonal skills	
13	Is an active community or team member, and contributes to the success of the group	
14	Stands up for others when they are treated unfairly, bullied, or ridiculed	
15	Is often chosen by others as a leader; is known to lead well	
16	Forgives easily those who offend him/her; does not hold grudges	
17	Doesn't like to be the center of attention and prefers others to shine	
18	Is careful and cautious, can anticipate risks and problems of his/her actions and responds accordingly	
19	Manages feelings and behaviors well in challenging situations; generally follows rules and routines	
20	Is moved deeply by beauty in nature, in art (e.g., painting, music, theatre) and/or in excellence in many fields of life	
21	Expresses thankfulness for good things through words and actions	
22	Hopes and believe that more good things will happen than bad ones	
23	Is playful and funny, and uses humor to connect with others	
24	Believes in a higher power and participates in religious or spiritual practices (e.g., prayer, meditation) willingly	

This worksheet was originally published in Rashid and Seligman's *Positive Psychotherapy: Clinician Manual.*

Reflect & Discuss

After completing this practice with your partner, reflect on and discuss:

- How was the process of labeling and affirming each other's strengths? Have you done similar things with your partner before?
- What behaviors, actions, or habits does your partner exhibit to denote the strengths you identified?
- Do you share strengths with each other? Discuss any your share as well as ones you don't.
- In what ways do your strengths complement each other?
- Did you also look at your partner's and your bottom strengths? What can you learn from those?

In Real Life: Rochelle, 33, female, Caucasian

Rochelle, married for four years, shares her experience with the *ACR* practice.

I love my husband. He is from an East Asian culture and was raised with the cultural expectations of not expressing emotions—positive or negative. He is a very polite person, but not very expressive. I was sure that the ACR practice would not work with him.

Despite being very accomplished, he is very modest. For example, I knew that he had submitted an application for a large grant proposal, and I knew the day he was going to find out if it came through. When he came home that afternoon, I asked about the grant, and he told me, smiling and happy, that he and his colleagues got the grant. So I found my moment to practice ACR. I responded positively and constructively, as follows. "I am so happy because I know how hard you worked for this grant, which will positively impact your research. You will now be able to hire staff to help you, which will free up your time for more important work. Your application must have been well written and well organized because not many people are successful in getting this grant." My husband, initially taken aback, started responding and gave detailed feedback—something he doesn't do very often. We decided to go out and celebrate. Although he did not explicitly express it, I could tell from his expression how proud he was feeling. This positive experience encouraged me to respond actively and constructively with our 12-year-old son and with my students, and I have found this to be quite beneficial. I also learned that I can address my concerns more effectively when I bring them up later and do not mix them with my active and constructive responses.

Tips to Maintain Your Progress

Discuss the following tips with your clinician to help you maintain your progress:

- In *ACR*, the authentic inquiry, not the volume of inquiry, matters. It is what is seen, felt, valued, and expanded authentically. These steps need practice in a variety of situations.
- *ACR* is about specificity. Each question builds on the next one. Even if the sharer dismisses or is evasive, the responder should keep acknowledging.
- *ACR* is about attunement, getting to know one another deeply and authentically, in which both parties feel understood, validated, and cared for.
- *ACR* is not only for partners. It can be used when friends or other family member share a good event.
- The impact of *ACR* is most likely to increase if you are able to set aside negative emotions, feeling, and doubts for a while and be with your loved one celebrating and sharing the positive moments. You can discuss negatives, complaints, doubts, or adverse impacts on you later on.
- *ACR* offers a concrete way to enhance the ability to recognize, understand, and respond to positive emotions, feelings, and experiences of loved ones. Ask your partner how this process can help the two of you to enhance your understanding of other issues, situations, events, or experiences that could also benefit from *ACR*.

RESOURCES

Readings

- Gottman, J. M. (2011). *The Science of Trust: Emotional Attunement for Couples*. New York: W.W. Norton.
- Pawelski, S. P., & Pawelski, J. (2018). *Happy Together: Using the Science of Positive Psychology to Build Love That Lasts*. New York: Penguin Random House.
- Socha, T. J., & Pitts, M. J. (2012). *The Positive Side of Interpersonal Communication*. New York: Peter Lang.

Videos

- YouTube: Active Constructive Responding:
  https://youtu.be/qRORihbXMnA?list=PLLBhiMXTg8qvQ4Ge94wRFYZhk66t_wm1e
- Shelley Gable explains Active Constructive Response (ACR):
  https://youtu.be/OF9kfJmS_0k
- It Is Not About the Nail: A hilarious illustration on the importance of "I just need you to listen":
  https://youtu.be/-4EDhdAHrOg

Websites

- People will like you:
  http://www.pbs.org/thisemotionallife/blogs/happiness-exercise-how-make-people-love-you
- Using positive psychology in your relationships:
  http://health.usnews.com/health-news/family-health/brain-and-behavior/articles/2009/06/24/using-positive-psychology-in-your-relationships
- Atlas of Emotions: Paul Ekman aims to build a vocabulary of emotions:
  http://atlasofemotions.org/#introduction/disgust

SESSION FOURTEEN: ALTRUISM

14

IN SESSION FOURTEEN, YOU WILL LEARN HOW being altruistic helps both you and others. The central positive psychotherapy (PPT) practice covered in this session is the *Gift of Time*.

THREE THINGS TO KNOW ABOUT *ALTRUISM*

1. **Creating meaning through altruism:** The final phase of PPT focuses on creating meaning, and altruism is one way to do that. Altruism is benefitting others, by your own free will, without being asked for it and without any financial reimbursement. You can create and pursue meaning by using your signature strengths to belong to and serve something that you believe is bigger than yourself. If you want to create and pursue meaning, you can shape your life or facets of your life that matter to the world and make a difference for the better.

2. **How can altruism help you?** Helping others shifts your focus from indulging in your own thoughts (i.e., brooding over depressive thinking) as your attention moves from unhealthy thinking to a healthier behavioral endeavor. While the former (brooding) may make you vulnerable and reinforces your self-perception as a victim, the latter (altruism) is more likely to boost your confidence that you can do something good.

3. **Purchases versus experiences:** If you buy and consume products with the goal of becoming happier, the odds are that you are not very likely to attain and maintain that goal because, over time, the products you purchase will lose their charm. However, positive experiential activities, over time, get better (Kasser & Kanner, 2004) because when you engage in experiences such as volunteering, you tend to reflect at a deeper level as to whether your involvement is worth it. Products are associated with utility, while experiences are linked with emotions. Experiences connect you with people (through interactions), while products and gadgets—especially all of today's technological devices—pull us away from the people around us. Indeed, you may connect with many people on Facebook and other social media platforms, but in reality, you are distancing yourself from your colleagues in the next office, from your neighbors next door, and from your loved ones in the next room.

START-OF-SESSION RELAXATION
At the start of the session, your clinician may begin with a brief relaxation exercise. To discover some of these practices on your own, go to Appendix A: Relaxation & Mindfulness Practices, which can be found at the end of this workbook.

IN-SESSION ACTIVITY: VIDEO CAPTURING THE PRACTICE OF THE *GIFT OF TIME*

The in-session practice for this session focuses on watching a video that captures the concept of altruism and illustrates the *Gift of Time* practice.

> *Gift: Singapore Inspiration Drama Short Film (Duration: 7:30):*
> https://youtu.be/1DUYlHZsZfc?list=PL8m
> This short film depicts a son who discovers a big secret about his father, one that changes the son's understanding of his father.

Reflect & Discuss

After watching the video, reflect on and discuss the following:

- What stood out for you in this video about altruism?
- Did the material remind you of anything from your own experiences regarding altruism?
- What specific actions, if any, did the video offer you to ponder regarding the cultivation of altruism in your daily life?
- Why did the father keep the secret of giving from his son?
- In the video, the father gives a lot, despite not having much. How can his example help people who may think that they have nothing or very little to offer?

After watching the video and discussing these questions in session, please complete Worksheet 14.1 as homework. Discuss with your clinician about when this assignment should be done.

WORKSHEET 14.1   *THE GIFT OF TIME*

The aim of this practice is for you to give someone you care about the Gift of Time by doing something for them that requires a fair amount of time and involves using one of your signature strengths.

It will make the exercise more gratifying for you if you use your signature strength to deliver the gift. For example:

- *Someone who is creative might write an anniversary note for a best friend.*
- *Someone who is playful and humorous might arrange a roast.*
- *Someone who is kind might prepare a four-course dinner for his or her sick roommate or partner.*

After completing this exercise, write about your experience giving the Gift of Time. Be sure to record exactly what you did and how long it took:

_____

_____

_____

_____

_____

_____

_____

_____

_____

_____

_____

_____

This worksheet was originally published in Rashid and Seligman's *Positive Psychotherapy: Clinician Manual.*

Reflect & Discuss

Reflect on and discuss the following:

- How did you feel as you were giving your gift?
- How did you feel after giving your gift?
- How did the recipient of your gift react?
- Were there any consequences (positive or negative) resulting from giving your gift?
- Did you use one or more of your signature strengths? If so, which one and how?
- Have you undertaken such an activity in the past? What was it? Did you find that it was different this time around? If so, what differences did you notice?
- Have there been times in the past when you were asked to give the *Gift of Time* and you did not want to?
- Have you been a recipient of someone else's *Gift of Time*? What was it?
- Are you willing to give the *Gift of Time* regularly for a particular cause? What cause might this be?
- Do you anticipate any adaptation? That is, after a while, do you think the *Gift of Time* might not provide as much satisfaction as it did the first time? If so, what steps can you take address this?

In Real Life: The following are illustrations of three clients who have used their *Gift of Time*:

- *Joshua, 22, male, Causation: Joshua struggled with self-image. From childhood on, he perceived himself as being overweight, unattractive, and unpopular. Discussing his signature strengths in his PPT group, he said that he developed humor—mostly by making fun of himself—and this made him popular. After completing his signature strengths and learning practical wisdom strategies, Joshua realized that he could also use humor to cheer up those who could really use it. He started volunteering at a school for children with special needs. He tells them stories and includes tons of humor.*
- *Nabeel, 28, male, who participated in a PPT workshop, immigrated to Canada from Bangladesh about 10 years before beginning PPT. Despite having lived in three cosmopolitan cities on two different continents, he initially struggled with the nuances of language—the cultural vernacular—which only the locals understand well. Teamwork and citizenship are among Nabeel's signature strengths. He finished his master's degree in public policy and now volunteers at a center for immigrants, educating them about government, civics, and ways they can understand public policy.*
- *Juanita, 39, female, Latina, participated in individual PPT. Tragically, she had lost her infant son due to a congenital heart problem 8 days after his birth, and, one year later, she lost her husband to a traffic accident. After many years of struggling with complicated grief and depression, helping others was the most effective intervention for Juanita. Kindness is one of her signature strengths. She now volunteers for an organization that raises funds to bring children from abroad who have congenital medical issues to Canada and the United States for treatment unavailable in their home countries.*

TIPS TO MAINTAIN YOUR PROGRESS

Discuss the following tips with your clinician to help you maintain your progress:

- Imagine a world where individuals are knowledgeable and equipped with skills for life-long engagement in philanthropy as givers of time, talent, and treasure for the common good. In order to be altruistic, we don't have to give big things. We can look for simple opportunities in everyday life to be generous with our time—by helping someone out or by complimenting someone for his or her positive behavior.

- Learn more about important altruists who, despite mental health issues, shared their strengths, skills, and kindness with others. Examples include Lady Diana (eating concerns), Martin Luther King (depression), and Mother Theresa (depression). Which one might you most identify with? What prompted those altruists to give to their causes? How did their actions change the world?
- Get involved in local school and community clubs and organizations, which provide opportunities to volunteer and donate time or skills.
- Start an altruistic endeavor on a small scale. Give it time consistently. Over a period of time, this endeavor will likely offer you purpose, meaning, and motivation to continue.
- Providing help to others will likely enable you to further refine your own social and personal intelligence, in terms of understanding subtleties of needs of others.
- Altruistic endeavors often connect us with networks of people who can help us learn skills needed for volunteering. This enlarges our social circles and teaches us about resources and services already present in the community, as well as how to utilize them effectively.

RESOURCES

Readings
- Keltner, D. (2009). *Born to Be Good: The Science of a Meaningful Life*. New York: W.W. Norton
- Post, S., & Neimark, J. (2008). *Why Good Things Happen to Good People: How to Live a Longer, Healthier, Happier Life by the Simple Act of Giving*. New York: Broadway.
- Ricard, M. (2016). *Altruism: The Power of Compassion to Change Yourself and the World*. New York: Hachette Books.

Videos
- Kindness Boomerang—"One Day": https://www.youtube.com/watch?v=nwAYpLVyeFU
- *Gift*, Singapore Inspiration Drama Short Film: https://youtu.be/1DUYlHZsZfc?list=PL8m
- The Science of Kindness: https://www.youtube.com/watch?v=FA1qgXovaxU

Websites
- The Random Acts of Kindness: https://www.kindness.org/
- Compassion Charter: https://charterforcompassion.org/
- Me to We: https://www.metowe.com/
- *Greater Good* magazine: https://greatergood.berkeley.edu/

15

SESSION FIFTEEN: MEANING AND PURPOSE

SESSION FIFTEEN FOCUSES ON THE SEARCH AND pursuit of meaningful endeavors for the greater good.

The central positive psychotherapy (PPT) practice in this session is *Positive Legacy*. This is the last session in Phase Three of PPT and the last session overall.

THREE THINGS TO KNOW ABOUT *MEANING* AND *PURPOSE*

1. **Meaning and purpose—the whole that is greater than the parts:** There are many ways to achieve a meaningful life: close interpersonal relationships (such as positive relationships and positive communication), generativity (creation, reproduction), altruism, social activism or service, and careers experienced as callings and spirituality. Feeling that your life has a purpose means that the world around you is not an empty vessel floating aimlessly in the vast universe. Absence of purpose, on the other hand, may make you see the world as a directionless mass that is aimlessly orbiting the sun, and this aimlessness can lead to sadness and anxiety. In short, a sense of meaning and purpose integrates parts of life in such a way that the whole is greater than the parts. Meaning does not have to be a grand, life-encompassing concept. Examples include getting a small task done, earning a promotion, completing a course, finishing a chapter in a book, and winning a game; these are relatively small events that can contribute toward a larger purpose, as long as similar small steps are taken with a specific goal in mind.
2. **Pursuing meaning and purpose:** Purpose and meaning give your life a sense of direction; once you have a sense of direction, you can set milestones to help you identify where you came from and where you are going.
3. **Meaning and interpersonal context:** Meaning tends to exist in interpersonal settings because we humans are such social animals. We tend to have goals that promote our group (e.g., "I want to become a doctor to help my community") or goals that are derived from the values of our group (e.g., "I want to become a doctor because that is a prestigious profession"). The essence of meaning is connection. Meaning can link two things even if they are physically separate entities, such as if they belong to the same category (banana and apple are both fruit), are owned by the same person (Sally has a guitar and a basketball), or are both used for a common goal (collecting warm blankets and food for the local homeless shelter).

START-OF-SESSION RELAXATION

At the start of the session, your clinician may begin with a brief relaxation exercise. To discover some of these practices on your own, go to Appendix A: Relaxation & Mindfulness Practices, which can be found at the end of this workbook.

IN-SESSION PRACTICE: A STORY FROM YOUR PAST AND ENVISIONING A FUTURE GOAL

Your clinician will be working with you on the in-session practices. Refer to Worksheet 15.1.

Recalling your Positive Introduction story from Session One, please answer the following questions. Feel free to draw upon other things you have learned about yourself throughout the course of treatment.

What meaning can you derive from the experience of resilience in your story?

_____

_____

_____

_____

_____

_____

Now that you have a much more sophisticated knowledge of character strengths, which character strengths do you think are most prominent in your story? Do you still use these strengths in your everyday life? If so, how?

_____

_____

_____

_____

_____

_____

Does your story of resilience tell you anything about your life's purpose?

_____

_____

_____

_____

_____

_____

In general, what creative or significant achievement would you like to pursue in the next 10 years?

_____

_____

_____

_____

_____

_____

Specifically, think of one achievement in art, science, relationships (social), or academics that you would like to accomplish that is good, both for you and for others.

_____

_____

_____

_____

_____

_____

What makes this achievement an important goal for you and why?

_____

_____

_____

_____

_____

_____

How does this goal make a difference for others?

_____

_____

_____

_____

_____

_____

What steps do you need to take to accomplish this goal in the next 10 years? What would you need to do, year by year?

_____

_____

_____

_____

_____

Which of your signature strengths will you use most often to accomplish your goal?

_____

_____

_____

_____

_____

_____

This worksheet was originally published in Rashid and Seligman's *Positive Psychotherapy: Clinician Manual.*

Reflect & Discuss

Reflect on and discuss the following:

- What was the experience of re-reading your story of resilience again?
- If you are given an opportunity to re-write your story of resilience, would you write in the same way you wrote a couple of months ago? If not, what would you change?
- In what ways have last few sessions of PPT influenced your thinking about the purpose and meaning of life?
- What was the process like for you of reflecting on and then writing about your goals for the future?
- What might happen if you accomplish your goals? What might happen if you do not accomplish your goals?

IN-SESSION PRACTICE: *POSITIVE LEGACY*

Your clinician will be working with you on the in-session practices. Refer to Worksheet 15.2.

Think ahead to your life as you would like it to be and how you would like to be remembered by those closest to you. What accomplishments and/or personal strengths would they mention about you? In other words, what would you like your legacy to be? Write this down in the space provided. Don't be modest, but be realistic.

_____

_____

_____

_____

_____

_____

_____

_____

_____

_____

Once you are finished, look back over what you wrote and ask yourself if you have a plan to create a legacy that is both realistic and within your power to do so.

After you've finished writing, put this worksheet aside and keep it somewhere safe. Read it again a year from now, or five years from now. Ask yourself whether you have made progress toward achieving your goals, and feel free to revise if new goals have emerged.

This worksheet was originally published in Rashid and Seligman's *Positive Psychotherapy: Clinician Manual.*

Reflect & Discuss
Reflect on and discuss the following:

- How was the process of writing your *Positive Legacy*?
- What was the most difficult part of this practice? Is the notion too abstract? Did it feel immodest to write something noteworthy about your future self? Are you not much concerned with how you will be remembered?
- Can you think of someone living or deceased who you knew well enough that you feel this person's life is an illustration of how you would like to be remembered? If you have someone in mind, think about what you would write to this person. If you don't have anyone in mind, please use a historical figure.
- What short- and long-term goals can you set to accomplish your *Positive Legacy*?
- What concrete actions would you like to undertake in order to accomplish your short- and long-term goals? What is the timeline for completion of these actions?
- In what ways can you use your signature strengths to do something that would enable you to leave a *Positive Legacy*?

In Real Life: Zainab, 38, female, Middle Eastern background

Zainab attended a PPT workshop and submitted the following *Positive Legacy*.
My Positive Legacy

- *I would like to be remembered as a person **who fights for her dreams and beliefs,** as well as for the **things that matter the most,** and who embraces all challenges in life—as a mother, a wife, a daughter, a sister, a friend, and as a professional—with bravery, zest, and authenticity, infecting others with this positive energy.*
- *I would like to be remembered as someone who lived life **with warm and caring relationships with family and friends,** showing genuine love and affection through her actions regularly.*
- *I would like to be remembered as **a grateful person** who does not take things for granted and gives thanks every day for what she receives.*
- *I also would like to be remembered as someone who is **able to help** those around her who need help.*
- *Especially for children, for whom I wish a safe and happy and easy life, I would like to be a symbol of a meaningful life. This involves love, ability to love, integrity and honesty, justice, kindness, and perseverance, all with the goal of giving my best in all that I do both in my professional and personal life.*
- *I would also like to be remembered as someone **whom friends can count on,** as a wise person to help them in difficult situations, and as someone who spreads positivity and serenity to the ones around me, as much as possible.*

Tips to Maintain Your Progress
Discuss the following tips with your clinician to help you maintain your progress:

- Meaning gives life coherence and increases self-efficacy. It is also associated with health and better relationships. Meaning can be global or local. To maintain a sense of meaning and purpose, select a global meaning. The global meaning refers to your goals and beliefs regarding issues in the larger world like justice, equality, and fairness. Meaning can also be maintained by working on a local issue that involves pursuing specific goals and objectives in your community or family.

- We can also maintain a sense of meaning and purpose by contemplating and discussing events that had a profound or significant impact on us but that we have not yet had a chance to reflect on. Such reflection can help us understand the meaning and purpose over time.
- Keep in mind that meaning is not constant; it may change with age, circumstances, or significant life events.
- To maintain a sense of purpose, one doesn't always have to do something. Meaning can also be maintained by reducing activities or by learning to say no to activities that do not feel purposeful to you. This could look like letting go of people, ideas, and things in your life that no longer make you happy. For example, take a look around your home. Are there clothes or books that you don't need anymore? Perhaps consider donating them. Do you have unhelpful or self-defeating thoughts that visit you frequently? Consider replacing those with more helpful ones. Are there people in your life who hurt you and who may be distracting you from your meaning? Can you think of ways to limit their importance in your life?

RESOURCES

Readings
- Aslan, R. (2017). *God: A Human History.* New York: Random House.
- Frankl, V. E. (1963). *Man's Search for Meaning: An Introduction to Logotherapy.* New York: Washington Square Press.
- Stager, M. (2007). *The untethered soul: The Journey Beyond Yourself.* Oakland, CA: New Harbinger.
- Valliant, G. (2008). *Spiritual Evolution: How We Are Wired for Faith, Hope, and Love.* New York: Broadway.

Videos
- YouTube: The Time You Have:
  https://www.youtube.com/watch?v=BOksW_NabEk
- YouTube: Hugo—Purpose:
  https://www.youtube.com/watch?v=7jzLeNYe46g
- YouTube: Peaceful Warrior—Everything Has a Purpose (Duration 3:20):
  https://youtu.be/w1jaPahTM4o?list=PL8m55Iz0Oco4BRLkwj9KM9yxbCsLC5mjb

Websites
- John Templeton Foundation:
  https://www.templeton.org/about
- Virtue, Happiness, and Meaning of Life:
  https://virtue.uchicago.edu/
- The Mind & Life Institute:
  https://www.mindandlife.org/

CONCLUSION

THE FULL LIFE

AS WE MOVE TO THE END OF our positive psychotherapy (PPT) journey, we hope that you have learned to focus on your own positive resources, such as your positive emotions, character strengths, positive relationships, accomplishments, and meaning and purpose. Change is not easy, and we hope that, through the PPT practices with which you have engaged during therapy, you have started the process of looking at your strengths as well as at your weaknesses. The challenge to integrate both negatives and positives in a balanced way that captures your essence—although quite challenging—is not impossible.

To focus exclusively on negatives, such as symptoms and weaknesses, OR to focus exclusively on positives, -such as strengths, talents, skills, abilities, and assets-4,444-might be easier. But focusing on both positives and negatives, in an authentic manner, is not easy. Hopefully after completing the PPT practices, you are better able to integrate your symptoms with strengths, your risks with resources, your weaknesses with virtues, and your deficits with skills. Hopefully you now understand that you are more than the sum of your symptoms or the embodiment of your strengths.

Even though you have completed the PPT practices, your brain has not "defaulted to neutral." The human brain attends and responds more strongly to negatives than to positives, but completing PPT practices will help you have more awareness and more tools to combat this tendency. Think back to early in the therapeutic process, when cultivating positives was harder and dwelling on negatives was easier. PPT has hopefully created a process to help you to rise above this "negativity bias" default and taught you valuable skills to authentically attend to and amplify the positives, so that you are able to reduce— or at least to better manage—your symptoms, as well as enhance your well-being. The toughest challenges in life require exploring and using our toughest internal resources, a process that builds resilience. By completing PPT practices, you have faced a tough challenge head on.

PPT's central point is that enhancing our strengths, along with improving our symptoms, is an effective therapeutic approach—much like health is better than sickness, security is better than fear, relaxation is better than stress, cooperation is better than conflict, and hope is better than despair. Indeed, there are exceptions when negatives may be more appropriate, but, generally, positives are more adaptive and functional than negatives.

Throughout the course of PPT, you have explored your strengths, and gradually you took deeper dives to reflect, acknowledge, attribute, and amplify these strengths, without (hopefully) dismissing, minimizing, or overlooking your problems. For example, PPT may have engaged you in discussions about an injustice you experienced. While attending fully to this experience, try to also recall an act of kindness you may have experienced. Similarly, along with insults and hurts that may have made you angry, use the PPT practice of *Active Constructive Responding* to look for experiences of genuine praise, humility, and harmony. Never dismiss or ignore the pain associated with adversities and trauma, but use the *One Door Opens, Another Door Closes* practice to explore potential growth and meaning from setbacks and trauma. You have hopefully mastered ways to use your strengths to solve problems that maintain your stress. Don't forget the practical wisdom strategies to figure out which character strength is relevant to your problem, whether it conflicts with your other strengths (e.g., should you be honest or kind?), and how can you translate abstract character strengths (e.g., hope, optimism, gratitude, self-regulation, and creativity) into concrete, attainable, and sustainable actions and habits.

We hope that these PPT practices have helped you direct your attention, memory, and expectations away from the negative and catastrophic and toward positive and optimistic outcomes. By keeping a *Gratitude Journal*, you have been able to counteract the negativity bias. Similarly, the *Gratitude Letter* and *Visit* may have shifted your memory from the unfavorable aspects of past relationships to savoring the good things about interactions with friends and family. Don't lose this reeducation of attention, memory, and expectation. Keep on writing about what goes well. This "spotting of good" will allow you to think more deeply about your positive qualities.

Like any therapeutic endeavor, PPT is not immune from triggering or even causing negative and uncomfortable emotions:

*   If during the course of treatment, you found something upsetting, which dampened your mood, don't let it linger. Whatever approach works, utilize it.
*   Some people going through PPT may be upset that their top strengths are kindness, forgiveness, and prudence, because these strengths can lead to problems. For example exercising too much kindness and forgiveness may allow others to take you for granted.

Continue to attend and remain attuned to nuances of your strength expressions, and invite creativity to develop insights to help you learn to behave differently and more adaptively. Don't conceive of PPT as being exclusively about positives. Rather, PPT is about developing a refined understanding of the integration of positives and negatives that can take you on the path toward achieving a full life.

Positive psychology in general has been criticized for overlooking the negatives. It would be naive and utopian to conceive of a life without negative experiences. As such, PPT does not deny negative emotions nor encourage people to see the world through rose-colored glasses. Rather, PPT aims to validate these experiences, while gently encouraging people to explore the effects of these negatives and seek out potential positives from difficult and traumatic experiences.

In conclusion, PPT is not a prescription; it is a descriptive approach based on converging scientific evidence that documents the benefits of paying attention to the positive aspects of human experience. PPT is not a panacea, nor is it appropriate for all people in all situations. It is not a "one-size-fits-all" approach. Some people may show a linear progression, others may move on a circular path, and still others may make no progress at all. Long-standing behavioral habits are hard to let go! But one has to begin from somewhere—and you certainly have made a very auspicious beginning.

APPENDIX A

Relaxation & Mindfulness Practices

CORE CONCEPTS

Mindfulness is maintaining a moment-by-moment awareness of our thoughts, feelings, bodily sensations, and surrounding environment, without being judgmental or being less judgmental. Mindfulness allows us to accept what we cannot change and enables us to see what can be changed.

Some specific events, experiences, and interactions stay in our heads. Whenever we think of them, emotions spring up and leave us feeling sad, happy, angry, or unsure. Sometimes we act on these feelings without much awareness. Mindfulness is being aware of this whole process by observing the flow of our thoughts and emotions without acting upon them immediately.

Mindfulness also helps us develop awareness of our actions and reactions in specific situations, especially situations that bother us. We also learn how our actions impact others. Developing awareness without judgment can help us be open and receptive to different perspectives.

For example, being mindful about a negative interaction with a friend can help us see the wider perspective. Perhaps the negative interaction was not caused by something we might have done. Instead, it could be that our friend might be upset about something completely unrelated to us. By being mindful, we break down a complex experience into its parts, allowing us to be open to widening our perspective. Mindfulness can strengthen our openness, self-regulation, and social intelligence.

IN-SESSION MINDFULNESS PRACTICES

Mindfulness can be developed, but it requires regular practice. The following are five mindfulness and relaxation practices that can be incorporated into positive psychotherapy (PPT) sessions or used at home.

PRACTICE ONE: A MINDFUL MINUTE

Instructions

1. Sit in a comfortable position with your hands resting on or close to your thighs and with your head, neck, and chest in a relaxed straight line. Rest your feet flat on the floor.
2. Bring your attention to your breath. Notice how it enters your body and how it leaves your body. Focus as you inhale and exhale, on how your chest expands and contracts.
3. Gently bring your breath deeper into your belly. Continue repeating this breathing cycle. Try to make each inhalation and exhalation last for 6 to 8 seconds. Start over after each breath.
4. Rather than trying to stop any other thoughts, keep your attention focused, and count very quietly or in your head. Your attention will wander, and your job is to gently bring it back and start again. Consider this a practice of not only focusing but also one in which you will make many starts—distraction, start again, distraction, start again. If doing this practice in session, when one minute is up, you will hear a sound.[1]

PRACTICE TWO: BREATHING

Instructions

1. Make sure you are sitting in a relaxed and comfortable position.
2. Keep your head, neck, and chest in a relaxed (not rigid) upright position.
3. Relax your shoulders. Bring your back toward the back of the chair.

4. Rest your hands softly on your thighs or wherever you feel comfortable.
5. If you feel comfortable, let your eyelids slowly and gently close, just as the curtain in a theatre closes.
6. Take a deep breath through your nose, hold it for a few seconds, and then exhale slowly and gently.
7. Repeat this breathing two more times, each time deepening it, from your chest down into your belly.
8. With every breath in and breath out, try to relax your whole body from head to toe.
9. Breathe smoothly, without pause.
10. Next, shape your breath; a good breath has three qualities (Sovik, 2005):
    • Smooth
    • Even (approximately equal duration of inhalation and exhalation)
    • Without sound
11. Relax the effort to breathe and let it naturally flow, as if your whole body is breathing.
12. Focus on your breath as it enters and exits through your nostrils.
13. Take 10 breaths that are smooth, even, and without sound. Open your eyes.

PRACTICE THREE: STRETCH & RELAX

Instructions

Sit in the Relaxation Position and practice the following stretches.

The Relaxation Position

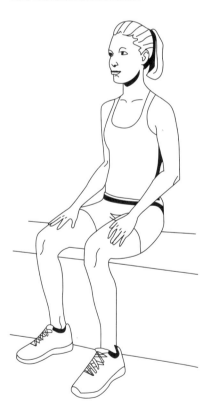

Sit with your head, neck, and chest aligned, legs uncrossed, feet flat on the floor, and hands on or close to knee caps (adapted from Cautela & Gorden, 1978).

Head

- Keeping your shoulders steady, bring your head slowly to the right.[2]
- Take three relaxed breaths, starting with exhaling.
- Repeat on the other side.

Ear

- Keeping your shoulders steady, bring your left ear to your left shoulder without moving the shoulder.
- Take three relaxed breaths.
- Repeat the same on the other side.

Neck

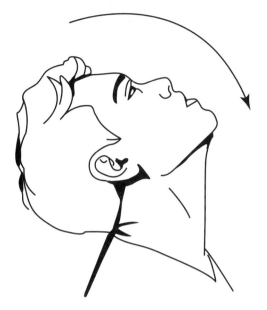

Align your head, neck, and chest, keeping your shoulders balanced. Slowly lift up your face toward the ceiling. Keep lifting until you reach a limit that is not comfortable. Holding your heady steady, stretch the front part of your neck and hold this stretch for as long as you can comfortably do so. Exhale and slowly bring your face back. Rather than stopping in the neutral position, bring your chin down into your chest. Hold the posture, and feel the stretch in the back of your neck. When you are ready, bring your face back to a neutral position.

Face Massage

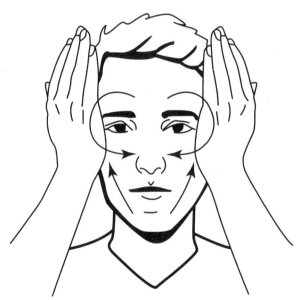

Place the lower parts of your palms on either side of your upper cheek bones, close to your temples. Begin to make small circular movements with your palms, moving downward. Once you reach your jaw bone, move upward, and then follow any bony parts of your face (adapted from Bellentine, 1977).

Eyes and Forehead Massage

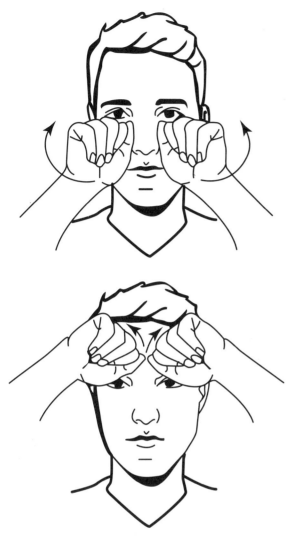

Make loose fists with your hands, placing palm and finger joings (the knuckles) at the bottom of your eye sockets and pressing gently against the socket bones. Move your knuckles slowly toward your temples. From the temples, move slightly up, pressing your eyebrows and forehead. Repeat this routine several times. Carry on pressing with your knuckles on any bony parts of your face.

PRACTICE FOUR: POSITIVE IMAGERY

Instructions

If you are doing this practice in session, your clinician can read the following script. If you are doing this practice at home, record the script so that you can listen to it while doing the practice. To begin, sit comfortably.

Close your eyes and imagine a place in your mind. This place can be indoors or outdoors, but it is a place where you effortlessly feel comfortable. Take a few relaxing breaths to fully feel that you have arrived here. See if you can focus on one sensation at a time. What things do you see? [pause] Look around slowly. [pause] What things do you hear? Notice the sounds—near, far, and perhaps very far away. Next, what do you smell? Natural smells, some artificial smells. [pause]. Now touch something, feel its texture—smooth or rough, hard or soft, heavy or light. Look around, and if there are any materials, colors, stones, features, or other materials, touch them. See if you can use them to make something. It doesn't have to be perfectly sized or symmetrical. Or you don't have to make anything. Feel at complete ease to do something or nothing. Relax. Take a few deep breaths. Try, but not too hard, to memorize details of this place, like a mental picture. This is your place, your place to relax. Gently and slowly trace you steps to leave, the same way you came in.

PRACTICE FIVE: LOVE & KINDNESS MEDITATION

Instructions

The following meditation practice has been adapted from Sharon Salzberg's (1995) book, *Love-Kindness*. This practice recites specific words and phrases evoking a "boundless warm-hearted feeling." The strength of this feeling is not limited to or by family, religion, or social class. The meditation begins with ourselves, and we gradually extend the wish for well-being and happiness to all.

Begin with the following phrases:

May I be happy. May I be well. May I be safe. May I be peaceful and at ease.

While saying these phrases, allow yourself to immerse into the intentions they express. Loving-kindness meditation helps us to connect our noble intentions with the well-being of others. Let feelings of love, kindness, openness, and acceptance embrace you, and let these feelings expand as you repeat these phrases. As you continue the meditation, you can bring in your own image and direct this love and kindness toward yourself.

After directing loving-kindness toward yourself, bring to your attention a friend or someone in your life who has deeply cared for you. Then slowly repeat phrases of loving-kindness toward that person:

May you be happy. May you be well. May you be safe. May you be peaceful and at ease.

As you say these phrases, immerse into their intention or heartfelt or heart full meaning. And, if any feelings of loving-kindness arise, connect the feelings with the phrases so that the feelings may become stronger as you repeat the words.

As you continue the meditation, you can enlarge the circle and bring to mind other friends, family members, neighbors, acquaintances, strangers, animals, and finally people with whom you have difficulty.

ADDITIONAL RESOURCES

The following are additional relaxation resources you may find useful.

Rolf-Solvik, a clinical psychologist, associated with the Himalayan Institute:
Learn Diaphragmatic Breathing for Deep Relaxation:
    https://youtu.be/Q82YnmL0Kr8

Jon Kabat-Zinn, one of the most distinguished practitioners in mindfulness, guides a 30-minute body scan meditation practice:
    https://youtu.be/_DTmGtznab4

Sharon Salzberg, a distinguished practitioner, teaches love and kindness:
    https://youtu.be/buTQP4Geabk

This animated video, based on Martin Boroson's book *One-Moment Meditation*, gives you the tools to find calm quickly and effectively. You can practice One-Moment Meditation at home by following along with this video:
    https://www.youtube.com/watch?v=F6eFFCi12v8

APPENDIX B

Gratitude Journal

Please write three blessings[1] (good things) each night before going to bed. Next to each blessing, write at least one sentence about:

• Why did this good thing happen today? What does this mean to you?
• What have you learned from taking the time to name this blessing or good thing?
• In what ways did you or others contribute to this blessing or good thing?

DAILY BLESSING: SUNDAY

Sunday	Date _____
First Blessing Reflection	
Second Blessing Reflection:	
Third Blessing Reflection:	

DAILY BLESSING: MONDAY

Monday	Date _____
First Blessing Reflection	
Second Blessing Reflection:	
Third Blessing Reflection:	

DAILY BLESSING: TUESDAY

Tuesday	Date: _____
First Blessing Reflection	
Second Blessing Reflection:	
Third Blessing Reflection:	

DAILY BLESSING: WEDNESDAY

Wednesday	Date: _____
First Blessing Reflection	
Second Blessing Reflection:	
Third Blessing Reflection:	

DAILY BLESSING: THURSDAY

Thursday	Date: _____
First Blessing Reflection	
Second Blessing Reflection:	
Third Blessing Reflection:	

DAILY BLESSING: FRIDAY

Friday	Date: _____
First Blessing Reflection	
Second Blessing Reflection:	
Third Blessing Reflection:	

DAILY BLESSING: SATURDAY

Saturday	Date: _____
First Blessing Reflection	
Second Blessing Reflection:	
Third Blessing Reflection:	

APPENDIX C

Positive Psychotherapy Inventory

The Positive Psychotherapy Inventory (PPTI) is the primary measure to assess client well-being based on the PERMA theory of well-being. The PPTI assesses well-being in terms of positive emotions, engagement, relationships, meaning, and accomplishment. It has been used in several published outcome studies (e.g., Schrank et al., 2014; Seligman, Rashid, & Parks, 2006; Uliaszek, Rashid, Williams, & Gulamani, 2016; Rashid et al., 2017), and it has been translated into Turkish (Guney, 2011), Persian (Khanjani, Shahidi, FathAbadi, Mazaheri, & Shokri, 2014), and German (Wammerl, Jaunig, Maierunteregger, & Streit, 2015). For psychometric properties of the PPTI, see Rashid and Seligman (2018, in the Clinician's Manual).

POSITIVE PSYCHOTHERAPY INVENTORY

*Please read each of the statements carefully. In the shaded box, rate yourself using the 5-point scale at the top of the form. Please **only mark the shaded box** in each line.*

Some questions are regarding strengths. Strengths are stable traits that manifest through thoughts, feelings, and actions; are morally valued; and are beneficial to self and others. Examples of strengths include optimism, zest, spirituality, fairness, modesty, social intelligence, perseverance, curiosity, creativity, and teamwork.

5: Very much like me	4: Like me	3: Neutral	2: Not like me	1: Not at all like me				
				P	E	R	M	A
1. I feel joyful.				☐				
2. I know my strengths.					☐			
3. I feel connected to people with whom I interact regularly.						☐		
4. What I do matters to society.							☐	
5. I am an ambitious person.								☐
6. Others say I look happy.				☐				
7. I pursue activities that use my strengths.					☐			
8. I feel close to my loved ones.						☐		
9. I feel that my life has a purpose.							☐	
10. The accomplishments of others inspire me to take actions to achieve my personal goals.								☐
11. I notice good things in my life and feel thankful.				☐				
12. I use my strengths to solve my problems.					☐			
13. During tough times, there is always someone I can turn to for support.						☐		
14. I participate in religious or spiritual activities.							☐	
15. I have done many things well in my life.								☐

5: Very much like me	4: Like me	3: Neutral	2: Not like me	1: Not at all like me				
				P	E	R	M	A
16. I feel relaxed.				☐				
17. My concentration is good during activities that use my strengths.					☐			
18. I have relationships that support me in growing and flourishing.						☐		
19. I do things that contribute to a larger cause.							☐	
20. When I set a goal, I am able to accomplish it.								☐
21. I laugh heartily.				☐				
22. Time passes quickly when I am engaged in activities that use my strengths.					☐			
23. There is at least one person in my life who listens well enough to understand my feelings and me.						☐		
24. I use my strengths to help others.							☐	
25. Achieving my goals motivates me to accomplish new goals.								☐
Total Score								

Please add up the scores from the boxes in each vertical column and transfer your scores to the following table. Note that at the start of the statements, there are five columns labeled P, E, R, M, and A. Those letters correlate to the letters in the left-hand column in the table.

Range	Clinical	Nonclinical	Your Score
P = Positive Emotions (5–25)	14	21	
E = Engagement (5–25)	16	21	
R = Relationships (5–25)	14	22	
M = Meaning (5–25)	14	19	
A = Accomplishment (5–25)	18	21	
Total (25–125)	76	104	

Scoring Instructions

Scale	Scoring—Add Items:	Definition of PERMA Elements
Positive Emotions	1 + 6 + 11 + 16 + 21	Experiencing positive emotions such as contentment, pride, serenity, hope, optimism, trust, confidence, gratitude
Engagement	2 + 7 + 12 + 17 + 22	Immersing oneself deeply in activities that utilize one's strengths to experience an optimal state marked by razor sharp concentration, optimal state of experience with intense focus, and intrinsic motivation to further develop

Scale	Scoring—Add Items:	Definition of PERMA Elements
Relationships	3 + 8 + 13 + 18 + 23	Having positive, secure, and trusting relationships
Meaning	4 + 9 + 14 + 19 + 24	Belonging to and serving something with a sense of purpose and belief that is larger than the self
Accomplishment	5+10+15+20+25	Pursuing success, mastery, and achievement for its own sake

REFERENCES

Schrank, B., Riches, S., Coggins, T., Rashid, T., Tylee, A., & Slade, M. (2014). WELLFOCUS PPT–modified positive psychotherapy to improve well-being in psychosis: Study protocol for a pilot randomised controlled trial. *Trials*, *15*(1), 203.

Seligman, M. E., Rashid, T., & Parks, A. C. (2006). Positive psychotherapy. *American Psychologist*. *61*(8), 774–788. doi:10.1037/0003-066X.61.8.774

Rashid, T., Louden, R., Wright, L., Chu, R., Lutchmie-Maharaj A., Hakim, I., . . . Kidd, B. (2017). Flourish: A strengths-based approach to building student resilience. In C. Proctor (Ed.), *Positive Psychology Interventions in Practice* (pp. 29–45). Dordrecht, The Netherlands: Springer.

Uliaszek, A. A., Rashid, T., Williams, G. E., & Gulamani, T. (2016). Group therapy for university students: A randomized control trial of dialectical behavior therapy and positive psychotherapy. *Behaviour Research and Therapy*, *77*, 78–85. doi:http://dx.doi.org/10.1016/j.brat.2015.12.003

TRANSLATIONS
Turkish
Guney, S. (2011). The Positive Psychotherapy Inventory (PPTI): Reliability and validity study in Turkish population. *Social and Behavioral Sciences*, *29*, 81–86.

Persian
Khanjani, M., Shahidi, S., FathAbadi, J., Mazaheri, M. A., & Shokri, O. (2014). The factor structure and psychometric properties of the Positive Psychotherapy Inventory (PPTI) in an Iranian sample. *Iranian Journal of Applied Psychology*, *7*(5), 26–47.

German
Wammerl, M., Jaunig, J., Maierunteregger, T., & Streit, P. (2015, June). *The Development of a German Version of the Positive Psychotherapy Inventory Überschrift (PPTI) and the PERMA-Profiler*. Presentation at the World Congress of International Positive Psychology Association, Orlando, FL.

APPENDIX D

Building Your Strengths

Stressors and strengths are part of daily life, although stressors (such as relationship challenges, problems at work or not having a job, work-life balance, being sick, constant traffic, or taxes) may stand out more than strengths (such as curiosity, integrity, kindness, fairness, prudence, and gratitude). This appendix looks at everyday experiences and identifies things you can do to incorporate strengths into your life. It also provides examples of movies, TED Talks, and other online resources that illustrate these strengths. The "therapeutic actions" in this appendix are not a substitute for psychotherapy, should you need that; rather, the material in this resource is meant to raise your awareness that while everyday life includes inevitable hassles, stressors, and problems, it also offers us opportunities to become proficient in learning about and using our strengths toward solving our problems and increasing our well-being.

ORGANIZATION OF THIS APPENDIX

The aim of this appendix is to translate abstract concepts of character strengths into concrete actions and to connect these strengths with relevant multimedia illustrations with which you can easily identify. This appendix is based on the VIA Classification of Character Strengths and Virtues (Peterson & Seligman, 2004). We are grateful to VIA Institute for generously allowing us the classification to devise strengths-based therapeutic resources.

According to Peterson and Seligman (2004), *character strengths* are ubiquitous traits that are valued in their own right and are not necessarily tied to concrete outcomes. Compared to symptoms, for the most part, character strengths do not diminish others; rather, they elevate those who witness the strength, producing admiration rather than jealousy. Clinically, character strengths manifest in many ways. Some are easy to spot and acknowledge in clinical settings (e.g., expressing gratitude or creativity), while other strengths are less visible (e.g., expressing humility or self-regulation; refraining from something that is not apparent). Like character strengths, *virtues* are also valued in every culture and are defined within cultural, religious, and philosophical contexts. In Peterson and Seligman's classification, virtues are clusters of strengths; in other words, virtues are broad routes to a good life.

Table D1 presents 24 character strengths divided into six virtue clusters. Each of these character strengths is discussed in this appendix and includes:

- A *description* of the strength presented
- A discussion of the "*golden mean*," for the strength
- An explanation of which other character strengths *integrate* with the strength under discussion
- Illustrations from *movies*—showing how characters embody the strength
- *Therapeutic actions*—what you can do to enhance your strength
- *Exemplars*—individuals who represent the strength, as presented in TED Talks
- *Books*—to help you delve more deeply into the strength
- *Websites* that expand the concept of the strength

Table D1.

CORE VIRTUES AND CORRESPONDING CHARACTER STRENGTHS

	Core Virtues					
	Wisdom & Knowledge	Courage	Humanity	Justice	Temperance	Transcendence
Character Strengths	Creativity Curiosity Open-mindedness Love of learning Perspective	Bravery Persistence Integrity Vitality & Zest	Love Kindness Social intelligence	Citizenship & Teamwork Fairness Leadership	Forgiveness & Mercy Humility & Modesty Prudence Self-regulation	Appreciation of Beauty & Excellence Gratitude Hope & Optimism Humor & Playfulness Spirituality

Table D2, located at the end of this appendix, presents an overview of the character strengths described throughout. This at-a-glance resource summarizes the 24 strengths by presenting their over- and underuse, a brief description of the balanced use of the strength (the golden mean), and how each strength potentially integrates with others.

This appendix is written directly for you (the client), although clinicians can also use it after clients have completed their signature strengths assessment (see Session 2). The resources in this appendix can help clinicians reinforce skills learned in individual sessions, as this appendix applies a strengths-based approach to deal with everyday challenges as well as cultivating more positive emotions, engagement, and positive relationships, helping to create and sustain meaningful goals.

THE GOLDEN MEAN

The "golden mean" is the Aristotelian concept that moral behavior is the mean (middle) between two extremes. In the context of strengths-based positive psychotherapy (PPT), the golden mean implies that a balanced use of strengths is both therapeutic and effective. For example, a balanced use of curiosity would be a mean between excessive use (prying or snooping) and absence (boredom, disinterest, or apathy).

INTEGRATION

Some character strengths share attributes with one another and often work well together. For example:

- To overcome symptoms of depression, you need to understand that not every future event will be negative (hope) and you also need to find practical ways to keep working on them (persistence).
- To deal with impulsive behavior, you need to find ways of regulating how you feel and what you do (self-regulation). In so doing, don't become too hard on yourself for past impulse-control lapses, because you also need self-care (self-forgiveness and self-compassion).
- To deal with relationship challenges, especially when told, "you don't understand me," try to become more aware of other people's feelings and motives, and try different strategies to better grasp the subtleties of complex interpersonal situations (social intelligence). However, you may also benefit from the strengths of playfulness, teamwork, and authenticity to achieve the same ends or to connect with others deeply, especially loved ones.

CORE VIRTUE: WISDOM & KNOWLEDGE

Cognitive strengths that entail the acquisition and use of knowledge

1. CREATIVITY

Description

If this is one of your top strengths, you can use creativity to devise new ways of solving problems that compromise your well-being, such as finding a creative and positive way to respond to ongoing stressors or dealing with a difficult person. Most creative expressions that include art (painting, pottery, graphic design), writing (poetry, stories, essays), and performance (singing, acting, playing an instrument) carry tremendous therapeutic potential. These expressions use attentional, cognitive, and emotional resources that might otherwise be spent brooding, wallowing, or blaming.

The Golden Mean

You are not content with doing most things as usual or blindly confirming to norms. Yet, your creative endeavors are not considered to be odd or weird, even by your closest friends. You also don't want to be merely content; rather, you want to be innovative. From a therapeutic standpoint, a balanced use of creativity entails trying new solutions to old problems that cause ongoing stress. Before you try these solutions, however, consider their impact on others. (For example, you can use your creativity to redesign your office—if it is your individual office—or on a project for which only you are responsible. However, redesigning a common space or infusing new and creative ideas into a group project—without involving others—is not a balanced expression of creativity.) When working with others, you will be best served by your own creativity when leading or facilitating a brainstorming session that is inclusive and open to new ideas.

- *Overuse of strength:* oddity, weirdness, eccentricity
- *Underuse of strength*: dullness, banality, conformity

Integration

You can use the strengths of curiosity, persistence, zest, and bravery to refine your creativity. Also, as noted above, if your creative expression impacts others, use the strengths of social intelligence, teamwork, and open-mindedness to include those others in finding co-creative solutions to problems that impact well-being.

Sadness and suffering are often cited as generators of creativity. However, there may be many paths and processes leading to creative expression. Consider when children are playing. They are happy (positive emotions) and often create role plays and imaginary characters and create new scenarios from existing settings. Strengths such as gratitude, appreciation of beauty, playfulness and humor—with relatively more explicit expressions of positive emotions—can facilitate creativity. Creative expression—from conception to fruition—needs support from persistence and self-regulation. Persistence is important to finish what is started, and self-regulation is needed to stay focused or to re-establish focus, if distracted.

Movies

- *Pianist (2002)*—Wladyslaw Szpilman's character is inspiring in this World War II movie. Despite the incredible cruelty of the Nazis, Szpilman relies on his creativity to survive.

- *Gravity (2013)*—This film presents an excellent illustration of creative problem solving as two astronauts work together to survive after an accident that leaves them stranded in space.
- *Julie & Julia (2009)*—Based on the celebrity chef Julia Child, the movie shows many facets of creativity both by Julia Child and another woman, Julie Powell.

Therapeutic Actions

- **Create new solutions for old problems:** Compile an original and practical list of solutions or tips that will address old, ongoing problems faced by you and your peers. Share this list with your friends through social media (or any other way you find appropriate) to elicit feedback.
- **Tackle boring tasks:** Make a list of tasks that you find boring yet have to do. Look for different and creative ways to accomplish these tasks. Find ways to incorporate them into your work or chores to make these times more enjoyable.
- **Offer creative solutions:** Offer at least one creative solution to the challenges of a sibling or friend. Share your relevant experiences, successes, and setbacks from when you tried something similar yourself. Practice being open to their creative ideas as well as to your own.
- **Use leftovers (food, paper, etc.) to make new products:** Consider the artistic or practical uses for items before you throw them away.
- **Collect and organize:** Collect and organize assorted materials (e.g., websites, online videos, sketchbooks, crayons, pastels, or flipcharts) that readily enable you to translate new ideas into concrete form.
- **Improve your attention:** If you experience attentional challenges—such as overlooking important details, getting distracted easily, being unable to keep in mind multiple pieces of information at the same time—pursuing a creative endeavor that engages you, can help you improve your attention.

Exemplars (TED Talks)

Visit https://www.ted.com/talks and search for the following talks to hear from individuals who represent the strength of creativity:

- **William Kamkwamba:** How I harnessed the wind
- **Isaac Mizrahi:** Fashion and creativity
- **Linda Hill:** How to manage for collective creativity
- **Kary Mullis:** Play! Experiment! Discover!
- **Richard Turere:** My invention that made peace with lions

Books

- Carlson, S. (2010). *Your Creative Brain: Seven steps to Maximize Imagination, Productivity, and Innovation in Your Life*. San Francisco: Wiley.
- Csikszentmihalyi, M. (1996). *Creativity: Flow and the Psychology of Discovery and Invention*. New York: HarperCollins.
- Edwards, B. (2013). *Drawing on the Right Side of the Brain: A Course in Enhancing Creativity and Artistic Confidence*. London: Souvenir Press.
- Drapeau, P. (2014). *Sparking Student Creativity: Practical Ways to Promote Innovative Thinking and Problem Solving*. Alexandria, VA: ASCD.

Websites

- Inspiring Creativity: A short film about creative thinking and behaviors: http://www.highsnobiety.com/2014/05/16/ watch-inspiring-creativity-a-short-film-about-creative-thinking-and-behaviors/

- The Imagination Institute: Focuses on the measurement, growth, and improvement of imagination across all sectors of society:
  http://imagination-institute.org/
- Shelley Carson's website: Complete a test to explore your creative mindset:
  http://www.shelleycarson.com/creative-brain-test
  https://www.authentichappiness.sas.upenn.edu/learn/creativity
- 25 things creative people do differently:
  http://www.powerofpositivity.com/25-things-creative-people-differently/
- The Artist's Way—tools to enhance your creativity, videos with the author Julia Cameron:
  www.theartistway.com

2. CURIOSITY

Description

Curiosity involves actively recognizing and pursuing challenging opportunities and seeking out new knowledge. In the therapeutic context, you can use curiosity to be open to experiences you may have been avoiding because these experiences make you feel afraid or anxious, such as riding in a crowded underground train, asking a question at an information desk, or talking to a stranger at a social gathering. Or maybe there are objects that make you uncomfortable, such as needles, germs in public washrooms, or specific foods. Curiosity has tremendous therapeutic potential especially if you have assumed that your fears cannot be changed. Instead of being fixated on these experiences, curiosity will enable you to be flexible. Its components, including being open and embracing uncertainty, the unknown, and the new, will help you understand the nuances and subtleties of your fears, which can facilitate both healing and growth.

The Golden Mean

We habituate to (i.e., get used to) almost all positive experiences and products. A balanced approach to curiosity helps to ward off boredom, apathy, and disinterest. Curiosity helps you seek out new or fresh aspects of an experience, process, or product, especially aspects you have not grasped fully. Also, without becoming anxiously preoccupied, curiosity can change the mundane aspects of your daily routine into engaged, interested, and motivated living. Balanced application of curiosity toward self-understanding is critical for growth. Instead of overanalyzing, being self-absorbed, or self-securitizing excessively, be sufficiently curious to challenge the limits of your knowledge—about yourself and about the world around you.

- *Overuse of strength*: prying, snooping, nosiness
- *Underuse of strength:* boredom, disinterest, apathy

Integration

Curiosity is closely tied with other strengths and attributes, such as creativity, persistence, and open-mindedness. Whenever you find yourself entangled in complex situation, use your curiosity, in concert with other strengths, to extract a balanced, yet optimal, use of your curiosity. At times, your curiosity needs courage to find its adaptive expression, especially when you feel ambivalent (part angry, part sad) and cannot identify a specific cause. It might be that your ambivalence is related to avoiding fears, confronting a person in authority who mistreated you, or emotionally numbing yourself from a traumatic experience. The curiosity to explore the root causes of your distress is a critical first step, before you can look for ways to manage this distress.

Movies

- *October Sky (1999)*—The curiosity of Homer Hickam, inspired by the launch of Sputnik, motivates him and his friends to build their own rockets, and eventually they get a spot in the National Science Awards competition.
- *10 Items or Less (2006)*—A "has-been" actor, in pursuit of a new role, goes to a grocery store in a small industrial town to observe a worker, displaying a high level of curiosity while interacting with a wide range of people.
- *Indiana Jones and The Raiders of the Lost Ark (1981)*—An archaeological adventure—covering a booby-trapped temple in Peru to the search for ancient artefacts—shows numerous aspects of curiosity.

Therapeutic Actions

- **Confront your fears:** Make a list of experiences or things that make you afraid, uncomfortable, or anxious. Make sure you list things that you fear and also *avoid*, either by not doing them (e.g., avoiding certain places, foods, or people) or by doing something else (e.g., taking a detour, eating substitute foods, or not interacting with people). Expand your knowledge about ways to deal with your fear by reading expert opinions, watching recommended videos, and speaking with someone who could help you with useful tips.
- **Deal with boredom through cultural explorations:** If you experience boredom and are tired of routine, try something new. For example, eat food from a different culture or engage in a cultural experience that carries an element of novelty for you. Explore the cultural context of the experience from someone familiar with the culture. Share your impressions with a friend or friends in person or through social media.
- **Cope with the anxiety of uncertainty:** We want to understand, manage, and predict events in our lives. However, it is almost impossible to do so, which often causes anxiety. Instead of coping with this anxiety through unhealthy means (e.g., by "filling in the blanks" with inaccurate information acquired impulsively), use curiosity to embrace uncertainty and be open to new information. This process will help you learn to tolerate uncertainty so that you will better be able to cope with anxiety. Rather than searching for certainty, be curious about the process that leads to certainty.
- **Overcome biases by diversifying social connections:** We often socialize with people who are like us. This helps us identify with them and hurts us by limiting our social exposure. Such limited exposure maintains or reinforces our biases toward people and cultures different from us. Arrange a face-to-face conversation or a coffee date with a person from a different culture, and spend an hour, at least once a month, learning about the person and his or her culture. Be inquisitive, nonjudgmental, and open about your own culture.
- **Develop curiosity about nature:** Nature holds tremendous therapeutic potential. Reallocate an hour that you would spend worrying, doubting, and stressing over your unsolved problems, to exploring nature. For at least one hour a week, explore the processes of nature, by being in the woods, or a park, or by a stream, in the yard, and so on. Write, draw, or paint in order to record your impressions and feelings.

Exemplars (TED Talks)

Visit https://www.ted.com/talks and search for the following talks to hear from individuals who represent the strength of curiosity:

- **Kary Mullis:** Play! Experiment! Discover!
- **Brian Cox:** Why we need the explorers
- **Taylor Wilson:** Yup, I built a nuclear fusion reactor
- **Jack Andraka:** A promising test for pancreatic cancer . . . from a teenager

Books

- Goldin, I., & Kutarna, C. (2016). *Age of Discovery: Navigating the Risks and Rewards of Our New Renaissance*. Bloomsbury, UK: St Martin's Press.
- Gruwell, E. (1999). *The Freedom Writers Diary: How a Teacher and 150 Teens Used Writing to Change Themselves and the World around Them*. New York: Doubleday.
- Grazer, B., & Fishman, C. (2015). *A Curious Mind: The Secret to a Bigger Life*. Toronto: Simon & Schuster.
- Kashdan, T. (2009). *Curious*. New York: William Morrow.
- Leslie, I. (2014). *Curious: The Desire to Know and Why Your Future Depends on It*. New York: Basic Books.

Websites

- Discover how cultivating an inquiring mind can help you lead a happier, healthier life: https://experiencelife.com/article/the-power-of-curiosity/
- Four reasons why curiosity is important and how it can be developed: http://www.lifehack.org/articles/productivity/4-reasons-why- curiosity-is-important-and-how-to-develop-it.html
- Curiosity prepares the brain for better learning: http://www.scientificamerican.com/article/curiosity-prepares-the-brain-for-better-learning/

3. OPEN-MINDEDNESS

Description

Open-mindedness is our ability to think things through and examine them from all sides. In the therapeutic context, open-mindedness entails a willingness to consider evidence against our own beliefs about ourselves. Psychotherapy is an interpersonal endeavor to evaluate one's beliefs, especially those that maintain symptoms and stress. Using the strength of open-mindedness, especially to grasp a complex personal situation, will encourage you to look at different perspectives not yet considered to solve problems. Open-mindedness will encourage you to maintain the "reality orientation," that is, being unbiased and perceiving problems objectively. You will therefore be better able to counteract the pervasive "my-side bias" that prevents many people from considering views other than their own.

The Golden Mean

For the most part, open-mindedness entails critical inquiry, sifting the quality of information carefully. In solving your everyday problems or tackling big challenges, a lack of open-mindedness prevents you from reflecting, and you likely perceive your problems in black and white. You likely are seen as being rigid, your stance would likely be called stubborn, and this stubbornness can exacerbate symptomatic distress. If you experience symptoms of depression and anxiety, and also face adversity, a setback, or a failure, you are more likely to attribute the challenge to your own shortcomings. You are likely to assume that the challenge will last forever and that it will adversely impact all aspects of your life.

Similarly, an overuse of this strength will make you overanalytical, cynical, and skeptical, and you won't be able to trust people or processes. A balanced use of open-mindedness requires that you exercise critical inquiry but do not discount emotional aspects of the situation that may not be fully explained by facts alone. (For example, after a break up, which you rationally justify is good for you, you may continue to feel sad and bad. It is important to mourn the loss, without being swept away by it.)

- *Overuse of strength:* cynicism, skepticism
- *Underuse of strength:* dogmatism, "unreflectiveness," rigidity, overly simplistic

Integration

Open-mindedness works synergistically with a number of strengths. For example, being open-minded and organically engaged in critical thinking allows you to be open to alternative explanations and innovative solutions—hallmarks of creativity and curiosity. Open-mindedness also entails being open to multiple perspectives and tapping into wisdom. Furthermore, the critical appraisal associated with open-mindedness reinforces fairness and integrity.

Movies

- *The Help (2011)*—Eugenia Skeeter, an open-minded white female writer, strives to tell the stories and perspectives of black maids in a clearly stratified and highly racist society.
- *The Matrix (1999)*—Neo, the protagonist, displays open-mindedness by questioning the meaning of reality.
- *The Social Network (2010)*—This movie tells how Mark Zuckerberg founded Facebook. A scene depicting the first meeting of a difficult college course shows the lack of open-mindedness of the professor, while the movie shows how Zuckerberg, despite experiencing social deficits, exercises his flexible and critical thinking strengths.
- *Apocalypse Now (1979)*—In an adaptation of Joseph Conrad's novel, *Heart of Darkness*, famed film director Francis Ford Coppola depicts a critical inquiry into primal madness, brought on by the Vietnam War.
- *Water (2005)*—This film displays the lives of three widows showing extraordinary judgment to remain open to new experiences confronting injustice and negative societal traditions.

Therapeutic Actions

- **Reflect on and rewrite your challenges:** Monitor and record at least three unhealthy thoughts and beliefs that make you sad, anxious, or ambivalent. (For example, *"My wife constantly leaves a mess everywhere and this really annoys me! I never say anything, but I feel like she doesn't respect me. Why does this always happen to me?"*) Reflect on and write about an alternative way of explaining these problems to yourself, one that includes some of the attributes of open-mindedness.
- **Reflect on and write about decisions that backfired:** Reflect on and write about three recent decisions you made that backfired or did not produce the desired and adaptive outcome. Share your reflections with a trusted and wise friend. Ask your friend to critically appraise your judgment. Commit to yourself that you will listen to this appraisal without getting angry or defensive.
- **Play devil's advocate:** Reflect on and select an issue about which you have strong opinions. Deliberately think through an argument for the other side. Dispassionately review credible sources that may support you to hold this opposing view. This exercise may open your mind to a new perspective you may not have considered before.
- **Mentor someone from a different ethnic or religious background:** Reflect on what skills or expertise you can teach someone from a disadvantaged or marginalized group. Approach this task with the expectation that you want to, and can, learn as much from the mentee as she or he can learn from you.
- **Reappraise causes of your failure:** Identify causes of three recent failures, set-backs, less than optimal results, or disappointments. Review the attributes of open-mindedness, and then appraise the situations again. Find patterns, if any, such as why you always feel bad or anxious or powerless when talking to this person, or if there is a specific cause that you typically endorse. (For example, *"I always miss something important before this meeting."*)

Exemplars (TED Talks)

Visit https://www.ted.com/talks and search for the following talks to hear from individuals who represent the strength of open-mindedness:

- **Alia Crum:** Change Your mindset, Change the game, TEDxTraverseCity
- **Adam Savage:** How simple ideas lead to scientific discoveries
- **Adam Grant:** The surprising habits of original thinkers
- **Vernā Myers:** How to overcome our biases? Walk boldly toward them
- **Dalia Mogahed:** What do you think when you look at me?

Books

- Costa, A. (1985). *Developing Minds: A Resource Book for Teaching Thinking.* Alexandria, VA: Association for Supervision and Curriculum Development.
- Hare, W. (1985). *In Defence of Open-Mindedness.* Kingston, UK: McGill-Queen's University Press.
- Markova, D. (1996). *The Open Mind: Exploring the 6 Patterns of Natural Intelligence.* Berkeley, CA: Conari Press.

Websites

- YouTube: Critical Thinking: A look at some of the principles of critical thinking: https://youtu.be/6OLPL5p0fMg
- YouTube: Top 5 Mind Opening and Quality Movies: https://youtu.be/gsjEX9lvAgY
- Open-mindedness, its benefits, its role as a "corrective virtue," and its exercises: https://www.authentichappiness.sas.upenn.edu/newsletters/authentichappinesscoaching/open-mindedness

4. LOVE OF LEARNING

Description

Love of learning involves enthusiastically studying new skills, topics, and bodies of knowledge. If this is one of your top strengths, you most likely enjoy learning, and, over time, you build a reservoir of knowledge of specific topics and domains. You don't need external prompts to "study;" rather, you are internally motivated to enhance and accumulate diverse dimensions of data and information to constantly strengthen your knowledge base on specific topics—from computers to culinary arts, from movies to museums, or from Lagos to literature. You create or are drawn to hubs of learning—be it a school, a book club, a discussion group, a lecture, a workshop, or even taking a course. Obstacles, challenges, and setbacks do not dampen your desire for learning.

The Golden Mean

Resisting learning and acquiring new knowledge and understanding most likely impedes one's growth and is often one of the signs of underlying depression. Going deeper into learning most likely brings about numerous benefits. However, knowledge is a concrete resource, and knowledge of statistics, facts, figures, historical events, scientific findings, and concrete evidence, can instill an air of over confidence and, in some cases, arrogance, which can easily create a division between those who know (or the know-it-all) and those who don't know, or don't know enough. Therefore, it is important that in a data-, information-, and knowledge-rich world, you not create or climb on a hierarchy of knowledge and learning and end up treating others (those without your quantity of knowledge) any less. More importantly, don't discount emotions. Having access to your worries, fears, and doubts is critical, as these emotions provide the context for your rationality and knowledge so that you can comprehend the wholeness of a situation to optimally solve your problems.

- *Overuse of strength:* "know it all"-ism
- *Underuse of strength:* complacency, smugness

Integration

Love of learning goes hand in hand with other strengths within the virtue of Knowledge & Wisdom. For example, love of learning accompanies curiosity and persistence. Without persistence, it is difficult to acquire a deeper understanding of any subject. Likewise, love of learning synergistically enhances critical thinking and widens perspective.

Movies

- *Theory of Everything (2014)*—An extraordinary story of one of the world's greatest living minds, the renowned astrophysicist Stephen Hawking displays love of learning despite extraordinary challenges.
- *Akeelah and the Bee (2006)*—The passion of an American adolescent to learn unfolds as she reluctantly participates and eventually wins the National Spelling Bee competition.
- *A Beautiful Mind (2001)*—This is the story of Noble Laurate John Nash and his passion for self-discovery and knowledge despite severe mental health challenges.

Therapeutic Actions

- **Reallocate time to learn about adaptive coping:** We often spend a lot of time thinking and brooding about our problems, and less time thinking about how to cope with them adaptively. Monitor yourself to estimate how much time you spend thinking about your problems. Reallocate that time to learn about how others have successfully coped with similar issues.
- **Share your learning:** Identify topics that you can share with your peers. Share information in a humble, conversational manner. Reflect afterwards. Most likely you will feel satisfied, and this will likely increase your self-efficacy.
- **Follow an ongoing situation:** Follow an ongoing local or global event about which you can personally identify or feel affinity for. Make a list of things you don't know about the event, and find credible sources to enhance your learning.
- **Learn through leisure:** Travel to new places and blend education with leisure. While you are there, take a tour, take a cooking class, or visit a local museum to learn more about the local culture and history.
- **Co-learn:** Learn with a friend with whom you share one or more areas of intellectual interest. Discuss specific areas that you each will study separately. Share your findings over a cup of coffee or tea, preferably in a café. You can also co-learn with a loved one, including your partner, parents, children, or extended family members. This will strengthen your relationships, and you will spend time together in a positive, rather than a potentially negative, way.

Exemplars (TED Talks)

Visit https://www.ted.com/talks and search for the following talks to hear from individuals who represent the strength of love of learning:

- **Salman Khan:** Let us Use Video to Reinvent Education
- **Bunker Roy:** Learning from a barefoot movement
- **Ramsey Musallam:** 3 rules to spark learning

Books

- Yousafzai, M., & Lamb, C. (2013). *I Am Malala: The Girl Who Stood Up for Education and Was Shot by the Taliban*. London: Hachette.
- Watson, J. C., & Watson, J. C. (2011). *Critical Thinking: An Introduction to Reasoning Well*. London: Continuum.
- Markova, D. (1996). *The Open Mind: Exploring the 6 Patterns of Natural Intelligence*. Berkeley, CA: Conari Press.

Websites

- Coursera offers a number of free online courses:
  https://www.coursera.org/
- Free course from Massachusetts Institute of Technology:
  http://ocw.mit.edu/index.htm
- Free courses online courses from Yale University:
  http://oyc.yale.edu/

5. PERSPECTIVE

Description

Perspective, which is often called wisdom, is distinct from intelligence and involves a superior level of knowledge and judgment. This strength allows you to provide wise counsel to others. A number of our psychological problems are characterized by assumptions. For example, we think that we can do many things, especially when it comes to things that require interacting with others. When others fall short of our expectations and don't (or are unable to) do what we desire, we become disappointed and, in some cases, depressed. (For example, "*I was hoping that my family would understand why I am making this difficult decision. . . .*") From a therapeutic standpoint, perspective helps you to evaluate what you can do, what you cannot do, what you can realistically expect, and what may not be realistic.

We experience ambivalence when we are unable to discern conflicting information or unable to balance competing positives (e.g., "*Should I work more to earn more money so that we can go on vacation, or should I use this time to play a board game with my loved ones, so that we can do something together now?*"). The strength of perspective will help you weigh an option for the greater good—be it related to self-care or caring for others. Perspective also allows you to address important and difficult questions about morality and the meaning of life. People with perspective are aware of broad patterns of meaning in their lives, their own strengths and weaknesses, and the necessity of contributing to their society.

The Golden Mean

Perspective, by definition, is the golden mean. That is, if it is one of your top strengths, you know how to strike a balance between your work and personal life. You are good at setting realistic expectations. You are good at separating positives from negatives and weighing them appropriately. With this strength, you can weigh personal factors (e.g., "*I always make a fool of myself*") versus situational factors (e.g., "*Yesterday, my presentation did not go well because my colleague did not provide the critical data that I needed.*) A balanced use of perspective entails having the ability to see both the forest from the trees and the trees in the forest. It is also about tolerating some short-term pain (e.g., confronting an anxious situation) for long-term gains (e.g., getting rid of your anxiety). However, be mindful that not all aspects of your life need perspective. Appraising and dealing with every mundane situation from the lens of perspective can make your decisions arcane or pedantic.

- *Overuse of strength:* elitism, arcane, pedantic
- *Underuse of strength:* superficiality

Integration

In some ways, perspective encompasses the strengths discussed previously. That is, perspective encompasses learning, curiosity, creativity, and understanding what proportion of your specific strengths best work together toward your satisfaction and well-being (e.g., a proportionate use of kindness and fairness).

Movies

- *Hugo (2011)*—Hugo, a 12-year-old boy living in the Gare Montparnasse train station in Paris, offers perspective on experiences with what really matters in life. The movie is also a brilliant illustration of resilience and social intelligence.
- *Peaceful Warrior (2006)*—Socrates, played by Nick Nolte, teaches Dan, an ambitious teenager, the strength of perspective, humility, and focus through actions and applied scenarios.
- *American Beauty (1999)*—Lester Burnham, a middle-aged businessman trapped in his own misery, undergoes a rapid transformation to realize what is truly important in his life.

Therapeutic Actions

- **Set goals for things that frustrate you:** Set five small goals That address your day-to-day stressors (such as feeling irritable at your partner for not bringing the dishes back into the kitchen from the dinner table, or feeling frustrated at forgetting passwords to important websites). Break down the goals into practical steps, accomplish them on time, and monitor your progress from week to week.
- **Choose a role model for problem-solving:** Select a role model who exemplifies perseverance, and determine how you can follow in her or his footsteps. Try to select a person who has dealt with challenges similar to yours, with whom you can identify. If this person is living and someone you know, speak with him or her about this strength.
- **Broaden your outlook and monitor temporary stressors:** Explain the broad outlook of your life in one or two sentences as a weekly exercise. Monitor whether temporary stressors have an impact on your overall perspective. If you do see this pattern, brainstorm ways that your perspective can remain constant through daily joys and struggles.
- **Volunteer the time you would otherwise spend analyzing your problems:** Pursue endeavors that have a significant impact on the world. Reallocate your time and resources to pursue this endeavor. This reallocation will positively distract your mind from thinking about your problems, some of which need fresh perspective. If you are unable to solve a problem right away, positive distraction allows you to reconsider from a fresh perspective.
- **Connect beliefs with emotions:** Connect your beliefs with your emotions by reading books or watching films of personal experiences on issues that matter to you personally. Put a human face on the issue and recall that when you feel your opinion on the issue is getting too heated.

Exemplars (TED Talks)

Visit https://www.ted.com/talks and search for the following talks to hear from individuals who represent the strength of perspective:

- **Barry Schwartz:** Using our practical wisdom
- **Joshua Prager:** Wisdom from great writers on every year of life
- **Rory Sutherland:** Perspective is everything

Books

- Frankl, V. (2006). *Man's Search for Meaning*. Boston: Beacon Press.
- Hall, S. (2010). *Wisdom: From Philosophy to Neuroscience*. New York: Random House.
- Sternberg, R. J., ed. (1990). *Wisdom: Its Nature, Origins, and Development*. Cambridge: Cambridge University Press.
- Vaillant, G. E. (2003*). Aging Well: Surprising Guideposts to a Happier Life from the Landmark Study of Adult Development*. New York: Little Brown.

Websites

- This website details the work of Thomas D. Gilovich, who studies beliefs, judgment and decision-making. He studies how these factors affect, and are affected by, emotions, behavior and perception:
  http://www.psych.cornell.edu/people/Faculty/tdg1.html
- Barry Schwarz studies practical wisdom and the paradox of choice. He discusses the disadvantages of having infinite choices, which he argues exhausts the society and the human psyche:
  https://www.ted.com/speakers/barry_schwartz

CORE VIRTUE: COURAGE

Exercising the will to accomplish goals in the face of opposition, external or internal

6. BRAVERY

Description

Bravery (courage) is the capacity to take action to aid others in spite of significant risks or dangers. When you are psychologically distressed and *also* face challenges, threats, or adversities—real or perceived—this can become a "double whammy," and the impact can therefore be two-fold. Sometimes our challenges, threats, and adversities themselves are overwhelming enough to cause psychological problems. If bravery is one of your top strengths, it can help you take action to deal with the challenge in an adaptive way. Bravery does not let you avoid or shrink from challenges, and you usually exercise this strength well aware of the risks involved. If bravery is one of your signature strengths, you place a high value on it. That is, when you feel stressed, sad, frightened, angry, or overwhelmed, the strength of bravery will most likely motivate you to take an action. Brave individuals avoid shrinking from the threats, challenges, or pain associated with attempting to do good works. Brave acts are undertaken voluntarily, with full knowledge of the potential adversity involved. Brave individuals place the highest importance on higher purpose and morality, no matter what the consequences.

The Golden Mean

To deal with your problems with the help of bravery, it is important that you not feel coerced or entirely extrinsically motivated. Courageous actions—physical or emotional—ought to be based on your own values. (For example, if you confront a family member who is being emotionally or physically abusive to another family member, or if you take a stand in support of a vulnerable or oppressed person, such action will be authentic if it is guided by your deeply held personal values that this action is the right thing to do.) A balanced use of courage requires the existence of a real threat or risk that can be averted by your courageous action. A balanced use of bravery also entails that you be aware of the consequences of your action or inaction. (For example, you will want to ensure that your use of bravery is not taking undue risk that comes with the cost of comprising your and other's safety.) Note that not using courage can often result in feelings of helplessness. Thus, overuse of bravery (e.g., disclosure, reputation, collective reprisals) and underuse of bravery (e.g., hopelessness, passivity, demotivation) can create problems both for yourself and others.

- *Overuse of strength:* risk-taking, foolishness
- *Underuse of strength:* debilitating fear, cowardice

Integration

Bravery can potentially interact with numerous other strengths. For example, bravery can entail *using* (i.e., committing) strengths such as fairness, authenticity, or perspective, or *not using* (i.e., omitting) strengths such as perspective, prudence, self-regulation, or forgiveness. Bravery also works well with strengths like zest, social and personal intelligence, persistence, and self-regulation. Examples include wanting to face your fear in spite of accessing uncomfortable emotions and memories, appraising with an open mind (judgment), taking action to halt the cycle of negativity or resisting impulses (self-regulation), and committing to adhere to your goal (persistence).

Movies

- *Milk (2008)*—This movie depicts Harvey Milks' courage to become the first openly gay person to be elected to public office in California.
- *The Kite Runner (2007)*—A moving tale of two friends, Amir and Hassan, whose friendship flourishes in pre-Soviet-invasion Kabul, in the mid to late 1970s. The film shows how Amir musters the courage to rescue Hassan's son from war-ravaged and Taliban-ruled Afghanistan.
- *Schindler's List (1993)*—Oskar Schindler is a German businessman whose bravery saves over a thousand Jews during World War II.
- *The Help (2011)*—Eugenia, also known as "Skeeter," is a courageous white female writer who strives to tell the stories and perspectives of black maids in a clearly stratified and highly racist society.

Therapeutic Actions

- **Resolve interpersonal distress with brave "one-to-ones":** Write about three interpersonal situations that cause you ongoing distress, such as fear or inhibition, especially with people in a position of authority and with whom you interact regularly. Reflect on how a balanced use of bravery can decrease your distress. (For example, *"I want to speak with my professor, alone after class, to bravely express myself."*)
- **Embrace darker and negative experiences with bravery:** Make a list of emotions from which you often run. Turn these into statements such as, *"I will make a complete fool of myself. I am so afraid of being rejected or being alone; I cannot do anything to stop him acting this way, so I just leave the situation altogether"* and evaluate the cost of not facing such emotions. Then, using bravery, visualize embracing the full range of your emotions, such as what might be the worst and the best scenarios if you were to stay and do something. Bravery can help you embrace the full range of your emotions, especially in distressful situations.
- **Speak the truth that will set you free:** Use bravery to share a truth about yourself with your closest relations. This is a truth that is important enough that it impacts your relationships in a negative way, is an important aspect of your life, and one you are not

sharing because of fear of rejection. (For example, *"I am really afraid to tell my parents that I am a lesbian. It is such an important part of me, but how will they take it? But if I don't tell them, then I am not being my authentic self with my family."*)

- **Ask difficult questions or question the status quo:** In group situations, such as at work, with your family, or among friends, use bravery to ask difficult questions or to question the status quo. Examples include questioning why do specific policies or rituals systematically keep specific people or groups on the fringes, not allowing them to assume leadership roles. Propose bold yet realistic solutions.
- **Stand up for someone or for a cause:** Stand up for someone who is unable to stand up for him- or herself, such as a younger sibling, a battered woman, a vulnerable immigrant, or a worker who is unaware of his rights. You can join an organization that courageously stands for those who need the support most.

Exemplars (TED Talks)

Visit https://www.ted.com/talks and search for the following talks to hear from individuals who represent the strength of bravery:

- **Ash Beckham:** We're all hiding something. Let's find the courage to open up
- **Clint Smith:** The danger of silence
- **Eman Mohammed:** The courage to tell a hidden story

Books

- Diener, R. (2012). *The Courage Quotient: How Science Can Make You Braver.* San Francisco: Jossey-Bass.
- Pury, C. (2010). *The Psychology of Courage: Modern Research on an Ancient Virtue.* Washington, DC: American Psychological Association.
- Pausch, R., & Zaslow, J. (2008). *The Last Lecture.* New York: Hyperion.

Websites

- The skill of bravery, its benefits, and the balance between fear and over-confidence: http://www.skillsyouneed.com/ps/courage.html
- Nine teens and their incredible acts of bravery: http://theweek.com/articles/468498/9-heroic-teens-incredible-acts-bravery-updated

7. PERSISTENCE

Description

Persistence is the mental strength necessary to continue striving for our goals in the face of obstacles and setbacks. From the therapeutic perspective, a number of psychological problems adversely impact attention and the ability to concentrate. Persistence (perseverance) is the strength that can help you deal with attentional problems because it enables you to remain goal-directed despite challenges, especially those due to distraction. With this strength, even if you are distracted, persistence brings you back to complete the task. You do your best to finish what you start and find ways to overcome hiccups and hardships. If you become bored and lackadaisical—another common feature of many psychological concerns—finding a task in which you can persist is an organic and therapeutic way to feel self-efficacious, uplifted, and satisfied when you finish the task.

The Golden Mean

The key to a balanced use of persistence is knowing when and where to persist and when to stop and cut your losses. To determine whether to persist or not, ask yourself what might happen if you do not finish this specific task. Equally important is your ability to adapt to changing situations. For example, in pursuing a desired career, you need to adapt to inevitable changes in market conditions, in technology, and in the larger socioeconomic framework. Finally, to optimally use this strength, you need to constantly be aware of your goal. (For example, to persist in successfully obtaining a social media certification that involves taking multiple courses in the evenings and on the weekends, you need to evaluate your goals and "keep your eyes on the prize.")

- *Overuse of strength:* obsessiveness, fixation, pursuit of unattainable goals
- *Underuse of strength:* laziness, apathy

Integration

To evaluate when persistence is adaptive versus when it enters the realm of obsessive and compulsive preoccupation, you need other strengths, such as perspective, social intelligence, judgment (open-mindedness), and prudence. To persist, especially if you experience setbacks, challenges, or obstacles, you need a good dose of hope and optimism. Without hope and optimism, motivation to persist will be sapped. However, you need to keep your hopes and optimism in the realm of what is realistic.

Movies

- *Life of Pi (2010)*—This movie presents the epic journey of a young man who perseveres and survives on the open sea to strike an unlikely connection with a ferocious Bengali Tiger.
- *127 Hours (2010)*—In a remarkable display of persistence and courage, Ralston, a mountain climber, becomes trapped under a boulder while canyoneering alone near Moab, Utah.
- *The King's Speech (2010)*—England's King George VI perseveres to overcome a speech impediment.

Therapeutic Actions

- **Tackle tasks that overwhelm you:** List five big tasks that you have to do, but that often overwhelm you, such as doing your taxes, responding to non-stop email, or preparing a holiday dinner for your partner's large family. Break these tasks into smaller steps, and congratulate yourself or celebrate—in small ways—when you finish each step. Monitor your progress step by step.
- **Find a role model who persisted despite challenges:** Select a role model who exemplifies perseverance and determine how you can follow in this person's footsteps. Try to find someone who has experienced mental health challenges similar to yours. Ideally meet this person face-to-face, or connect with him or her through other ways, to explore how he or she overcame challenges and perseverance.
- **Persist while acquiring new skills:** Your persistence may come to a halt simply because you do not have the next skill level to move forward. (For example, after designing a product, don't hesitate to ask for help in either learning new skills or having someone work with you, so that you can finish the project and produce it.)
- **Incorporate elements of "flow":** If you struggle to persist, explore flow, an intrinsically motivated state of deep immersion. Explore activities that induce flow; you will persist, and, in the process, you will grow.

- **Work with others:** A potentially therapeutic use of persistence is working with other like-minded individuals. The company of others can increase your skills and your motivation to persist.

Exemplars (TED Talks)

Visit https://www.ted.com/talks and search for the following talks to hear from individuals who represent the strength of persistence:

- **Angela Lee Duckworth:** Grit: The power of passion and perseverance
- **Elizabeth Gilbert:** Success, failure and the drive to keep creating
- **Richard St. John:** 8 secrets of success

Books

- Duckworth, A. (2016). *Grit: The Power of Passion and Perseverance.* New York: Simon & Schuster.
- Luthans, F., Youssef, C., & Avolio, B. (2007). *Psychological Capital: Developing the Human Competitive Edge.* New York: Oxford University Press.
- Tough, P. (2012). *How Children Succeed: Grit, Curiosity, and the Hidden Power of Character.* New York: Houghton Mifflin Harcourt.

Websites

- Self-determination theory discusses intrinsic motivation, values and how they affect well-being and goals:
  http://www.selfdeterminationtheory.org/
- Edward L. Deci studies motivation and self-determination and their effects on different facets of life, such as mental health, education, and work:
  http://www.psych.rochester.edu/people/deci_edward/index.html

8. INTEGRITY

Description

The strength of integrity (authenticity) is manifested by speaking the truth and presenting oneself in a genuine way. From a therapeutic standpoint, a number of psychological conditions entail ambivalence, inhibition, fear, embarrassment, and rejection, which keep us from sharing our emotions, thoughts, and, more importantly, needs, in an authentic manner. Integrity helps you to be open and honest about your thoughts and emotions. If integrity and authenticity are your top strengths, you easily take ownership of your actions, which enables you to behave in accordance with your values. In other words, there is little dissonance and alienation, which, in turn, improves your reality testing and social reasoning. An individual high on integrity is less likely to experience cognitive distortions and social fears. She is better able to understand and handle the context of complex dilemmas often posed by psychopathology.

A person of integrity is open and honest about his own thoughts, feelings, and responsibilities, being careful not to mislead others through action or omission. This strength allows you to feel a sense of ownership over your own internal states, regardless of whether those states are popular or socially comfortable, and to experience a sense of authentic wholeness.

The Golden Mean

Living in accordance with your values and taking ownership of your emotions and thoughts in an interpersonally complex world are not easy tasks, given the impact of cultural, religious, political, economic, ecological, and even technological (especially social media) influences. Therefore, a balanced use of integrity depends on the context. (For example, not every situation is amenable to authentic expressions like, *"I am not as good as others;" "Often I feel worthless," "I am too embarrassed to ask for help; others will see me as weak."* Also, sharing whatever you are thinking on Facebook or Twitter may not be the optimal way to represent yourself authentically.) To live an authentic and honest life, courage to withstand external pressures is indeed necessary. An authentic life also entails being credible, being real, and speaking the truth. Note that authenticity and fairness are not applicable in absolute terms; cultures differ vastly in terms of authentic representation of the self. Therefore, a balanced use of authenticity, honesty, and integrity can better be appraised within the cultural context. However, whatever the cultural framework might be, underuse of authenticity could lead to not expressing your emotions, interests, and needs. This in turn could limit your self-efficacy—if you cannot own your needs, how can you meet them? Furthermore, underuse of this strength forces you to adopt different roles in different situations, causing a fragmented personality that is more controlled or influenced by external forces than by yourself.

- *Overuse of strength:* righteousness
- *Underuse of strength:* shallowness, phoniness

Integration

Integrity works well when you are also attuned to your needs and motivations. Zest and vitality nicely complement integrity, and perspective and social intelligence are two key strengths that can help you understand context. In addition, emotional intelligence (as a sub-domain of social intelligence) provides you cues to feel, own, and express your internal states in a way that feels appropriate and authentic to you. Kindness and love are two other attributes that go hand in hand with integrity. Genuine love marked by caring and sharing encourages authenticity and vice-versa.

Movies

- *Separation (2011, Iran)*—During the dissolution of a marriage, this film presents an inspiring display of integrity and honesty by a person who is accused of lying.
- *Erin Brockovich (2000)*—The lead character's deep sense of integrity to bring the truth to light eventually results in one of the biggest class-action lawsuits in U.S. history.
- *The Legend of Bagger Vance (2000)*—Rannulph Junnah, once the best golfer in Savannah, Georgia, overcomes alcoholism to reconstruct both his golf game and his life through the strengths of authenticity and integrity.
- *Dead Poet Society (1989)*—English teacher John Keating, teaches boys about the joys of poetry, but in essence, they learn and eventually show the strengths of honesty and integrity.

Therapeutic Actions

- **Evaluate inhibitions, judgments, and rejection—lack of authenticity:** Reflect on and write about five situations that stressed you. Evaluate each situation as to whether it was partly due to inhibition, fear of judgment, or rejection, especially those caused by social norms and expectations. With a close friend or family member, discuss ways of finding how you can express yourself authentically.
- **Look for situations that facilitate your authenticity:** Reflect on and write about situations that naturally allow you to be yourself. Pay close attention to both internal and

external factors that facilitate your authenticity. Discuss with a confidant how you can create more such situations.

- **Foster authentic interaction:** A number of our psychological stressors spring from our inability to authentically relate to others with integrity. Review models of feedback that are both authentic and constructive, and that build—not block—the relationship.
- **Seek authentic roles:** Seek roles with clear structure that allow you to be authentic and honest, especially if you feel inhibited at work. Pursue positions in organizations that foster honest, forthright communication.
- **Clarify moral convictions:** Identify your area of strongest moral conviction. (For example, doing your job optimally and giving it your best.) How can you bring these convictions into other areas of your life where you tend to struggle? (For example, obeying traffic rules, always opting for environmentally friendly options, standing up for some being mistreated.) Set small, measurable goals to improve your behavior that lead to greater integrity.

Exemplars (TED Talks)

Visit https://www.ted.com/talks and search for the following talks to hear from individuals who represent the strength of integrity:

- **Brené Brown:** The power of vulnerability
- **Malcolm McLaren:** Authentic creativity vs. karaoke culture
- **Heather Brooke:** My battle to expose government corruption

Books

- Brown, B. (2010). *The Gifts of Imperfection: Let Go of Who You Think You're Supposed To Be and Embrace Who You Are.* Center City, MN: Hazelden.
- Cloud, H. (2006). *Integrity: The Courage to Meet the Demands of Reality.* New York: Harper.
- Simons, T. (2008). *The Integrity Dividend Leading by the Power of Your Word.* San Francisco: Jossey-Bass.

Websites

- Profiling voices, victims and witnesses of corruption and work toward a world free of corruption:
  https://www.transparency.org
- The International Center for Academic Integrity works to identify, promote, and affirm the values of academic integrity among students, faculty, teachers, and administrators:
  http://www.academicintegrity.org/icai/home.php

9. VITALITY & ZEST

Description

Vitality is an approach to life marked by an appreciation of energy, liveliness, excitement, and zest. From a psychological perspective, a lack of vitality breeds depression, passivity, and boredom. Vitality includes positive emotions such as joy, exuberance, and excitement, as well as contentment, satisfaction, and gratification. If vitality and zest are among your top strengths, you approach life whole-heartedly. You have both emotional and physical vigor when pursuing everyday activities. You often feel inspired and turn this feeling into creative projects and initiatives. You give your best to your projects, and this engagement often encourages others. A life of vigor allows you to experience the overlap of the mental and physical realms of experience as stress decreases and health increases.

The Golden Mean

A balanced use of vitality is critical, but it is not easy to distinguish between balance and overuse. Both of these states can easily be viewed as passion. However, when vitality is overused, it can become a passion that is internalized so deeply that it becomes part of your identity. On the other hand, not using vitality would leave you passive and unmotivated. For a balanced use, it is important that zest and vitality become part of your personality, but only a part, among many other parts. A balanced use of vitality means that you pursue many activities with enthusiasm, but you do not neglect your other responsibilities.

- *Overuse of strength:* hyperactivity
- *Underuse of strength:* passivity, inhibition

Integration

Vitality is a strength that works best with strengths from other virtues such as prudence, self-regulation, curiosity, playfulness, and appreciation of beauty, which are also utilized to create experiences that are wholesome. (For example, learning a musical instrument may require you to establish a practice routine [self-regulation], to appreciate music already created [appreciation of beauty and excellence], to enjoy the learning process [curiosity], to improvise and have fun with it [playfulness, creativity], and to learn music as well fulfilling other responsibilities [prudence].)

Movies

- *Hector and the Search for Happiness (2014)*—This movie presents a quirky psychiatrist's quest to feel alive and search for the meaning of life. The film displays a number of character strengths including zest, curiosity, love, perspective, gratitude, and courage.
- *Silver Lining Playbook (2012)*—The main character, Pat, has a motto—*excelsior* (which is a Latin word meaning *forever upward*)—which embodies zest and vitality, as Pat recovers from setbacks and becomes determined, energetic, and more attentive.
- *Up (2009)*—An uplifting story (literally and metaphorically) of 78-year-old Carl, who pursues his lifelong dream of seeing the wilds of South America, along with an unlikely companion.
- *My Left Foot (1993)*—Born a quadriplegic in a poor Irish family, Christy Brown (with the help of his dedicated mother and teacher) learns to write using the only limb he has any control over: his left foot. This character displays vitality, zest, and enthusiasm for life.

Therapeutic Actions

- **Engage in a "have to do" activity:** A number of psychological conditions sap our motivation. Select a "have to do" activity—one that you have to do (such as completing homework, exercising, or washing the dishes) but that you don't feel like doing. Use your strength of creativity to do the activity in a different and exciting way. You can select a partner and do it with him or her.
- **Go outdoors:** For an hour each week, do at least one outdoor activity, such as hiking, biking, mountain climbing, brisk walking, or jogging. Enjoy both the outdoors and your own internal sensations. Nature carries immense therapeutic potential.
- **Get better sleep:** Improve your sleep hygiene by establishing a regular bed time. Don't eat any later than three or four hours before bed time, and avoid doing any work in bed, ingesting caffeine late in the evening, and so on. Notice changes in your energy level.

- **Join a club:** Get involved with a dance club, go to a concert, or join a performing arts group—at least a monthly event. If there is singing or dancing involved, join in. Alternatively, use your smart phone to take pictures that represent your concept of vitality and zest.
- **Socialize more with happy people:** Spend time with friends who like to laugh heartily. Notice how laughter can be infectious. Alternatively, watch a sitcom on television or go to a comedy club with your friends.

Exemplars (TED Talks)

Visit https://www.ted.com/talks and search for the following talks to hear from individuals who represent the strength of vitality & zest:

- **Dan Gilbert:** The surprising science of happiness
- **Ron Gutman:** The hidden power of smiling
- **Meklit Hadero:** The unexpected beauty of everyday sounds
- **Matt Cutts:** Try something new for 30 days

Books

- Buckingham, M. (2008). *The Truth About You.* Nashville, TN: Thomas Nelson.
- Elfin, P. (2014). *Dig Deep & Fly High: Reclaim Your Zest and Vitality by Loving Yourself from Inside Out.* Mona Vale, NSW: Penelope Ward.
- Peale, V. N. (1967). *Enthusiasm Makes the Difference.* New York: Simon & Schuster.

Websites

- Robert Vallerand explains what passion is and what differentiates obsessive passion from harmonious passion:
  https://vimeo.com/30755287
- Website of self-determination theory, which is concerned with supporting our natural or intrinsic tendencies to behave in effective and healthy ways:
  http://www.selfdeterminationtheory.org
- Four Reasons to Cultivate Zest in Life:
  https://greatergood.berkeley.edu/article/item/four_reasons_to_cultivate_zest_in_life

CORE VIRTUE: HUMANITY

Emotional strengths that show the exercise of will in the face of opposition or internal threat

10. LOVE

Description

Love includes both the capacity to love and be loved. The defining characteristic of this strength is valuing and caring for others, in particular those with whom sharing and caring is reciprocated. If love is among your top strengths, giving and receiving love comes easily to you. You can express your love toward those who you depend on and toward those who you romantically, sexually, and emotionally love. This strength allows you to put trust in others and make them a priority in your decision-making. You experience a sense of deep contentment from the devotion of those you love.

The Golden Mean

Love is arguably the wellspring from which your numerous other strengths flow. That makes striking a balance between love and other strengths challenging, especially when you may be feeling sad, anxious, ambivalent, or upset. If you tend to avoid (likely due to anxiety) instead of confront a repeat offender, you may be exercising your strength of love, possibly overlooking or even forgiving the offender. Likewise, the fear of loss of a relationship (likely due to depression) may compromise your strength of love, and you may tolerate unfair treatment. Relatedly, a skewed and selective expression of love can develop for one specific person—a romantic partner, parent, child, sibling, or friend—hurting others with whom you have to relate. Note that a balanced application of love is quintessentially framed within the cultural context of the individual: In interdependent cultures, this balance is to love the family as a whole, whereas in individualistic cultures, this implies balancing love and work appropriately.

- *Overuse of strength:* emotional promiscuity
- *Underuse of strength:* isolation, detachment

Integration

Love, a universal need to forge mutually caring relationships, acts like "super glue" that can integrate almost any number of other strengths. In this book, Session 3: Practical Wisdom, discusses numerous strategies to adaptively integrate strengths. Because of love's all-encompassing and idiosyncratic nature, it is important to be aware of which guiding principles integrate various strengths most adaptively, given the situation or challenge at hand. (For example, if you are experiencing relationship distress, you may integrate love with social intelligence and courage to relieve the distress, whereas someone else with a similar challenge can resolve it by integrating love with playfulness and creativity.)

Movies

- *Doctor Zhivago (1965)*—An epic story showing love—the capacity to love and be loved—of a physician who is torn between love of his wife and love of his life, set amidst the Russian Revolution.
- *The English Patient (1996)*—Set during World War II, this film tells a powerful story of love, when a young nurse cares for a mysterious stranger.
- *The Bridges of Madison County (1995)*—Francesca Johnson, a married mother, falls in love with a traveling photographer; the romance lasts only four days, but it changes her life drastically.
- *Brokeback Mountain (2005)*—This film presents the deep love story between two cowboys who fall in love almost by accident, set in the conservative landscape and social milieu of the 1960s, when gay love was still largely unaccepted.

Therapeutic Actions

- **Love is a learnable skill:** If your love is causing you distress, evaluate the sources and consequences of your distress. Love is an acquired skill that needs practice. Explore specific evidence-based skills, such as looking at the strengths of your loved ones (see the *Tree of Positive Relationships* practice in Session 12: Positive Relationships; and the *Active Constructive Responding* practice in Session 13: Positive Communication).
- **Keep up-to-date with your partner/loved ones:** Stay connected with your loved ones. Take five minutes out of your work day to send a text, or call to ask how their day is going,

especially on important days. Regularly ask your loved ones about current stressors, worries, projects, hopes, dreams, friends, and adversaries.

- **Avoid "relationship fatigue":** Most relationships start on a positive note. Over time, however, partners start assuming that they have figured each other out, and the negativity bias tends to minimize the positives and accentuate the negatives. This bias slows the growth of relationships, while anger and resentment accumulate. Use love, together with creativity and curiosity, to explore something new about your partner, and do something the two of you have not tried previously.
- **Share a deep sense of meaning:** Flourishing relationships grow when couples and families play and laugh together, and when they share a deep sense of meaning. Such meaning can be shared in a number of ways, such as having values in common (e.g., autonomy, familial harmony, and career success) and understanding the actions that express these values.
- **Spend time together:** Arrange regular family leisure activities, such as walking, hiking, biking, or camping together; taking family yoga or dance classes; or attending sporting events, retreats, concerts, or cultural festivals as a family. These activities will build pleasant, instead of toxic, memories.

Exemplars (TED Talks)

Visit https://www.ted.com/talks and search for the following talks to hear from individuals who represent the strength of love:

- **Robert Waldinger:** What makes a good life? Lessons from the longest study on happiness
- **Helen Fisher:** Why we love, why we cheat
- **Yann Dall'Aglio:** Love—you're doing it wrong
- **Mandy Len Catron:** Falling in love is the easy part

Books

- Fredrickson, B. L. (2013). *Love 2.0.* New York: Plume.
- Gottman, J. M., & Silver. N. (1999). *The Seven Principles for Making Marriage Work.* New York: Three Rivers Press.
- Pileggi Pawelski, S., & Pawelski, J. (2018). *Happy Together: Using the Science of Positive Psychology to Build Love That Lasts.* New York: TarcherPerigee.
- Vaillant, G. E. (2012). *Triumphs of Experience: The Men of the Harvard Grant Study.* Cambridge, MA: Belknap Press of Harvard University Press.

Websites

- The Gottman Institute offers research-based assessment techniques and intervention strategies as well as information about training in couple's therapy: https://www.gottman.com/
- The Attachment Lab: The Research on attachment focuses on understanding the conscious and unconscious dynamics of the attachment behavioral system: http://psychology.ucdavis.edu/research/research-labs/adult-attachment-lab
- The Centre for Family Research, at the University of Cambridge, has a worldwide reputation for innovative research that increases understanding of children, parents and family relationships: https://www.cfr.cam.ac.uk

11. KINDNESS

Description

Kindness includes numerous attributes such as being considerate, courteous, and caring. If kindness is among your top strengths, you translate these attributes into actions, deeds, and endeavors for others, without being asked and without expecting tangible outcomes. Kindness is not merely what you want to do. You are also aware of your motives, skills, and the likely impact of your efforts. Although the act of kindness is done without the expectation of personal gain, from a psychotherapeutic perspective, the person receiving the act of kindness experiences positive emotions and so does the person doing the act. Thus kindness can act as a buffer for a person in distress, by re-directing attention from oneself to others in adaptive ways. If kindness is your strength, you find joy in helping others. It doesn't matter if you know the other person or not; you are motivated to help unconditionally.

The Golden Mean

Indeed, there is value and importance in undertaking spontaneous and random acts of kindness that address immediate needs. Such acts may include resolving someone's technological glitch, providing an injured person with first aid, listening mindfully to someone who needs to share his or her distress, or cooking a meal for a sick friend. However, some consideration is needed in doing acts of kindness that may require a lot of effort, energy, and time. (Examples include tutoring, helping with a household construction or building project, and assisting with professional expertise such as accounting, legal, or medical.) For all such situations, explain any potential risks and outcomes. Also consider whether the help you are offering is actually needed; is accepted; is offered respectfully; is pragmatic; and is not contingent on any direct, indirect, or secondary gains. Ensure that you consult with the recipient about the process and logistics, as a number of factors may not be obvious. Also make sure that your kindness is not perceived as leniency or does not evolve into dependency. Always connect your acts of kindness with your deeper values. It is very important to understand that kindness also includes being kind to the self. Kindness devoid of self-compassion can be an excuse to avoid or suppress your own harsh inner critic. A balanced use of kindness entails that you are not being unduly critical of yourself.

- *Overuse of strength:* intrusiveness
- *Underuse of strength:* indifference, cruelty, mean-spiritedness

Integration

Kindness works well with a number of other strengths. For example, deploying facets of emotional intelligence can help you appraise the nuances of situations such as: Is kindness relevant to the situation, or could some other strength bring about a better outcome? If, for example, a task requires a very specific skill set that you yourself can only accomplish in part, you can ask someone else to help you (teamwork), or clarify the extent of what you know so that the recipient is aware of what you can and cannot accomplish (authenticity), and then get the rest of the task done elsewhere. If you are eager to help someone and you have the skills to deliver the help but you are afraid of making mistakes, consult and collaborate with the recipient, and utilize other strengths such as prudence, judgment, and open-mindedness to create an optimal experience of expressing your kindness.

Movies

- *Blind Side (2009)*—Based on a true story of kindness and compassion, Michael Oher, a homeless and traumatized boy, is adopted by Sean and Leigh Anne Tuohy—a connection that leads Michael to play in the National Football League.

- *Children of Heaven (1997, Iran)*—This movie shows kindness and compassion, rather than traditional sibling rivalry, between a brother and sister who share a pair of shoes.
- *The Secret Life of Bees (2008)* –A moving story that shows a powerful connection between strangers. A 14-year-old girl escapes a troubled world to find care and love in the home of the Boatwright sisters and their engrossing world of beekeeping.
- *The Cider House Rules (1999)*—Homer, a youth residing in an orphanage in Maine, learns both medicine and the value of kind actions over blind deference to rules.

Therapeutic Actions

- **Build self-efficacy:** Commit to doing at least one act of kindness to help others. When you help others genuinely, you do so without the expectation of any reward or other benefit. However, you are likely to reap psychological benefits as helping others builds your own self-efficacy, which in turn, decreases psychiatric distress.
- **Be kind to yourself:** Psychologically distressed people—especially those battling depression—harshly criticize themselves and think of themselves as the cause of their distress. If you are like this, start to use self-compassion, that is, be kind to yourself. Instead of exclusively focusing on your deficits, affirm your strengths in an authentic manner.
- **Express kindness through communication:** Use kinder and softer words to people when interacting through email, writing letters, talking on the phone, or interacting on social media. Create a list of tips and strategies for being kind on social media. Post this list and elicit responses and suggestions from you friends and family.
- **Expand your kindness and cultural connections:** Select one specific and distinct culture. Using different sources, including a few from within the culture, devise a list of cultural expressions that are often misunderstood by people outside the culture. Share the list with your social circles.
- **Engage in spontaneous acts of kindness:** While driving, give way to others, and be courteous toward pedestrians and bicyclists. When entering or exiting buildings, hold the doors for others. Help fix someone's flat tire, or offer your cell phone to a stranded motorist. Carry jumper cables and flares in your trunk in case you need to help someone on the road.
- **Share belongings and expertise:** Share your belongings with others (c.g., lawn mower, snow blower, or jumper cables). Offer to help them if they don't know how to operate the equipment or to go about accomplishing a task.

Exemplars (TED Talks)

Visit https://www.ted.com/talks and search for the following talks to hear from individuals who represent the strength of kindness:

- **Karen Armstrong:** Charter of Compassion
- **Matthieu Ricard:** How to let altruism be your guide
- **Robert Thurman:** Expanding our circle of compassion
- **Hannah Brencher:** Love letters to strangers
- **Abigail Marsh:** Why some people are more altruistic than others

Books

- Keltner, D., & Marsh, J., & Smith, J. A. (Eds.). (2010). *The Compassionate Instinct: The Science of Human Goodness.* New York: W. W. Norton.
- Rifkin, J. (2009). *The Empathic Civilization: The Race to Global Consciousness in a World in Crisis.* New York: Penguin.
- Ferrucci, P. (2007). *The Power of Kindness: The Unexpected Benefits of Leading a Compassionate Life.* Paperback edition. New York: Penguin.

- A list of 35 little acts of kindness you can do:
  http://www.oprah.com/spirit/35-Little-Acts-of-Kindness
- The Random Acts of Kindness, an internationally recognized non-profit organization that provides resources and tools that encourage acts of kindness:
  https://www.randomactsofkindness.org
- The Roots of Empathy and Compassion; Paul Ekman describes some of the necessary components of empathy and compassion:
  https://youtu.be/3AgvKJK-nrk
- Evidence-based article showing the benefits of a compassionate mind
  http://www.psychologicalscience.org/index.php/publications/observer/2013/may-june-13/the-compassionate-mind.html
- How to Increase Your Compassion Bandwidth:
  Bandwidthhttp://greatergood.berkeley.edu/article/item/how_to_increase_your_compassion_bandwidth

12. SOCIAL INTELLIGENCE

Description

People with social intelligence (which also includes emotional and personal intelligence) are aware of their own emotions and intentions as well as those of others. If this is one of your top strengths, you are most likely well aware of your own emotions, motives, and reactions (personal intelligence), as well as keenly aware of others (social intelligence). You have an uncanny ability to notice a shift in emotions in others and are able to make necessary adjustments to ensure a cordial milieu is maintained. While working with others, you make sure everyone feels comfortable, included, and valued, especially in endeavors that include a group. From a therapeutic standpoint, social intelligence offers you access to your own feelings as well as to feelings of others. This access can work in fostering, maintaining, and deepening healthy relationships.

The Golden Mean

A balanced use of social intelligence enables you to notice nuanced differences among other people, especially when their mood or motivation changes. This strength lets you respond in ways that are appropriate to the situation. You connect with others almost effortlessly. You react appropriately, and when needed, you express sympathy, empathy, or simply are able to put yourself in another's shoes. (For example, if something triggers sadness in your friend, your social intelligence will notice it, and you will be able to say or do something that doesn't make your friend feel isolated.) You have the ability to know the whole person. Much like love and kindness, social intelligence is one of the key strengths for a healthy life.

Deficit and excess of this strength are associated with psychological problems. A lack of social intelligence doesn't allow you to connect with others on a deeper level. Therefore, you are unable to forge connections that can be therapeutic and supportive, especially when you are stressed, sad, and/or anxious—states that are, by default, isolating and do not easily enable you to open up to others. You may also feel that sharing your psychological distress with others is embarrassing because they may not understand it and you may be burdening them unnecessarily. However, if you have deep and secure relationships due to your social intelligence, it is relatively easy for you to open up to others and seek support. In this way, your social intelligence offers you buffers, especially during difficult times.

There are also severe deficits of social intelligence. These manifest through conditions like autism, Asperger's syndrome, and schizoid personality disorder. These conditions, which have strong biological roots and need specialized, sustained treatment, do benefit from buildable aspects of social intelligence.

An excess of social intelligence can also be problematic. For example, knowing and understanding others, amidst complex social contexts, is time consuming and requires considerable emotional investment. If you invest these resources excessively, you may not have time for yourself. Second, you may garner a flattering reputation of being available for everyone but may very likely set up unrealistic expectations in others who would like to confide in you. You may become the "one pseudo-therapist" for many, and this could, and most likely would, exhaust you emotionally. Your social intelligence may become over-taxed; you might start showing signs of irritability and being less emphatic—having heard the same story from many—and ultimately you may start feeling inadequate. Therefore, a balanced use of social intelligence entails that you are mindful of your own well-being.

- *Overuse of strength:* psycho-babbling, self-deception
- *Underuse of strength:* obtuseness, cluelessness

Integration

To accomplish a balanced use of social intelligence, you will need to use it along with other strengths, such as perspective, which is critical. In deploying social and personal intelligence in any endeavor, always keep the big picture (the meaning and purpose) front and center. Social intelligence works well when you also use your judgment and open-mindedness to examine the situation from all possible angles to catch any potential biases. Vitality and zest can accentuate social intelligence, especially when an event or situation needs motivation and hope. Social intelligence can also resolve many tense situations if you are able to spot a lighter, playful, and humorous aspect of the situation to break the impasse or relieve the tension.

Movies

- *Monsieur Lazhar (2011)*—Bahir Lazhar, an Algerian immigrant and replacement teacher, uses his social intelligence to connect with students in a class that just lost their teacher in a traumatic way.
- *Children of a Lesser God (1986)*—This film beautifully depicts social and personal intelligence as the relationship between a speech therapist and a woman with hearing challenges evolves in understanding one another's emotions, intentions, and actions.
- *K-Pax (2001)*—A mysterious patient in a mental hospital claims to be an alien from a distant planet, demonstrating a remarkable display of social intelligence in relating to the other patients.
- *I am Sam (2002)*—Sam, a man with significant psychological challenges, fights for custody of his young daughter, arguing successfully that it is not brains but love and relationships that count the most.

Therapeutic Actions

- **Tackle uncomfortable situations with emotional intelligence:** Consider tackling a social situation that typically produces feelings of anxiety and depression for you.

(Examples may include sharing your thoughts in a work meeting on issues you disagree with, discussing an unresolved issue that continues to bother you with family members, and communicating feedback to a friend about something you disagree with and feel strongly about.) Use your social and personal intelligence and take turns to clarify points not previously clarified. Share your motivation and underlying values, and ask others to do the same. At the very least, this process will help you and others to ascertain values.

- **Listen without interruption:** Listen to your loved ones, especially to those with whom you interact frequently and frankly. Let them know you would like to listen from start to finish, without interrupting or preparing a rebuttal. Make mental notes of points to clarify, and address those when the person is done speaking. Then share your thoughts, and also elicit feedback from the sharer.
- **Unpack offenses**: If someone offends you, attempt to find at least one positive element in his motives. Using notions associated with social intelligence, consider reasons why the offensive behavior may have resulted from temporary, situational factors, rather than from the person's disposition or nature.
- **Elicit feedback:** Ask someone close to you about times when you did not emotionally understand her and also about how she would like to be emotionally understood in the future. Think of a few small, practical steps that you can take when next interacting with this person.
- **Be plain and direct:** In your close relationships, speak plainly and directly about your needs and wishes. Allow others to do the same without judging them or responding with rebuttals.

Exemplars (TED Talks)

Visit https://www.ted.com/talks and search for the following talks to hear from individuals who represent the strength of social intelligence:

- **Daniel Goleman:** Why aren't we more compassionate?
- **Joan Halifax:** Compassion and the true meaning of empathy
- **David Brooks:** The social animal

Books

- Cassady, J. C., & Eissa, M. A. (Eds.) (2008). *Emotional Intelligence: Perspectives on Educational and Positive Psychology.* New York: P. Lang.
- Goleman, D. (2006). *Social Intelligence: The New Science of Human Relationships.* New York: Bantam Books.
- Livermore, D. A. (2009). *Cultural Intelligence: Improving Your CQ to Engage Our Multicultural World.* Grand Rapids, MI: Baker Academic.

Websites

- Yale's Center for Emotional Intelligence: http://ei.yale.edu
- Emotional Intelligence Consortium: http://www.eiconsortium.org
- Marc Brackett—Yale Center for Emotional Intelligence: https://youtu.be/62F9z1OgpRk

CORE VIRTUE: JUSTICE

Interpersonal strengths that involve tending and befriending others

13. CITIZENSHIP & TEAMWORK

Description

The character strength of citizenship, also called teamwork, involves working as a member of a group for the common good. If this is one of your top strengths, you are most likely willing to make sacrifices for the common good of the groups you are involved with, such as your neighborhood, religious community, cohort at school, professional networks, and cultural circles. You feel affinity and closely identify with your neighborhood, city, province or state, and your country, in an adaptive manner, without being xenophobic. These groups and units form sources of identity for you. If citizenship and teamwork are among your top strengths, you manifest them by fulfilling and/or going over and above your civic responsibilities.

People who participate in activities that build citizenship and teamwork generally have good mental health because these activities connect them with like-minded people, which in turn builds their social trust. Having social trust provides assurance that the world around you is not an unsafe place. Furthermore, participating in community-building activities enhances self-efficacy.

The Golden Mean

A balanced use of citizenship and teamwork entails that you connect with your group or team and find ways of utilizing your strengths, expertise, knowledge, and resources for the welfare of the group. However, citizenship does not mean that you blindly follow the rules and regulations of those in power. A balanced and well-adjusted use of citizenship means that almost every member of the team feels included and is intrinsically motivated to work for the success of the group. Citizenship and teamwork function optimally when team goals take precedence, despite inevitable individual differences. Indeed, each team member maintains his or her own identity, but the collective identity creates group cohesion and solidarity. You may have heard expressions such as, "band of brothers" and "sisterhood," which symbolically represent family.

A balanced use of citizenship also entails that you do not become a spectator. If a few individuals assume a greater role that could diminish your participation, you need to use strengths such as courage and fairness to ensure that the group's harmony is not compromised. A lack of teamwork and citizenship may leave you isolated and deprived of social and community support that can make a significant difference, especially when you experience psychological distress.

- *Overuse of strength:* mindless and automatic obedience
- *Underuse of strength:* selfishness, narcissism

Integration

To optimally use citizenship and teamwork, you will need numerous other strengths, such as knowing yourself and others (emotional and social intelligence). When working with a group of diverse individuals (e.g., in terms of ethnicity, educational background, dispositions, or preferences), you will benefit from open-mindedness, fairness, and being aware and respectful of differences.

Almost every team or group experiences tensions and conflicts. Therefore, you can spark the creativity of group members to brainstorm solutions for the common good and optimal team performance. Well-intentioned humor and playful relieve group tensions, and the task becomes easier if group members share a common purpose (perspective) to increase solidarity. Furthermore, teamwork greatly benefits when the strengths of group members are spotted, acknowledged, and supported.

Movies

- *Field of Dreams (1989)*—An excellent depiction of citizenship and teamwork, this film shows the collaborative efforts of an Iowa farmer who interprets a mysterious message, *if you build it, they will come.*
- *Invictus (2009)*—This is the inspiring true story of a rugby team that wins the World Cup on the field and also unites post-apartheid South Africa off the field.
- *Hotel Rwanda (2004)*—An extraordinary display of social responsibility by Paul Rusesabagina, a hotel manager who, during the Rwanda Genocide, housed over a thousand Tutsi refugees, shielding them from the Hutu militia.
- *Blind Side (2009)*—A homeless and traumatized boy becomes an All American football player and first round NFL draft pick with the help of a caring woman and her family.

Therapeutic Actions

- **Avoid civic alienation:** Many of us disengage from civic participation, assuming that whatever we do, nothing will change. This is a hopeless and pessimistic view—two hallmarks of depression. Get involved in community work and bring your friends along. Indeed, your work will benefit the organization, and, more so, civic engagement will connect you with a noble cause and company, both of which are potent predictors of mental well-being.
- **Build an online community:** Build a web-based community whose members share a noble purpose, such as saving a specific endangered species; raising funds for refugees; or taking civic action against discrimination such as Islamophobia, homophobia, or xenophobia. Share this online hub to build a community.
- **Become involved with a community garden:** Start or join a community garden, which can offer you a supportive, safe, and calming environment. You can interact with others who may (or may not) be struggling with mental health issues. Sharing the space and task (gardening) helps you become part of a community.
- **Join a community mental health support group:** Start or join a community-based mental health organization. Using multimedia resources, you can present illustrations of how others have successfully dealt with mental health challenges. Explore the most effective treatments for specific mental health issues.
- **Decorate a communal place with the art of "lived experiences":** In an available community space, invite individuals with mental health challenges to present their "lived experiences." These would be people who are willing to share their experiences through any number of artistic forms. Individuals can submit their art expression online as well.

Exemplars (TED Talks)

Visit https://www.ted.com/talks and search for the following talks to hear from individuals who represent the strength of citizenship & teamwork:

- **Jeremy Rifkin:** The empathic civilization
- **Douglas Beal:** An alternative to GDP that encompasses our wellbeing
- **Hugh Evans:** What does it mean to be a citizen of the world?
- **Bill Strickland:** Rebuilding a neighborhood with beauty, dignity, hope

Books

- Putnum, R. (2001). *Bowling Alone: The Collapse and Revival of American Community.* New York: Simon & Schuster.

- Kielburger, C., & Keilburger, M. (2008). *Me to We: Finding Meaning in a Material World.* New York: Simon & Schuster.
- Ricard, M. (2015). *Altruism: The Power of Compassion to Change Yourself and the World.* New York: Little Brown.

Websites

- Me to We, a non-profit organization that advocates connecting with others, building trust, and getting involved in community building initiatives:
  http://www.metowe.com
- Harvard sociologist, Robert Putnum's websites on the decline and rise of community, with resources:
  http://bowlingalone.com
  robertdputnam.com/better-together/

14. FAIRNESS

Description

Fairness involves treating everyone according to universal ideals of equality and justice. If fairness is one of your top strengths, you generally do not let your personal feelings bias your moral or ethical decisions about others, and instead you rely on a broad set of moral values. Your sense of fairness incorporates both a respect for moral guidelines and a compassionate approach to caring for others. This is a strength you can apply across all aspects of your life—personal, professional, leisure, and community—in everyday interactions with social justice issues.

The Golden Mean

A balanced application of fairness entails that you generally abide by the principle of taking the welfare of others into consideration, even if you do not know them. The challenge you may face is the definition of "welfare." You may struggle to decide what is fair and what is right, as the cultural context may pose conflicts between the two and how they represent underlying core values. For example, female attire (a behavioral expression) and modesty (an underlying value) vary vastly from culture to culture and even within the same culture. A woman wearing a bikini in a conservative Muslim country could be considered a sign of immodesty, while such swimwear is perfectly acceptable in a Western country. Likewise, wearing a hijab for Muslim women is expected and admired in Muslim countries, while this veil or headscarf could be perceived by some as a forced choice or a religious or cultural obligation in some Western countries. Therefore, to strike a balance of fairness among competing rights, rituals, and values, interpret fairness in light of each context. Before applying fairness, ask about and understand the sociocultural cues. Seek wise council to interpret them. Fairness, perhaps more than any other strength, is not black and white, and you should therefore be prepared to navigate the grey areas.

Before applying fairness, always explore what the ultimate aim is. For example, look at equity and equality. In the context of fairness, equity is treating everyone in a way in which they are successful or not harmed, while equality is treating everyone the same, even though not everyone needs the same sort or levels of support. Along the same lines, if you treat everyone equally, know that unless you construct a Utopian society, not everyone will be treated fairly. Therefore, rather than applying fairness in absolute terms, use it contextually.

- *Overuse of strength:* impartiality without perspective or empathy, detachment
- *Underuse of strength:* prejudice, partisanship

Integration

For a balanced use of fairness, you will need a number of strengths such as leadership, citizenship, and teamwork, which will enable you to apply fairness easily. Likewise, honesty and authenticity will reinforce a sense of fairness. Kindness should also be considered in applying fairness. (For example, if a teacher keeps punishing a student who exhibits hyperactive behavior due to an underlying attention deficit hyperactivity disorder, punishing this student will likely lose its impact and may leave him more irritable and resentful. But if the teacher uses kindness and offers appropriate modifications to the student, the odds are better that he will improve his behavior.)

Movies

- *The Emperor's Club (2002)*—William Hundert, a principled Classics professor, comes into conflict with a pupil at a prestigious academy, as his attempts to teach the young man to act fairly and morally have mixed results.
- *Philadelphia (1993)*—Andrew Beckett, fired from his law firm for being both gay and HIV-positive, hires homophobic lawyer Joe Miller to act on his behalf. During the legal proceedings, Miller comes to view Beckett as a person worthy of respect and fair treatment, rather than as a stereotype.
- *The Green Zone (2010)*—This is a chilling depiction of fairness and social justice. Roy Miller, a senior CIA officer, unearths evidence of weapons of mass destruction in the Iraq war and realizes that operatives on both sides of the conflict are attempting to spin the story in their favor.
- *Suffragettes (2015)*—This film is an excellent depiction of fairness. It tells a story of ordinary women during the first part of the 20th century who are loving wives, mothers, and daughters. Their main concern is gender inequality. They face sexual harassment in the workplace, domestic violence, and violation of their parental rights, and their salaries are much lower than those of their male colleagues.

Therapeutic Actions

- **Understand biases and preconceptions:** To promote fairness, become aware of the discrimination you witness or experience firsthand. This discrimination may manifest in many ways, including ageism, ableism, gender, sexual orientation, accent, language fluency, religion, and xenophobia. Use your strength of fairness to do something to stop these biases and preconceptions.
- **Increase fairness in everyday life:** Make a list of everyday tasks, interactions, and activities that can use a dose of fairness—things that will increase your stress if they don't become more equitable. (For example, speak with your partner about taking over some of the daily cooking and household tasks.) Find culturally and contextually appropriate ways to apply fairness with the goal of decreasing stress.
- **Identify social issues that bother you:** Make a list of societal issues that upset you the most, focusing on issues that could be resolved by fairness. (For example, does it bother you that females continue to earn significantly less than males for the same work? Does it bother you that indigenous peoples struggle with basic amenities? Or that, despite clear evidence, supermarkets continue to sell harmful, synthetic food products?)
- **Monitor your judgments:** Self-monitor to see whether your judgments are affected by your personal likes and dislikes or if they are based on principles of justice and fairness. Try to minimize the influence of your personal preferences when making future judgments.
- **Speak up for your group:** Be a voice for the rights of others in a manner that respects people from other groups.

Exemplars (TED Talks)

Visit https://www.ted.com/talks and search for the following talks to hear from individuals who represent the strength of fairness:

- **Daniel Reisel:** The neuroscience of restorative justice
- **Paul Zak:** Trust, morality—and oxytocin?
- **Jonathan Haidt:** The moral roots of liberals and conservatives
- **Bono:** My wish: Three actions for Africa

Books

- Sun, L. (2009). *The Fairness Instinct: The Robin Hood Mentality and Our Biological Nature.* New York: Prometheus Books.
- Harkins, D. (2013). *Beyond the Campus: Building a Sustainable University Community Partnership.* Charlotte, NC: Information Age.
- Last, J. (2014). *Seven Deadly Virtues: 18 Conservative Writers on Why the Virtuous Life Is Funny as Hell.* West Conshohocken, PA: Templeton Press.

Websites

- The difference between equality and equity:
  http://everydayfeminism.com/2014/09/equality-is-not-enough/
- With more than 100 national chapters worldwide, Transparency International works with partners in government, business, and civil society to put effective measures in place to tackle corruption:
  https://www.transparency.org
- Roméo Antonius Dallaire: commandeered the United Nations Assistance Mission for Rwanda in 1993. Since his retirement, he has become an outspoken advocate for human rights, genocide prevention, mental health, and war-affected children:
  http://www.romeodallaire.com

15. LEADERSHIP

Description

Leadership is the process of motivating, directing, and coordinating members of a group to achieve a common goal. If this is one of your top strengths, you assume a dominant role in social interaction; however, effective leadership also requires listening to the opinions and feelings of other group members as much as it involves active direction. As a leader, you are able to help your group achieve goals in a cohesive, efficient, and amiable manner.

The Golden Mean

We see a balanced use of leadership when a person is able to find common ground in a group, despite differences among its members. This common ground is communicated effectively and in different ways, so that group members stay motivated. Some leaders who are remarkable in instilling hope and reinvigorating the spirts of their followers may lack the skills needed to translate their vision into clear, concrete, and tangible tasks and outcomes. Therefore, a balanced use of leadership incorporates the will and motivation plus the concrete steps needed to be successful.

Also, a balanced use of leadership requires following as well as leading. That is, without humility and the ability to listen, a leader can easily evolve into an authoritarian figure. In addition, a balanced use of leadership requires that you be able to build genuine and trusting relationships with the people you lead. Through trust, you have the highest chance of bringing out the best in your group. Relationships based on fear or the abuse of power or authority will induce fear, and, instead of being their best, people in such a group are more likely operate out of fear and mistrust.

- *Overuse of strength:* despotism, bossiness
- *Underuse of strength:* compliance, acquiescence

Integration

Leadership can use any number of strengths to foster well-being and resilience. For example, social intelligence, teamwork, and kindness can build strong ties within your group, and humility and gratitude can make your leadership humane and accessible. Together these strengths can create synergy, which may enable you to stay attuned to your group.

Movies

- *Gandhi (1982)*—The life of Mohandas Gandhi offers the model of leadership based on the ethos of nonviolence, social justice, and humility, ideas that inspired the likes of Martin Luther King Jr.
- *Iron Lady (2011)*—This movie is based on the life of Margaret Thatcher, the British stateswoman and politician who became the first ever female (and longest-serving) prime minister of the United Kingdom in the 20th century.
- *Mandela: Long Walk to Freedom (2013)*—This film chronicles Nelson Mandela's epic leadership journey, starting from his early life, through his coming of age, education, and 27 years in prison, to become the president of post-apartheid South Africa.
- *Lincoln (2012)*—This movie about Abraham Lincoln recounts his extraordinary number of strengths, especially his leadership and courage to go against the current and emancipate slaves despite continuing unrest on the battlefield and strife within his own ranks.

Therapeutic Actions

- **Stand up for someone or champion a cause**: Stand up for someone who is being treated unfairly. Encourage other leaders to emphasize fairness in their group processes. Alternatively, you can champion a cause that you find meaningful. This could involve many issues, such as child labor, underemployment of marginalized groups, school bullying (including cyber-bullying), or the use of environmentally unhealthy chemicals.
- **Read a biography of a leader who struggled with mental health challenges:** Read a biography and/or watch a film about a famous leader who suffered from mental health challenges and who dealt with them through the strength of leadership (e.g., Queen Victoria, Abraham Lincoln, Winston Churchill). What insights can you draw from this leader that may boost your own strength of leadership?
- **Mentor a child:** Mentor a child in your neighborhood or in your circles who could benefit from your skills (e.g., academic, technical, athletic). Assess your mood before and after each mentoring session and also as you see the impact of your efforts.
- **Mediate between two feuding friends:** When two people are in an argument, become a mediator. Invite them to meet with you together, and, after setting some ground rules, which you can enforce, let them share their points of view. Emphasize problem-solving through discussion.
- **Lead a family activity:** Organize and lead a family event that includes both young and old relatives. Use your leadership skills to invite family members to participate in this

activity, especially those who may not be on speaking terms or may be holding grudges against one another. Also involve everyone in the conversation, rather than allowing age groups to self-segregate. Draw people's attention to cross-generational similarities.

Exemplars (TED Talks)

Visit https://www.ted.com/talks and search for the following talks to hear from individuals who represent the strength of leadership:

- **Roselinde Torres:** What it takes to be a great leader
- **Simon Sinek:** How great leaders inspire action
- **Simon Sinek:** Why good leaders make you feel safe

Books

- Avolio, B. & Luthans, F. (2006). *The High-Impact Leader.* New York: McGraw-Hill.
- Csikszentmihalyi, M. (2004). *Good Business: Leadership, Flow, and the Making of Meaning.* New York: Penguin.
- Rath, T. & Conchie, B. (2009). *Strengths-Based Leadership.* New York: Gallup Press.

Websites

- The top 10 qualities that make good leaders:
  http://www.forbes.com/sites/tanyaprive/2012/12/19/top-10-qualities-that-make-a-great-leader/
- 20 ways to become a leader right now:
  http://www.inc.com/john-brandon/20-ways-to-become-a-better-leader-right-now.html
- Uma Jogulu's work on leadership, and its cultural influences:
  http://www.buseco.monash.edu.my/about/school/academic/management/uma-jogulu-dr
- Kim Cameron's work revolves around organizational structures and positive leadership:
  http://michiganross.umich.edu/faculty-research/faculty/kim-cameron
- Gilad Chen studies team and leadership effectiveness, as well as work motivation:
  http://www.rhsmith.umd.edu/directory/gilad-chen
- Centre for Health Leadership and Research led by Dr. Ronald R. Lindstrom:
  http://sls.royalroads.ca/centre-health-leadership-and-research

CORE VIRTUE: TEMPERANCE

Strengths that protect against excess

16. FORGIVENESS & MERCY

Description

Forgiveness is a process of gradual change, not a one-time decision and event. In forgiveness, you are willing to forsake your right and desire to take revenge; in fact, you are willing to cease the cycle of revenge, and you will likely be able to find a healthier path toward self-growth. This strength involves forgiving those who have wronged or offended you. Through forgiveness you accept the shortcomings of others; give offenders a second chance; and deliberately put aside the temptation to hold a grudge, ill-feelings, and vindictiveness. Moreover, forgiveness enables you to process the self-destructive negativity that keeps your anger simmering and your other strengths at bay. In order to enact forgiveness, you need mercy. To motivate yourself to go through the process of forgiveness, you need to exercise mercy in terms of accepting the shortcomings of others and making cognitive and emotional space to offer a gift to the transgressor. Mercy is important in initiating the process of forgiveness and holding onto it.

The Golden Mean

To achieve a balanced use of forgiveness, it is also important to thoroughly understand what forgiveness is *not* and what constitutes mercy. In using the strength of forgiveness, you are not absolving, avoiding, overlooking, or ignoring the impact of the offence; nor are you minimizing the need for justice, swapping negative emotions with positive ones, resorting to fate, compromising, opting to resolve unilaterally, or hoping to attain the high moral ground. Forgiveness is not an outcome; rather, it is a process of prosocial change. This often gradual, complex, and difficult process is one in which the person offended willfully decides to stop the cycle of revenge and move beyond the offense, such that the offense—although not expunged from memory—no longer causes ongoing pain.

Attaining forgiveness is exceedingly difficult. However, it is worth pursuing a balanced notion of forgiveness because its lack (being "unforgiving") will likely make you hard-hearted and can leave you embittered by memories of the past. Forgiveness becomes easier when you are able tap into your mercy and kindness. Lack of forgiveness and mercy may impact your relationships as your trust may be tarnished forever. Furthermore, whenever the offence is triggered, this can drain you emotionally and can leave you once again dwelling for days on the negative memories. Too much forgiveness and mercy, on the other hand, can lead to you becoming a non-assertive and vulnerable "doormat." And if you are trying to forgive something that should not be forgiven—such as abuse, gross and repeated violation of other's rights, or offenses that hurt you but the actual victim may be someone else—sometimes the process of forgiveness is not effective.

You most likely need a number of strengths—whether or not these are among your top ones—to optimally use forgiveness. You need courage to overcome internal fear and let go of the anger and revenge. Judgment and open-mindedness can allow you to examine the situation thoroughly from all sides. Kindness can enable you to offer forgiveness, which is an altruistic gift.

- *Overuse of strength:* permissiveness
- *Underuse of strength:* mercilessness, vengefulness

Integration

A regular dose of gratitude—to fill your head and heart with authentic and realistic positive events in your life—can help counteract the bitter memories. Once you decide to forgive, you also need persistence and social support to hold on to forgiveness.

Movies

- *Incendies (2010, France/Canada)*—In a series of flashbacks, twins (a brother and sister) uncover the mystery of their mother's life, which unsettles them, but the strength of forgiveness helps them to reconcile with the past.
- *Pay it Forward (2000)*—Seventh-grader Trevor McKinney undertakes an intriguing assignment—to change the world for the better—which starts a chain of acts of kindness and forgiveness.
- *Dead Man Walking (1995)*—This film tells the tale of a convicted murderer on death row who befriends a nun, who helps him understand that forgiveness is possible even under the worst circumstances.
- *Terms of Endearment (1983)*—Amidst the ups and downs of life, a mother and daughter find ways to see past resentments and transgressions and find joy in their relationship.

Therapeutic Actions

- **Evaluate the effect on you of "unforgiveness":** Explore how not forgiving and resentment torture you emotionally. Do these produce disruptive emotions, such as anger, hatred, fear, worry, sadness, anxiety, or jealousy? Reflect on and write about how these disruptive emotions affect your behavior. Assess their collective impact, especially on your mental health.
- **Let go of negative emotions through forgiveness:** Review Session 6: Forgiveness, which stresses that the process of forgiveness allows you to replace negative emotions with positive ones. Using your strength of perspective, reflect on the benefits of "letting go" of negative emotions through forgiveness.
- **Search your motivation for forgiveness:** You need to feel willing to forgive internally. Mindfully attune yourself to the feelings of holding on to negative emotions related to the offense, and also to emotions that may come from enacting forgiveness.
- **Recall when you were forgiven:** Recall vividly and write about situations in which you offended someone and were forgiven. If the person who forgave you is a loved one, ask what helped him or her to apply forgiveness as a relationship corrective or as a restorative act. Reflect on what it would take for you to apply a similar corrective or restorative action.
- **Plan your response for the next time someone offends you:** Create a plan, and rehearse it if possible. Periodically affirm to yourself, "No matter how he or she offends me, I will respond as I have planned."
- **Move from brooding to empathy:** Are ruminating or brooding getting in the way of your path to forgive? When you brood, then anger, sadness, and ambivalence take over your thinking. Deliberately see if you can replace your thoughts of brooding to empathize with the offender. Try to understand from the offender's perspective why she or he offended you. Then assess whether your reaction is hurting you more than the offender, especially when you slip into brooding.

Exemplars (TED Talks)

Visit https://www.ted.com/talks and search for the following talks to hear from individuals who represent the strength of forgiveness and mercy:

- **Aicha el-Wafi and Phyllis Rodriguez:** The mothers who found forgiveness, friendship
- **Joshua Prager:** In search of the man who broke my neck
- **Shaka Senghor:** Why your worst deeds don't define you

Books

- Enright, R. D., & Fitzgibbons, R. (2001). *Forgiveness Is a Choice: A Step-by-Step Process for Resolving Anger and Restoring Hope.* Washington, DC: APA Books.
- Nussbaum, M. C. (2016). *Anger and Forgiveness: Resentment, Generosity, Justice.* New York: Oxford University Press.
- Tutu, D. (2015). *The Book of Forgiving: The Fourfold Path for Healing Ourselves and Our World.* New York: HarperOne.
- McCullough, M. (2008). *Beyond Revenge: The Evolution of the Forgiveness Instinct.* New York: Wiley.

Websites

- Psychologist Evertt Worthington, a leader in the forgiveness research: http://www.evworthington-forgiveness.com/

- Ten Extraordinary Examples of Forgiveness:
  http://listverse.com/2013/10/31/10-extraordinary-examples-of-forgiveness/
- Ten Inspiring Stories of Extreme Forgiveness:
  http://incharacter.org/archives/forgiveness/ten-great-moments-in-forgiveness-history/
- Great Moments in Forgiveness History:
  http://incharacter.org/archives/forgiveness/ten-great-moments-in-forgiveness-history/

17. HUMILITY & MODESTY

Description

Humility and modesty entail letting your accomplishments and your accolades speak for themselves. You are aware of them but don't feel the need to make others explicitly aware of them. You are also aware of your limitations. If this is one of your top strengths, you do not perceive yourself as being better than others, although your self-esteem is uncompromised. In contemporary culture, which is often blinded by the social media spotlight on one's accomplishments and happiness, you avoid seeking the spotlight. As a humble person, you are honest with yourself, with your fallibility, and with what you cannot do, and you are open to asking for help.

The Golden Mean

A balanced use of humility entails the attributes noted previously, but be aware that an overuse of humility and modesty (being too humble or overly modest) can be hard to spot. To distinguish a balanced versus overuse of humility and modesty, you need to assess the specific situation to determine if you are really fine with it, or if your mental health challenges are leading you to be too unassuming and quiet, while others take advantage of the situation. (For example, you may have been overlooked for a job promotion or leadership role—despite deserving it on the basis of merit—simply because your humility won't allow you to speak up for yourself, or because you have a modest opinion of yourself. It could also be that humility and modesty don't allow you to pursue higher positions that you deserve). To achieve a balance, you need to figure out if you are okay with the status quo, and if you are not, you need to tamp down your humility and assert your rights. If you are unsure about what to do, consult with someone wise and impartial.

On the other hand, if you lack humility and modesty (or if you have been told so), ask a trusted friend to give you honest feedback. Select someone who is not afraid of providing this feedback, and who you are not afraid of hearing it from. Think at length about what this friend has to say, and select a few areas to work on. (For example, resist the need to share your accomplishments with people who are not your closest friends, those to whom you feel the need to prove yourself.) You may also feel a heightened desire to be acknowledged, but this may not be entirely due to a lack of humility. Rather, you might have had experiences of being put down by others, especially older siblings or parents, or being repeatedly told that you, compared to other siblings, may not accomplish much. It is equally plausible that your expression of zest and playfulness may be perceived as a lack of humility and modesty. The golden mean of humility and modesty cannot be appraised and appreciated without understanding all the nuances of the context.

- *Overuse of strength:* self-deprecation
- *Underuse of strength:* foolish self-esteem, arrogance

Integration

Humility, by default, melds well with kindness, social intelligence, self-regulation, and prudence. However, it is important that similar strengths work synergistically to continue the status quo. (For example, if you are known at work to be a humble person, and if kindness, prudence, and humility and modesty are among your top strengths, the combination of these strengths could reinforce nonassertive, unassuming, and down-to-earth tendencies that may not serve you well. You might be better off using strengths such as zest and curiosity, so that you achieve an optimal balance.) As a humble and modest person, you are open to the views of others, so seek opinions about yourself from a trusted friend who will likely highlight your accomplishments. Accept compliments with grace and, of course, humility.

Movies

- *Forest Gump (1994)*—Despite a low IQ, Forest Gump accomplishes a lot: meeting presidents, winning an All American football player award, receiving the Congressional medal of honor, and being featured on magazine covers. Displaying humility, he experiences all of his accomplishments in stride.
- *Peaceful Warrior (2006)*—Dan, brimming with pride for being an elite gymnast, thinks that he has figured out life, until a surprising mentor, Socrates, teaches him humility and wisdom.
- *The Passion of the Christ (2004)*—This film shows the final hours of Jesus Christ and numerous, moving examples of humility.

Therapeutic Actions

- **Cultivate humility through other strengths:** You can deploy your other strengths to cultivate humility. For example, be sensitive (social and emotional intelligence) as to how your inadvertent "showing off" can make others feel. After sharing news of an accomplishment with your family members or close friends, ask a confidant how the news was received. Did it feel like bragging or showing off? Did it draw an inadvertent comparison with someone present, making him or her feel uncomfortable?
- **Listen more, speak less:** If you are aware (or have been told) that you speak more than others in a group situation, concentrate on listening to the words of other people rather than simply waiting for your turn to talk.
- **Acknowledge your mistakes:** Acknowledge your mistakes, especially those that have created a rift between you and your loved ones. Apologize even to those who are younger than you. Be aware of your place as a role model to the next generation.
- **Let others discover your skills, talents, and accomplishments:** Resist showing off your accomplishments, talents, and skills. Allow others to notice them on their own.
- **Compliment sincerely:** Compliment sincerely if you find someone is authentic and better than you in some ways. Accept compliments from others humbly.

Exemplars (TED Talks)

Visit https://www.ted.com/talks and search for the following talks to hear from individuals who represent the strength of humility and modesty:

- **Feisal Abdul Rauf:** Lose your ego, find your compassion
- **Robert Wright:** Progress is not a zero-sum game
- **Graham Hill:** Less stuff, more happiness
- **Sam Richards:** A radical experiment in empathy

Books

- Hess, E. D., & Ludwig, K. (2017). *Humility Is the New Smart: Rethinking Human Excellence in the Smart Machine Age.* Oakland, CA: Berrett-Koehler.
- Nielsen, R., Marrone, J. A., & Ferraro, H. S. (2014). *Leading with Humility.* New York: Routledge.
- Worthington, E. L. (2007). *Humility: The Quiet Virtue.* West Conshohocken, PA: Templeton Press.

Websites

- How to develop and maintain humility:
  https://www.bigquestionsonline.com/content/how-do-we-develop-and-maintain-humility
- Best Leaders are Humble Leaders: *Harvard Business Review*:
  https://hbr.org/2014/05/the-best-leaders-are-humble-leaders
- How we develop and maintain humility:
  https://www.bigquestionsonline.com/content/how-do-we-develop-and-maintain-humility

18. PRUDENCE

Description

Prudence is a practical orientation toward future goals. If it is your top strength, you are generally quite careful about your choices. You don't take undue risks, and you keep long-term goals in mind when making short-term decisions. Therefore, you are a good planner and also anticipate unexpected outcomes. You generally arrive early or on time. When you are late due to circumstances beyond your control, you find ways to inform those waiting. You drive carefully and follow traffic rules and regulations. When you make a decision or plan, you remove unnecessary distractions. You take your time to clear your mind and gather your thoughts. You monitor and control impulsive behavior and anticipate the consequences of your actions. You refrain from making snap judgments, and you do not yield easily or spontaneously to proposals and ideas.

The Golden Mean

A balanced use of prudence requires making decisions and approaching important tasks with caution and deliberation. However, an overuse of this strength can manifest itself in the form of preoccupation with details and analysis, which may appear like an obsession. Indeed, there are tasks that require meticulous detail—such as performing brain surgery, entering your credit card number on your phone's key pad, and doing a spell check before submitting an editorial to the newspaper. But there are tasks that do not require such meticulous detail—such as perfectly loading the dishwasher, spending more time arranging everything on your desk and far less time on actual the work to be done, and focusing more on the formatting than on the content of a critical report. Utilizing prudence in such situations would be an overuse of the strength. A balanced use of prudence can help you plan well, arrive early or on time, motivate you to follow rules and regulations, and buffer against feeling overwhelmed when unexpected situations surface.

This strength is not synonymous with stinginess or timidity and instead involves an intelligent and efficient perspective toward achieving major goals in life. However, an excessive use of prudence may lead to ambivalence and indecisiveness. You may experience "decision paralysis." On the other hand, a lack of prudence can lead to rushed decisions, overlooking risks, or being lax about rules and regulations. There are always exceptional situations due to extenuating circumstances, but a lack of prudence may not let you adequately assess the situation, and you may make a decision sooner than you should. (For example, if someone asks that you extend the deadline for a grant or job application, a lack of prudence will manifest in you making a decision without fully exploring the ground on which such an exception should be granted, because it may not be fair to those who submitted their applications on time.)

- *Overuse of strength:* prudishness, stuffiness
- *Underuse of strength:* recklessness, sensation-seeking

Integration

You can use any number of strengths to achieve a balanced use of prudence. Social intelligence can help you determine the motives of others. Curiosity can help you explore more to make a prudent decision. Persistence and self-regulation can help you follow through on your prudent decision. Open-mindedness and kindness can help you do a thorough cost-and-benefit analysis and also explore the human dimensions of your decisions.

Movies

- *Shawshank Redemption (1995)*—Andy Dufresne, wrongly convicted of a double murder and serving his sentence at the Shawshank State Prison in Maine, uses his strengths of prudence, social intelligence, and resilience to improve the conditions of the prison, which enhances the dignity of the prisoners.
- *Driving Miss Daisy (1989)*—Daisy Werthan, a wealthy 72-year-old Jewish widow, slowly builds trust and friendship with her African-American chauffer, Hoke Colburn. Their friendship develops through the mutual strength of prudence.
- *The Queen (2006)*—Helen Mirren portrays Queen Elizabeth II and brilliantly captures her strengths, especially her prudence, sense of duty, and stoicism.

Therapeutic Actions

- **Make important decisions when you are relaxed:** Making big decisions when relaxed enables you to consider all the possibilities, rather than making a snap decision that could backfire later on. If you must make a decision under pressure (such as when you are anxious or depressed), take a few seconds to breathe deeply and clear your mind.
- **Remove distractions:** Remove all extraneous distractions before you make your next three important decisions. Take the time to clear your mind and gather your thoughts.
- **Anticipate long-term consequences:** Visualize the consequences of your decisions in 1, 5, and 10 years' time. Take these long-term consequences into account when making short-term choices.
- **Reflect before speaking:** Think twice before saying anything. Do this exercise at least 10 times a week and note its effects.
- **Drive cautiously or follow traffic rules:** Drive cautiously and note that there are fewer time-bound emergencies than you think. Make highway safety a priority, especially during busy times such as rush hour and holiday weekends.

Exemplars (TED Talks)

Visit https://www.ted.com/talks and search for the following talks to hear from individuals who represent the strength of prudence:

- **Naomi Klein:** Addicted to risk
- **Paolo Cardini:** Forget multitasking, try monotasking
- **Gary Lauder's** new traffic sign: Take Turns

Books

- Hariman, R. (2003). *Prudence: Classical Virtue, Postmodern Practice.* University Park: Pennsylvania State University Press.
- McKeown, G. (2014). *Essentialism: The Disciplined Pursuit of Less.* New York: Crown.
- Gracian, J., & Robbins, J. (2011). *The Pocket Oracle and Art of Prudence.* London: Penguin

Websites

- Virtue First Foundation:
  http://virtuefirst.org/virtues/prudence/
- In Praise of Prudence, by Kathryn Britton:
  http://positivepsychologynews.com/news/kathryn-britton/2013031225590

19. SELF-REGULATION

Description

Self-regulation is one's ability to exert control over oneself in order to achieve goals or meet standards. If this is one of your top strengths, you are most likely able to control instinctive responses such as aggression and impulsivity, and instead, you respond according to well-thought-out standards of behavior. In the context of psychological distress, self-regulation allows you to regulate your feelings, thoughts, and actions. When you become overwhelmed, this strength helps you redirect your emotions in a healthy manner. Even when others react strongly, you keep your poise and composure. You do not become incited easily, and you know how to keep your composure.

The Golden Mean

A balanced use of self-regulation depends on the context. You don't underestimate the impact of a serious situation and assume that it will somehow resolve, nor do you overestimate the situation and panic. A balanced use of self-regulation also requires that you are aware of what you are regulating. From a therapeutic perspective, take these three situations: (a) setting concrete goals for losing weight, (b) refraining from spiraling into negativity, and (c) avoiding getting into unhealthy relationships. To lose weight, you need a balanced application of self-regulation to eat healthy foods and to exercise. However, this does not imply becoming overly focused on food labels or, when visiting others, feeling disappointed when they have different eating habits. To counter the negativity spiral, rather than brooding over experiences and events beyond your control, you redirect your thoughts to events and experiences that are within your control, or to positive ones that can provide scaffolding to help prevent negativity. To establish healthy relationships, you look for character and value it, rather than being charmed by looks and other superficial features.

A balanced use of self-regulation also requires you to have a concrete goal, one that can ensure your self-regulation is adaptive, without harming you physically or cognitively. Losing weight in a healthy manner is one thing, but excessive exercising and an extremely controlled diet may make you ill. Excessive emotional control is associated with feelings of isolation. On the other hand, lack of self-regulation is associated with impulsive behavioral patterns, including smoking, drug abuse, and sexual promiscuity. Psychologically, a lack of self-regulation overwhelms us and we tend to make poor choices that often leave us with negative emotions, ruminations, and impulsivity (saying or doing things without thinking) that may offend others and harm our relationships.

- *Overuse of strength:* inhibition, reticence
- *Underuse of strength:* self-indulgence, impulsivity

Integration

A number of strengths work well with self-regulation to produce favorable behaviors and outcomes. Perhaps the most important is persistence, without which self-regulation is hardly possible. Likewise, prudence, fairness, authenticity, perspective, and courage can help you effectively self-regulate. Having the knowledge of a desirable behavior is not sufficient to make it happen; putting this knowledge into concrete action is important. To manage the hurdles in reaching your goal, you will need a healthy dose of optimism, creativity, and courage, along with self-regulation.

Movies

- *Twelve Years a Slave (2013)*—Solomon (Chiwetel Ejiofor), a free black man from upstate New York, is abducted and sold into slavery. He displays extraordinary strength of self-regulation and poise for 12 years, enduring abuse and cruelty, yet retaining his dignity.
- *Black Swan (2010)*—This psychological thriller shows the electrifying, and at times scary, journey of a young ballerina who displays an extreme sense of self-regulation and discipline to give a near-perfect performance.
- *The King's Speech (2010)*—England's Prince Albert ascends the throne as King George VI and has to overcome a severe speech impediment. The movie shows the king's strengths of courage and self-regulation in learning to speak with confidence.

Therapeutic Actions

- **Eliminate objects of temptation:** When dieting, don't keep junk food around; when you want to spend time with others, turn off the television; when abstaining from alcohol, don't socialize in bars or attend events with an open bar; when quitting smoking, replace cigarettes with chewing gum or another adaptive chewing item; or when cutting back on shopping, leave your credit cards or money at home. However, once a month, enjoy a yummy dessert, take a credit card with you, and so on. Otherwise, you may experience burnout. Ask others who you interact with to respect your removal of tempting items and to encourage your positive lifestyle changes.
- **List triggers:** Make a list of situations that trigger intense emotions in you, when you automatically "lose it." Write at least one strategy to neutralize these intense emotions. Keep these strategies accessible for use the next time you feel intense emotions.
- **Try to control your feelings:** The next time you get upset, try to control your emotions and focus on positive attributes of the situation. Become aware of the degree to which you can control your feelings and reactions.
- **Create routines:** Carefully create routines that you can systematically follow. These routines should be therapeutically helpful, such as going to bed at a regular time, exercising three times a week, and so on. Make minor adjustments as needed, but keep the core elements intact.
- **Engage in progressive relaxation when upset:** When you get upset, do a progressive relaxation. Allow your upset thoughts to be interrupted momentarily so that they don't get out of control.
- **Tolerate distress:** List things that regularly upset you. Set a goal to gradually tolerate the distress, and, if you can, completely eliminate it. If you get upset by a certain colleague's behavior, or when the subway is late and then very crowded, or when speaking in public, find ways to decrease this distress. Set specific, measurable goals to lower the distress. (Here are two examples: Avoiding a coworker you don't like could adversely impact your work. So rather than avoiding her, set a goal of not focusing on her personal attributes and instead work with her on a small project you can do together. Or instead of always being annoyed by your teenage son because of the food, music, and attire he currently favors, focus on what you love about him, rather than on the things you don't.)
- **Determine your optimal waking time:** Pay close attention to your biological clock, and do your most important tasks when you are the most alert.

Exemplars (TED Talks)

Visit https://www.ted.com/talks and search for the following talks to hear from individuals who represent the strength of self-regulation:

- **Judson Brewer:** A simple way to break a bad habit
- **Carol Dweck:** The power of believing that you can improve
- **Michael Merzenich:** Growing evidence of brain plasticity
- **Arianna Huffington:** How to succeed? Get more sleep

Books

- Berger, A. (2011). *Self-Regulation: Brain, Cognition, and Development.* Washington, DC: American Psychological Association.
- Shanker, S. (2012). *Calm, Alert and Learning: Classroom Strategies for Self-Regulation.* Toronto: Pearson.
- Vohs, K. D., & Baumeister, R. F. (Eds.). (2016). *Handbook of Self-Regulation: Research, Theory, and Applications* (3rd ed.). New York: Guilford Press.

Websites

- Canadian Self-Regulation Initiative: http://www.self-regulation.ca/about-us/canadian-self-regulation-initiative-csri/
- How to develop focus and feel better: https://www.psychologytoday.com/blog/anger-in-the-age-entitlement/201110/self-regulation
- Wilhelm Hofman studies self-regulation in different contexts as well as looking at why people act impulsively in certain contexts: http://hofmann.socialpsychology.org/publications
- The MEHRIT Centre presents books, videos, info sheets, and other resources highlighting Dr. Shanker's work in self-regulation: www.self-reg.ca/

CORE VIRTUE: TRANSCENDENCE

Strengths that forge connections to the larger universe and provide meaning

20. APPRECIATION OF BEAUTY & EXCELLENCE

Description

Individuals with an appreciation of beauty feel a sense of awe at the scenes and patterns around them. If appreciation of beauty and excellence is one of your top strengths, you take pleasure in observing natural and physical beauty, you admire the skills and talents of other people, and you appreciate the beauty inherent in virtue and morality. You can find beauty in almost every area of life, from nature to the arts to mathematics to science to everyday experience. Observing and admiring natural and physical beauty and experiencing elevated feelings produce positive emotions, which from a therapeutic standpoint, counteract negative emotions. When we observe someone performing an act of courage or self-sacrifice, when a person exhibits composure in a stressful situation or is kind and compassionate, not only do we admire these actions, but sometimes we feel inspired to do the same. Thus, witnessing excellence motivates us to do something similar. This is an organic way of being motivated for positive action—instead of being steeped in the negative feelings associated with a number of psychological disorders.

The Golden Mean

A balanced use of appreciation of beauty and moral excellence requires that we are sensitive and open to noticing, acknowledging, appreciating, and appraising positive experiences. This sensitivity can vary from person to person and can be culturally bound. (For example, you may experience awe while listening to Mozart's opera *Marriage of Figaro* or to Beethoven's *Ninth Symphony,* whereas someone else may experience awe when listing to classical Indian music or Georgian chants, or while watching dancers performing an Argentinian tango or Irish step dance.) Some life-altering events, such as birth and death, a miraculous and unexpected recovery, or a surprising and significant achievement, also have a cultural subtext. To fully appreciate the elevation and awe associated with such events, you need to understand that cultural context—both the macro level (the broader cultural norms, such as practices at Irish funerals) and the micro level (the funeral norms practiced by a specific Irish family). If you see someone moved at a social gathering and you are unable to comprehend it, politely asking the person to explain the importance will help you to understand the awe that is being experienced. Acts of moral courage that involve putting oneself in danger to save others, are more universally understood, even without knowing the language, and can be morally elevating. An artistic expression (e.g., music, dance, acting, painting) can also cultivate elevation as you witness a deeply moving performance. Such elevation can occur when you attend a concert or witness great art in a museum; it can also happen while watching or hearing something on popular media, through programs like *America's* or *Britain's Got Talent, Idol Competitions,* or *Dancing with the Stars*—all can leave us awe struck.

A balanced use of appreciation of beauty and excellence also entails that it is not exercised, expressed, or shared as snobbery, nor is it expressed with the intention of earning external recognition and rewards. A lack of appreciation of beauty and excellence may keep your daily life filled with boredom and lack of motivation, although such lack could be due to a number of factors, such as physical, cultural, or economic barriers.

- *Overuse of strength:* snobbishness, pretentiousness
- *Underuse of strength:* oblivion, unconsciousness

Integration

Appreciation of beauty integrates naturally with numerous strengths, such as creativity and gratitude. You are able to appreciate the creative nature of painting, sculpture, artistic performance, and so on. The very act of appreciation is a hallmark of gratitude. Appreciation almost always connects us with others—in person or virtually—thereby strengthening our social trust and sparking our inspiration, in particular, our moral elevation. This can occur when we see someone going out of her way to save a life, when a first-responder puts his life at risk to save others, or when we witness an exceptional artistic performance by someone unknown or not formally trained. This elevation infuses motivation, zest, and persistence in us to emulate what we have experienced at a deeper level.

Movies

- *Avatar (2009)* –The human/Na'vi hybrids, called Avatars, connect with human minds to explore the beauty of Pandora because the environment is otherwise toxic to humans.
- *Out of Africa (1985)*—Karen Blixen goes to Africa from Denmark in order to start a coffee plantation. Amidst a dysfunctional marriage, she begins to appreciate the beauty of her surroundings.
- *The Color of Paradise (1999, Iran)*—The film centers on a visually impaired boy who explores beauty in nature through his remaining senses, with a dramatic and emotionally powerful ending.

Therapeutic Actions

- **Explore the fullness of your emotions:** Become aware of your negative emotions—when they surface, how they persist, and how they impact your behavior. At the same time, notice at least one instance of natural beauty around you every day (such as the sunrise, sunset, clouds, sunshine, snowfall, rainbows, trees, moving leaves, chirping birds, flowers, fruits, and vegetables). At the end of the day, critically appraise both the negative and positive emotions, and write about ways to increase the positive ones, especially when you feel distress.
- **Start projects that buffer against negativity:** Think about and then select three projects to do that use creativity, persistence, and appreciation of beauty. Spend time on these projects instead of worrying, being anxious, or feeling stressed. Make sure each project really involves you, especially at times or in ways that buffer you from sliding into negativity.
- **Pay attention to expressions:** Notice how other people appreciate beauty and excellence through specific words, expressions, gestures, and actions. See if you notice these individuals admiring aspects of life that you aren't typically aware of. Incorporate that expression in your vocabulary.
- **Catalogue positive behaviors:** Note weekly how the goodness of other people affects your life. Appreciate the beauty of positive human behavior. Catalogue it, review it weekly, and draw motivation to do something similar.
- **Reflect and write:** Reflect on and write about three aspects of natural beauty, three instances of human creativity or artistic expression, and three experiences of seeing someone do something positive that you can identify with and see yourself doing.
- **Apply appreciation of beauty and gratitude to your close relationships:** Applying this appreciation will likely replace negative feelings. In particular, if you have a slightly biased view or hold a grudge against someone, focusing on positives and genuinely admiring that person will reduce negativity and replace it with trust and intimacy.

Exemplars (TED Talks)

Visit https://www.ted.com/talks and search for the following talks to hear from individuals who represent the strength of appreciation of beauty & excellence:

- **Louie Schwartzberg:** Nature. Beauty. Gratitude.
- **Bernie Krause:** The voice of the natural world
- **Mac Stone:** Stunning photos of the endangered Everglades

Books

- Cold, B. (2001). *Aesthetics, Well-Being, and Health: Essays within Architecture and Environmental Aesthetics.* Aldershot, UK: Ashgate.
- Murray, C. A. (2003). *Human Accomplishment: The Pursuit of Excellence in the Arts and Sciences, 800 B.C. to 1950.* New York: HarperCollins.
- Wariboko, N. (2009). *The Principle of Excellence: A Framework for Social Ethics.* Lanham, MD: Lexington Books.

Websites

- Fringe Benefits of Appreciation of Beauty and Excellence: http://positivepsychologynews.com/news/sherri-fisher/2014091529973
- How to appreciate beauty and enjoy its benefits: http://feelhappiness.com/how-to-appreciate-beauty/

21. GRATITUDE

Description

Gratitude is an awareness of and thankfulness for the good things in one's life. If gratitude is one of your top strengths, you take time to express thanks and contemplate all that you have been given in life. When you look back on your life, you don't become paralyzed or preoccupied by negative memories; rather, you are likely to re-evaluate and reappraise your negative memories and extract meaning from them. You never take things for granted, and you express your gratitude to a specific person, to divinity, or simply to nature. Therefore, you generally view the world as more positive than negative, and this trust helps you extend the gratitude to others. In fact, gratitude is often "other-oriented." That is, you express gratitude to someone, with someone, or for someone, and this process builds positive relationships. You are more likely to focus on positive aspects when relating with others.

The Golden Mean

A balanced use of gratitude requires that you neither feel entitled to receive a positive outcome nor that you take any positive event or outcome for granted. A balanced and adaptive use of gratitude is generally not compatible with negative emotion. That is, when you are genuinely grateful, you don't feel anger, bitterness, envy, greed, impoverished, or inferior/superior to others. An appropriate use of gratitude, in fact, thwarts such feelings. However, there are situations—such as becoming pregnant after trying for several years, only to learn that the child will likely have significant developmental delays; or the relief experienced at the end of an abusive relationship, the memories of which still bother you; or miraculously surviving an accident but losing mobility—that encapsulate multiple emotions, some positive, some negative.

Also, be mindful that if you effusively express gratitude for every little thing, the receiver of such gratitude may get used to this expression, may take it for granted, and may not acknowledge it appropriately. Others may feel uncomfortable with an elaborate and public expression of thanks. Therefore, it is important to understand the personal disposition and situational dynamics before expressing gratitude. On the other hand, not expressing gratitude when you should can give the impression that you have a sense of entitlement, or that you are too self-absorbed to take notice of positive things around you.

A sensible use of gratitude promotes a balanced self-image. You are happy with what you have and refrain from social comparisons. However, this doesn't imply that you don't strive and instead become complacent—but you don't strive in relation to others or feel resentful at their progress and want to catch up. You find your own inner measures of competence.

- *Overuse of strength:* ingratiation
- *Underuse of strength:* entitlement, privilege

Integration

Gratitude works well with a number of strengths, such as kindness, love, and social and emotional intelligence, to help you be perceptive and sensitive to other's needs and to express your care through actions. Gratitude also fosters savoring of positive experiences. You are able to exercise mindful attention to notice a positive event or experience and share it with others. Using your strength of appreciation of beauty and excellence, you also notice the positive events and attributes of others, and you genuinely share this feedback with them, thereby strengthening social ties. Like most positive emotions, gratitude opens your cognitive and attentional channels, allowing you to incorporate diverse and fresh perspectives in problem-solving and undertaking a creative endeavor. A balanced use of gratitude also inhibits social comparisons.

Gratitude helps us cope with stress and trauma. It fosters positive reinterpreting or reframing. After the initial shock, gratitude helps us evaluate what is most important in our lives. Expressing gratefulness during personal adversity, loss, or trauma might be hard and may seem irrelevant at the time. However, such expression may be the most important thing that you can do, as it may help you to adjust, cope, and grow. Another marker of the balanced application of gratitude is prosocial behavior; that is, gratitude promotes moral behavior. You become sensitive and caring about other's needs and share your resources with them.

Movies

- *The Fault in Our Stars (2014)*—Two teenagers with cancer fall in love, rather miraculously. This movie is a reminder to be grateful for the love and beauty around us, as we may not be around forever to enjoy it.
- *Amélie (2001, France)*—Amélie approaches life with an inquisitive nature and an appreciation for the little things. She befriends a shut-in neighbor, plays pranks, and returns lost items to their owners.
- *Sunshine (1999)*—This epic film follows the lives of three generations of Jewish men living in Hungary. The movie ends with the grandson's ultimate realization of his gratitude toward his family and his heritage, regardless of the pain of the past.

Therapeutic Actions

- **Cultivate gratitude:** Simultaneous expression of gratitude and negative emotions is incompatible. In other words, if you are feeling grateful, it is highly unlikely that you also feel angry, ambivalent, stressed, or sad. Using the strategies that follow (e.g., express thanks, unlearn self-pity), cultivate gratitude on daily basis. The more you experience positive emotions, the less you will feel negative emotions, or the time you are stuck in negative emotions will decrease.
- **Express thanks:** Express thanks to everyone who has contributed to your success, no matter how small such contribution might have been. Be aware of the degree to which your success is a product of others' helpful influence in addition to your own hard work. Express thanks without just saying "thanks"—be more descriptive and specific (e.g., *"I appreciate your prudent advice"*). Closely observe how other people express gratitude.
- **Unlearn self-pity:** Gratitude helps you appreciate what you have, what you have accomplished, and what resources and support you enjoy. This, in turn, makes you more confident and effective. This process can help you unlearn habits like self-pity and feeling victimized.
- **Deal with trauma:** Gratitude also helps you cope with stress and trauma. It enables you to positively reinterpret or reframe events from the past that still bother you.
- **Practice daily gratitude:** Set aside at least 10 minutes a day to savor a pleasant experience. Decide to withhold any conscious decisions during these ten minutes.

Exemplars (TED Talks)

Visit https://www.ted.com/talks and search for the following talks to hear from individuals who represent the strength of gratitude:

- **David Steindl-Rast:** Want to be happy? Be grateful
- **Laura Trice:** Remember to say thank you
- **Chip Conley:** Measuring what makes life worthwhile

Books

- Emmons, R.A. (2007). *THANKS! How the New Science of Gratitude Can Make You Happier.* Boston: Houghton-Mifflin.

- Sacks, O. (2015). *Gratitude* (1st ed.). Toronto: Alfred A. Knopf.
- Watkins, P. C. (2013). *Gratitude and the Good Life: Toward a Psychology of Appreciation.* Dordrecht: Springer.

Websites

- A practical guide to cultivating gratitude:
  http://www.unstuck.com/gratitude.html
- Robert Emmon's lab on Gratitude:
  http://emmons.faculty.ucdavis.edu
- Alex Wood studies the good in other people, as well as himself:
  http://www.alexwoodpsychology.com/
- Adam Grant studies the advantages of give and take in workplace interactions, and for success:
  https://adam-grant.socialpsychology.org/publications

22. HOPE & OPTIMISM

Description

Hope and optimism is the expectation that good things will happen in the future. Although "hope" and "optimism" are sometimes used interchangeably, research has shown subtle differences. From a therapeutic standpoint, depression can develop when an individual explains the causes of failure in pessimistic terms, whereas an optimist looks at failure differently. For example, a person with depression might think that a single failure (a) is likely to ruin her entire life, (b) impacts every area of her life, and (c) persists forever. An optimist, on the other hand, will understand that (a) a single failure doesn't mean that he will fail in every endeavor, (b) failure happens but it doesn't last forever, and (c) failure doesn't ruin everything in life. Likewise, if you are experiencing depressive symptoms, working on hope will help you boost your will and, at the same time, will provide you with specific strategies to harness your will or motivation into action. Hope and optimism can lead you to explore and expect the best from yourself.

The Golden Mean

A balanced use of hope and optimism requires that you don't set unrealistic expectations or goals, especially if you are psychologically distressed. Start with realistic and achievable goals, particularly ones for which you have support.

One of the guiding principles of PPT is fundamentally believing in your own strengths, and your act of seeking help (i.e., engaging in PPT) is an act of hope and optimism. You have the courage to acknowledge that you need help, and you have made a very good start. In many ways, PPT is an effort to set personalized goals. Using your strengths, both you and your clinician can set goals that are meaningful for you, and together you will monitor progress as therapy progresses. The more realistic the goals, the faster your recovery and journey toward well-being will be. Celebrate as you accomplish each goal or part thereof.

For a balanced use of hope and optimism, it is important that you establish goals early in therapy because the odds of change in your symptoms are much higher in the first five weeks or sessions. If you fail to establish goals, or are too spontaneous in goal selection, you may lose your motivation to change, and, over time, your symptoms may worsen. Writing about a positive future version of yourself (see Session Four: A Better Version of Me) will also likely help you set and revise realistic goals. Lastly, hope and optimism should also be viewed within the cultural context.

- *Overuse of strength:* Panglossian outlook
- *Underuse of strength:* pessimism, despair

Integration

A number of strengths can meld with hope and optimism to offer optimal therapeutic benefits. For example, turning hope and optimism into goals is important, and you need strengths like courage and persistence to accomplish these goals. Optimism, in particular, needs a good dose of courage and zest because sometimes we really want to do something but our inner critic and criticism from others derail our progress. We may not believe in our strengths and pay more attention to our deficits.

Movies

- *The Diving Bell and the Butterfly (2007)*—This is the remarkable tale of Jean-Dominique Bauby, a French editor, who suffered a stroke and became paralyzed; his only way of communicating with the outside world was by blinking one eye. His hope and optimism helped him learn to speak through his seemingly irrelevant gestures, and he began to produce words.
- *Cinderella Man (2005)*—During the depths of the Great Depression, legendary athlete Jim Braddock—a once-promising light heavyweight boxer—uses his hope and optimism to find his way back into the ring and pull off a surprising third-round win.
- *Gone with the Wind (1939)*—Scarlett O'Hara is living during the tumultuous years of the Civil War in a society torn by every sort of strife. In addition, she must contend with the trials of unrequited love and romantic frustration. In spite of all these obstacles, Scarlett maintains her sense of hope and continues to strive toward a better future for herself.
- *Good Will Hunting (1997)*—Will Hunting, a janitor at MIT, has a gift for mathematics. To deal with his difficult past and articulate his sense of hope and optimism, he needs the good counsel of a compassionate therapist who believes in him.

Therapeutic Actions

- **Apply optimism and hope:** List three things that deplete your hope and optimism. Using the ideas and strengths discussed earlier, apply hope and optimism to decrease your distress.
- **Cultivate optimistic company:** Surround yourself with optimistic and future-minded friends, particularly when you are facing a setback. Accept their encouragement and help, and let them know that you will be there for them when they face obstacles.
- **Succeed after struggle:** Recall a situation in which you—or someone close to you—successfully overcame a difficult obstacle. Remember this precedent if you are faced with a similar situation in the future.
- **Visualize your life:** Reflect on where and what you want to be in 1, 5, and 10 years. Sketch a pathway that you can follow to get there. Include manageable steps and ways to chart your progress.
- **Tackling adversity:** When facing adversity, focus on how you overcame a similar situation in the past. Let your successes set the precedent for your future endeavors.

Exemplars (TED Talks)

Visit https://www.ted.com/talks and search for the following talks to hear from individuals who represent the strength of hope & optimism:

- **Tali Sharot:** The optimism bias
- **Martin Seligman:** The new era of positive psychology
- **Douglas Beal:** An alternative to GDP that encompasses our well-being
- **Laura Carstensen:** Older people are happier
- **Carlos Morales** Finds Hope After Tragedy While Raising Quadruplets on His Own

Books

- Gillham, J. (2000). *The Science of Optimism and Hope*: West Conshohocken, PA, Templeton Press.
- Seligman, M. (2006). *Learned Optimism: How to Change Your Mind and Your Life.* New York: Vintage Books.
- Tali Sharot, T. (2011). *The Optimism Bias: A Tour of the Irrationally Positive Brain.* Toronto: Knopf.
- Snyder, C. R. (1994). *The Psychology of Hope: You Can Get There from Here.* New York: Free Press.
- Seligman, M. (2018). *The Hope Circuit: A Psychologist's Journey from Helplessness to Optimism.* New York: Hachette Book Group.

Websites

- Overview of hope research:
  http://www.thepositivepsychologypeople.com/hope-research/
- Shane J. Lopez, PhD:
  http://www.hopemonger.com/

23. HUMOR & PLAYFULNESS

Description

Humor involves an enjoyment of laughing, friendly teasing, and bringing happiness to others. As an integral part of social play, humor offers us a different perspective. If humor and playfulness is one of your top strengths, you know how to take the edge off a stressful situation while maintaining group cohesion. From a therapeutic standpoint, humor offers a viable way to release negative emotions. With this strength, you are able to see the lighter side of life for many situations, finding things to be cheerful about rather than letting adversity get you down. Humor means more than just telling jokes; rather, humor is a playful and imaginative approach to life.

The Golden Mean

Too much humor can make you look like a fool, whereas a severe lack of this strength can make you too serious and boring. A balanced use of humor and playfulness, although not easy, is very desirable. Without sacrificing empathy and cultural sensitivity, a well-delivered joke, quick retort, observation, or comment can offer a fresh and different perspective, and can expand your thinking and improve your sense of self. Context, however, is crucial in using humor and playfulness. For example, in situations that may benefit from a little burst of humor with a quick shift to serious deliberations, overusing humor can give the impression that you are not being serious, and hence are unreliable. On the other hand, a serious tone and stoic expression that cannot be penetrated by a quick joke or light-hearted comment can isolate you from others and keep them from freely sharing their thoughts and feelings with you.

- *Overuse of strength:* buffoon-like, clown-like
- *Underuse of strength:* cheerlessness, grimness

Integration

A number of strengths can help harness playfulness, such as social intelligence, zest, curiosity, teamwork, kindness, authenticity, and fairness. If a playful remark, joke, or anecdote is shared mindfully, it can amiably relieve a stressful situation without offending others and offer a new perspective. Note that a balanced and adaptive use of humor and playfulness requires that this joke or funny story be relevant, engaging, and culturally sensitive.

Movies

- *Patch Adams (1999)*—Patch Adams commits himself to a psychiatric ward and finds joy in helping his fellow patients. Disturbed by the staff's cold approach to the patients, he vows to change the system and enrolls in medical school. His unorthodox blend of medicine and humor brings him both praise and at times condemnation.
- *Life is Beautiful (1998, Italy)*—Guido, a charming Jewish man, never loses his cleverness, hope, or humor, especially in protecting his young son from the horrors of the Holocaust by pretending the whole affair is a game.
- *Amadeus (1984)*—This film depicts the humor and laughter of young Mozart, who in addition to his creativity and perseverance shows his lighter side when engaging in practical jokes.

Therapeutic Actions

- **Use cognitively distracting humor:** If you feel stressed, depressed, or angry, create a playlist of funny YouTube or other online videos. Make sure the content engages you so that you are disengaged from negative emotions. Keep the list updated.
- **Cheer up a gloomy friend:** Cheer up someone whose likes and dislikes you know well. This will also help you in dealing with your own distresses.
- **Befriend someone who is funny:** Become friends with someone who has a great sense of humor. Watch how he or she uses this strength to deal with difficult situations and bad news.
- **Look for the lighter side of a serious situation:** When something serious happens, try to find a fun and lighter side to the situation. Strike a balance between taking things seriously enough and not taking them too seriously.
- **Engage in outdoor fun:** Go out with your friends at least once a month to run, hike, cross-country ski, bike, and so on. Note how the group dynamic improves when you laugh together.

Exemplars (TED Talks)

Visit https://www.ted.com/talks and search for the following talks to hear from individuals who represent the strength of humor & playfulness:

- **Jane McGonigal:** The game that can give you 10 extra years of life
- **Liza Donnelly:** Drawing on humor for change
- **John Hunter:** Teaching with the World Peace Game
- **Cosmin Mihaiu:** Physical therapy is boring—play a game instead
- **Ze Frank:** Nerdcore comedy

Books

- Akhtar, M. C. (2011). *Play and Playfulness: Developmental, Cultural, and Clinical Aspects.* Lanham, MD: Jason Aronson.
- McGonigal, J. (2011). *Reality Is Broken: Why Games Make Us Better and How They Can Change the World.* New York: Penguin Press.
- Schaefer, C. E. (2003). *Play Therapy with Adults.* Hoboken, NJ: Wiley.
- Russ, S. W., & Niec, L. N. (2011). *Play in Clinical Practice: Evidence-Based Approaches.* New York: Guilford Press.

Websites

- Cognitive neuroscientist Scott Weems talks about his book *HA! The Science of When We Laugh and Why*:
http://www.scientificamerican.com/podcast/episode/humor-science-weems/
- Scientists discover the secret of humor:
http://www.telegraph.co.uk/news/science/science-news/7938976/Scientists-discover-the-secret-of-humour.html
- The Science of Humor: This website contains detailed information on humor research:
http://moreintelligentlife.com/story/the-science-of-humour;
- Signs you have a good sense of humor:
http://www.huffingtonpost.com/2014/08/29/good-sense-of-humor_n_5731418.html

24. SPIRITUALITY

Description

Spirituality is a universal part of human experience involving knowledge of one's place within the larger scheme of things. Spirituality can include—but is not limited to—religious belief and practice. With the help of this strength, you become aware of both the sacred and secular in everyday life. This is a strength that offers you a sense of comfort in the face of adversity and the experience of transcending the ordinary to reach something fundamental. You feel the comfort that there is someone or something greater than you, a force to rely on. Having a sense of spirituality offers you emotional support that you can handle adversity. To enhance your sense of spirituality, you take specific actions that generally follow established spiritual or religious norms. While following these actions, you feel that your life has meaning.

The Golden Mean

A balanced sense of spirituality indicates that your life is imbued with meaning and purpose, although the meaning and purpose do not have to be grand and earth-shattering. A balanced use of spirituality, meaning, and purpose can be accomplished through tangible prosocial activities, such as volunteering at a food bank, a center for children with disabilities, or a home for senior citizens. Becoming involved with a religious institution (such as a church, mosque, or temple), professional association, leisure or sports club, non-profit organization, environmental task force, or humanitarian group all offer opportunities to connect with something larger. Regardless of the particular way in which you establish a spiritual and meaningful life, ensure that the aim or meaning is always clear. There are multiple paths to spirituality. Each path could lead you to something greater than yourself—your purpose. Before embarking on any path, reflect on where and to what end this path will bring you. A total lack of spirituality, meaning, and purpose could leave you feeling empty, unfulfilled, and existentially anxious about the aimlessness of your life.

- *Overuse of strength:* fanaticism, radicalism
- *Underuse of strength:* anomie, isolation

Integration

A number of strengths integrate naturally with spirituality, including gratitude, self-regulation, persistence, authenticity, appreciation of beauty, and hope. In addition to specific strengths, a number of strengths-based actions can offer you soothing and satisfying experiences of spirituality. These include mentoring, going on a retreat with your partner or close friend, meditating or praying together or sharing the same space, and periodically reviewing your life to reflect on its meaning and how your actions and habits are congruent with this meaning.

Movies

- *Contact (1997)*—Dr. Eleanor Arroway, a scientist working on the search for extraterrestrial intelligence, discovers a signal from a faraway star. This discovery throws society into turmoil as the age-old conflict erupts between reason and belief.
- *Priest (1994, Britain)*—Fr. Greg Plinkington lives two lives, one as a conservative Catholic priest and the other as a gay man with a lover. When a girl in his confessional tells him about sexual abuse at the hands of her father, his frustration with the laws of the Catholic Church boils over, and he must reconcile his inner beliefs with the tenets of his doctrinal faith.
- *Eat Pray Love (2010)*—Despite having a home and successful career, Liz's divorce leaves her confused and at a crossroads. She ventures out on a quest of self-discovery and travels to different places in the world, where she steps out of her comfort zone to learn more about herself.

Therapeutic Actions

- **List experiences that make you feel detached and ones that forge connections:** Make a weekly or monthly list of experiences that leave you feeling fragmented, distracted, and detached. Next to each such experience, write about a potential experience that would forge strong connections in your life.
- **Fine-tune your quest**: If you find yourself steeped in negative feelings (such as sadness, stress, or anger), deliberately immerse yourself in nature, art, music, poetry, or literature that instills a sense of awe and wonder in you. Gradually fine-tune your awareness. These experiences can connect you with your spiritual quest.
- **Practice relaxation:** Spend 10 minutes daily breathing deeply, relaxing, and meditating (emptying the mind of thoughts by focusing on breathing). Observe how you feel afterward.
- **Explore different religions:** Take a class, do online research, meet someone from a different religion, or attend a congregation of a different religion. Speak to people who practice this faith, and get to know them as people.
- **Explore your purpose:** If you feel lost, ambivalent, or empty, explore a fundamental purpose of your life, and link your actions to this purpose. Each day, ask yourself if you accomplished anything toward fulfilling this purpose.
- **Write your own eulogy:** Write your eulogy or ask your loved ones how they would like to remember you. Do they mention your signature strengths?

Exemplars (TED Talks)

Visit https://www.ted.com/talks and search for the following talks to hear from individuals who represent the strength of spirituality:

- **Lesley Hazleton:** On reading the Koran
- **Dan Dennett:** Let's teach religion—all religion—in schools
- **Julia Sweeney:** Letting go of God
- **Kwame Anthony Appiah:** Is religion good or bad? (This is a trick question)

Books

- Aslan, R. (2017). *God: A Human History*. New York: Random House.
- Newberg, A., & Waldman, M. R. (2006). *Why We Believe What We Believe: Uncovering Our Biological Need for Meaning, Spirituality, and Truth*. New York: Free Press.
- Valliant, G. (2008). *Spiritual Evolution: How We Are Wired for Faith, Hope, and Love*. New York: Broadway.

Websites

- How to get in touch with your spiritual side:
  http://www.actionforhappiness.org/take-action/get-in-touch-with-your-spiritual-side
- Research on spirituality by Michael McCullough:
  http://www.psy.miami.edu/faculty/mmccullough/
- Research on spirituality by Kenneth I. Pargament:
  http://www.bgsu.edu/arts-and-sciences/center-for-family-demographic-research/about-cfdr/research-affiliates/kenneth-i-pargament.html

Table D2.
BALANCED USE OF CHARACTER STRENGTHS

Strength	Overuse (too much)	Underuse (lack of, or too little)	Golden mean	Integration (interaction with other strengths)
Wisdom & Knowledge				
Cognitive strengths that entail the acquisition and use of knowledge				
Creativity	Oddity, weirdness, eccentricity	Dullness, banality, conformity	Adaptive, positive, and innovative ways of doing things	Curiosity, open-mindedness, and zest
Curiosity	Prying, snooping, nosiness	Boredom, disinterest, apathy	Exploration and openness that is neither boring nor intrusive	Persistence, open-mindedness, and courage
Open-mindedness	Cynicism, skepticism	Dogmatism, "unreflectiveness," rigidity, overly simplistic	Unbiased critical inquiry toward adaptive change, if needed	Perspective, curiosity, and fairness
Love of learning	"Know-it-all"-ism	Complacency, smugness	Deepening knowledge to better understand self and society	Curiosity, open-mindedness, and persistence
Perspective	Elitism, arcane, pedantic	Superficiality	Synthesis of knowledge to understand context	Social intelligence, integrity, and courage
Courage				
Exercising the will to accomplish goals in the face of opposition, external or internal				
Bravery	Risk-taking, foolishness	Debilitating fear, cowardice	Facing and responding to threats and fear without jeopardizing safety and well-being	Self-regulation, integrity, and persistence
Persistence	Obsessiveness, fixation, pursuit of unattainable goals	Laziness, apathy	Finishing what is started and needs be finished	Courage, perspective, and zest
Integrity	Righteousness	Shallowness, phoniness	Being real and true, without external pressures or rewards	Fairness, courage, and perspective
Vitality & Zest	Hyperactivity	Passivity, inhibition	Enthusiasm that is not obsession or too much inhibition	Self-regulation, hope, and courage
Humanity				
Emotional strengths that show the exercise of will in the face of opposition or internal threat				
Love	Emotional promiscuity	Isolation, detachment	Genuinely loving and caring for others without making extreme sacrifices	Kindness, Social intelligence, and hope
Kindness	Intrusiveness	Indifference, cruelty, mean-spiritedness	Doing actions for others that are needed, are not asked for, and don't carry tangible rewards	Social intelligence, citizenship & teamwork, and perspective
Social Intelligence	Psycho-babbling, self-deception	Obtuseness, cluelessness	Nuanced understanding of emotions, motives, and corresponding changes.	Kindness, love, and self-regulation

Justice
Interpersonal strengths that involve tending and befriending others

Citizenship & Teamwork	Mindless and automatic obedience	Selfishness, narcissism	Being inclusive and harmonious for the common good	Social intelligence, leadership, and hope
Fairness	Impartiality without perspective or empathy, detachment	Prejudice, partisanship	Doing the right thing, without being influenced by personal and societal biases	Integrity, courage, and open-mindedness
Leadership	Despotism, bossiness	Compliance, acquiescence	Aspiring and bringing others toward a positive common goal	Zest, teamwork, and social intelligence

Temperance
Strengths that protect against excess

Forgiveness & Mercy	Permissiveness	Mercilessness, vengefulness	Willingly ceasing cycle of revenge	Kindness, social intelligence, and integrity
Humility & Modesty	Self-deprecation	Foolish self-esteem, arrogance	Without compromising self-care, not seeking spotlight despite deserving it	Gratitude, integrity, and spirituality
Prudence	Prudishness, stuffiness	Recklessness, sensation-seeking	Being cautious without being preoccupied or nonchalant about potential and realistic risks	Persistence, self-regulation, and curiosity
Self-Regulation	Inhibition, reticence	Self-indulgence, impulsivity	Regulating emotions and actions without feeling stifled or restrained	Perspective, persistence, and hope

Transcendence
Strengths that forge connections to the larger universe and provide meaning

Appreciation of Beauty & Excellence	Snobbishness, pretentiousness	Oblivion, unconsciousness	Intrinsically appreciating beauty and excellence without snobbery	Gratitude, zest, and creativity
Gratitude	Ingratiation	Entitlement, privilege	Deep and genuine sense of thankfulness without feeling obligated	Kindness, love, and social intelligence
Hope & Optimism	Panglossian outlook	Pessimism, despair	Being optimistic within realistic bounds	Open-mindedness, courage, and zest
Humor & Playfulness	Buffoon-like, clown-like	Cheerlessness, grimness	Expressing lighter and playful aspects of a situation with good intentions	Zest, social intelligence, and integrity
Spirituality	Fanaticism, radicalism	Anomie, isolation	Pursuing adaptive paths through meaningful actions	Gratitude, humility, and kindness

NOTES

CHAPTER 1

1. The **In Real Life** stories are based on feedback from actual clients and people who have taken PPT workshops. The specific details have been changed to protect privacy.

2. "Blue Sky" is the name of this client's *Gratitude Journal*. She has left dancing, and, with the support of her family, she is pursuing a degree after a year of inpatient rehab. She never forgets to write in her journal about what she is grateful for.

APPENDIX 1

1. If this practice is done in session, the clinician should gently bring the client out of the exercise with a soothing sound.

2. Or preferred side; from here on, please include the preferred side in your directions. For the sake of balance, we alternate between sides, from posture to posture.

APPENDIX 2

1. To make additional copies of this *Gratitude Journal*, go to the companion website www.oup. com/ppt. to print them out.

REFERENCES

Akhtar, M., & Boniwell, I. (2010). Applying positive psychology to alcohol-misusing adolescents: A group intervention. *Groupwork: An Interdisciplinary Journal for Working with Groups, 20*(3), 6–31.

Bellentine, R. M. (1977). *Joints and glands exercises: As taught by Sri Swami Rama of the Himalayas.* Honesdale, PA: Himalayan Institute Press.

Cautela, R. J., & Gorden, J. (1978). *Relaxation: A comprehensive manual for adults, children and children with special need.* Champaign, IL: Research Press.

Csillik, A., Aguerre, C., & Bay, M. (2012). Positive psychotherapy of depression: Specificities and clinical contributions. *Medico-Psychological Annals, Psychiatric Review, 170*(8), 541–546.

Emmons, R. (2007). *Thanks! How the new science of gratitude can make you happier.* New York: Houghton Mifflin.

Finlay, W. M. L., & Lyons, E. (2000). Social categorizations, social comparisons and stigma: Presentations of self in people with learning difficulties. *British Journal of Social Psychology, 39*, 129–146.

Folkman, S., & Moskowitz, J. T. (2000). Positive affect and the other side of coping. *American Psychologist, 55*(6), 647–654.

Forgeard, M. J. C., & Seligman, M. E. P. (2012). Seeing the glass half full: A review of the causes and consequences of optimism. *Pratiques Psychologiques, 18*(2), 107–120. https://doi.org/10.1016/j.prps.2012.02.002

Fowers, B. J. (2005). *Virtue and psychology: Pursuing excellent in ordinary practices.* Washington, DC: American Psychological Association.

Froh, J. J., Emmons, R. A., Card, N. A., Bono, G., & Wilson, J. A. (2011). Gratitude and the reduced costs of materialism in adolescents. *Journal of Happiness Studies, 12*(2), 289–302.

Gable, S. L, Reis, H. T., Impett, E. A., & Asher, E. R. (2004). What do you do when things go right? The intrapersonal and interpersonal benefits of sharing positive events. *Journal of Personality and Social Psychology, 87*, 228–245.

Gilman, R., Schumm, J. A., & Chard, K. M. (2012). Hope as a change mechanism in the treatment of posttraumatic stress disorder. *Psychological Trauma: Theory, Research, Practice, and Policy, 4*, 270–277. doi:10.1037/a0024252

Guney, S. (2011). The Positive Psychotherapy Inventory (PPTI): Reliability and validity study in Turkish population. *Social and Behavioral Sciences, 29*, 81–86.

Jayawickreme, E., & Blackie, L. E. (2014). Post-traumatic growth as positive personality change: Evidence, controversies and future directions. *European Journal of Personality, 28*(4), 312–331.

Kahneman, D. (2011). *Thinking fast and slow.* London: Allen Lane.

Kasser, T., & Kanner, A. D. (Eds.). (2004). *Psychology and consumer culture: The struggle for a good life in a materialistic world.* Washington, DC: American Psychological Association. http://dx.doi.org/10.1037/10658-000

Kelly, J. R. (1997). Changing issues in leisure-family research—Again. *Journal of Leisure Research, 29*(1), 132–134.

Khanjani, M., Shahidi, S., FathAbadi, J., Mazaheri, M. A., & Shokri, O. (2014). [The factor structure and psychometric properties of the Positive Psychotherapy Inventory (PPTI) in an Iranian sample]. *Iranian Journal of Applied Psychology, 7*(5), 26–47. (In Persian)

Langston C. A. (1994). Capitalizing on and coping with daily-life events: Expressive responses to positive events. *Journal of Personality and Social Psychology, 67*(6). 1112–1125. doi:10.1037/0022-3514.67.6.1112

Maisel, N. C., & Gable, S. L. (2009). The paradox of received support: The importance of responsiveness. *Psychological Science, 20*, 928–932.

Markus, H., & Nurius, P. (1986). Possible selves. *American Psychologist, 41*(9), 954–969.

Meyer, P. S., Johnson, D. P., Parks, A., Iwanski, C., & Penn, D. L. (2012). Positive living: A pilot study of group positive psychotherapy for people with schizophrenia. *The Journal of Positive Psychology, 7*, 239–248. doi:10.1080/17439760.2012.677467

Morganson, V. J., Litano, M. L., & O'Neill, S. K. (2014). Promoting work–family balance through positive psychology: A practical review of the literature. *The Psychologist-Manager Journal, 17*(4), 221–244. https://doi.org/10.1037/mgr0000023

Peterson, C., & Seligman, M. E. (2004). *Character strengths and virtues: A handbook and classification* (Vol. 1). New York: Oxford University Press.

Rashid, T., & Seligman, M. E. P. (2018). Positive psychotherapy. In D. Wedding & R. J. Corsini (Eds.), *Current psychotherapies* (pp. 481–526). Belmont, CA: Cengage.

Roepke, A. M. (2015). Psychosocial interventions and posttraumatic growth: A meta-analysis. *Journal of Consulting and Clinical Psychology, 83*(1), 129–142.

Salzberg, S. (1995). *Loving-kindness: The revolutionary art of happiness.* Boston: Shambhala.

Schrank, B., Brownell, T., Jakaite, Z., Larkin, C., Pesola, F., Riches, S., . . . Slade, M. (2015). Evaluation of a positive psychotherapy group intervention for people with psychosis: Pilot randomised controlled trial. *Epidemiology and Psychiatric Sciences, 25*(3), 235–246. doi:10.1017/S2045796015000141

Schrank, B., Riches, S., Coggins, T., Rashid, T., Tylee, A., & Slade, M. (2014). WELLFOCUS PPT–modified positive psychotherapy to improve well-being in psychosis: Study protocol for a pilot randomised controlled trial. *Trials, 15*(1), 203.

Schwartz, B. (2004). *The paradox of choice: Why more is less* (1st ed.). New York: ECCO.

Schwartz, B., Ward, A., Monterosso, J., Lyubomirsky, S., White, K., & Lehman, D. R. (2002). Maximizing versus satisficing: Happiness is a matter of choice. *Journal of Personality and Social Psychology, 83*(5), 1178–1197. doi:10.1037/0022-3514.83.5.1178

Seligman, M. (1991). *Learned optimism: How to change your mind and your life.* New York: Vintage Books.

Seligman, M. E. P. (2012). *Flourish: A visionary new understanding of happiness and well-being.* New York: Simon & Schuster.

Seligman, M. E., Rashid, T., & Parks, A. C. (2006). Positive psychotherapy. *American Psychologist, 61,* 774–788. doi:10.1037/0003-066X.61.8.774

Sovik, R. (2005). *Moving inward: The journey to meditation.* Honesdale: PA: Himalayan Institute Press.

Uliaszek, A. A., Rashid, T., Williams, G. E., & Gulamani, T. (2016). Group therapy for university students: A randomized control trial of dialectical behavior therapy and positive psychotherapy. *Behaviour Research and Therapy, 77,* 78–85. http://dx.doi.org/10.1016/j.brat.2015.12.003

Van Dillen, L. F., Koole, S. L., Van Dillen, L. F., & Koole, S. L. (2007). Clearing the mind: A working memory model of distraction from negative mood. *Emotion, 7*(4), 715–723.

Vázquez, C. (2015). Beyond resilience: Positive mental health and the nature of cognitive processes involved in positive appraisals. *The Behavioral and Brain Sciences, 38,* e125.

Wammerl, M., Jaunig, J., Maierunteregger, T., & Streit, P. (2015, June). *The development of a German version of the Positive Psychotherapy Inventory Überschrift (PPTI) and the PERMA-Profiler.* Presentation at the World Congress of International Positive Psychology Association, Orlando, FL.

Watkins, C. E. (2010). The hope, promise, and possibility of psychotherapy. *Journal of Contemporary Psychotherapy, 40*(4), 195–201. doi:10.1007/s10879-010-9149-x

INDEX

Worksheets and Tables are indicated by an italic *w* and *t* following the page number respectively.

integration, character strengths, 128
integrity, 143–145, 182*t*
interpersonal contact, meaning and, 104

J

justice, 128*t*, 155–161, 183*t*
  citizenship & teamwork, 155–157, 183*t*
  fairness, 157–159, 183*t*
  leadership, 159–161, 183*t*

K

kindness, 150–152, 182*t*
Know-How of Strengths, 2*t*, 30–36, 31–34*w*

L

leadership, 159–161, 183*t*
love, 147–149, 182*t*
love of learning, 135–137, 182*t*

M

Markers of Your Signature Strengths, 22*w*
Maximizing versus Satisficing, 3*t*, 55–62
  The *Gift of Time,* 4*t*, 100–103, 101*w*
  in-session practice: Are You a Maximizer of
    a Satisficer?, 55–57, 56*w*
  in-session practice: *Toward Satisficing,* 3*t*,
    57, 58–60*w*
  maintenance, 61
  in real life, 61
  reflect & discuss, 57, 61
  resources, 62
  three things to know, 55
Meaning and Purpose, 4*t*, 104–110
  in-session practice, 104–110
  in-session practice: A Story from your Past
    and Envisioning a Future Goal, 104–107
  in-session practice: *Positive Legacy,* 4*t*,
    107–109, 108*w*
  in-session practices, 104–110
  maintenance, 109–110
  in real life, 109
  Recalling Your Story and Envisioning a
    Future Goal, 105–106*w*
  reflect & discuss, 107, 109
  resources, 110
  three things to know, 104
memories, open and closed, 43
Mindful Minute, A, 113
mindfulness, 113
mindfulness practices, 113–118. *See also*
    relaxation and mindfulness practices
  Breathing, 113–114
  Love & Kindness Meditation, 118
  A Mindful Minute, 113
  Positive Imagery, 117–118

resources, additional, 118
  Stretch & Relax, 114–117
motivation, 6
multitasking, 77

N

negative events, responding to, 93
negatives, 111–112
negativity bias, 111

O

One Door Closes, Another Door Opens, 3*t*,
    68–71, 69*w*, 111
Open and Closed Memories, 2*t*, 43–47
  in-session practice, 43–47, 45*w*
  maintenance, 46–47
  Positive Appraisal, 2*t*, 7, 45*w*
  in real life, 46
  reflect & discuss, 44, 46
  resources, 47
  three things to know, 43
open memories, 43
open-mindedness, 133–135, 182*t*
optimism, 68
other-oriented gratitude, 63

P

persistence, 141–143, 182*t*
perspective, 137–139, 182*t*
Planned Savoring Activity, 81
positive, brain responses to, 111
positive appraisal, 43
  negatives integration with, 111
Positive Appraisal, 2*t*, 7, 45*w*
Positive Communication, 4*t*, 93–98
  in-session practice: *Active Constructive
    Responding,* 4*t*, 93–95, 94*w*, 111
  maintenance, 97
  in real life, 97
  reflect & discuss, 95, 97
  resources, 98
  three things to know, 93
  Your Partner's Strengths, 96*w*
positive events, responding to, 93
Positive Imagery, 117–118
Positive Introduction and *Gratitude Journal,*
    2*t*, 8–13, 112
  Gratitude Journal, 119–121
  Gratitude Journal: in real life, 11
  Gratitude Journal: in-session practice,
    2*t*, 11–12
  Gratitude Journal: maintenance, 12
  Gratitude Journal: reflect & discuss, 11
  Gratitude Journal: resources, 13
  Gratitude Journal: three things to know, 11